Javanese Gamelan and the West

Eastman/Rochester Studies in Ethnomusicology

Ellen Koskoff, Series Editor
Eastman School of Music

(ISSN: 2161-0290)

*Burma's Pop Music Industry:
Creators, Distributors, Censors*
Heather MacLachlan

*Yorùbá Music in the Twentieth Century:
Identity, Agency and Performance Practice*
Bode Omojola

Javanese Gamelan and the West
Sumarsam

Javanese Gamelan
and the West

Sumarsam

UNIVERSITY OF ROCHESTER PRESS

Copyright © 2013 by Sumarsam

All Rights Reserved. Except as permitted under current legislation, no part of this work may be photocopied, stored in a retrieval system, published, performed in public, adapted, broadcast, transmitted, recorded, or reproduced in any form or by any means, without the prior permission of the copyright owner.

First published 2013
Reprinted in paperback 2015

University of Rochester Press
668 Mt. Hope Avenue, Rochester, NY 14620, USA
www.urpress.com
and Boydell & Brewer Limited
PO Box 9, Woodbridge, Suffolk IP12 3DF, UK
www.boydellandbrewer.com

ISSN: 2161-0290
Hardcover ISBN: 978-1-58046-445-1
Paperback ISBN: 978-1-58046-523-6

Library of Congress Cataloging-in-Publication Data

Sumarsam, author.
　Javanese gamelan and the West / Sumarsam.
　　pages cm. — (Eastman/Rochester studies in ethnomusicology Volume 3)
　Includes bibliographical references and index.
　ISBN 978-1-58046-445-1 (hardcover : alkaline paper) 1. Gamelan music—Indonesia—Java—History and criticism. 2. Gamelan music—Western countries—History and criticism. I. Title. II. Series: Eastman/Rochester studies in ethnomusicology.
　ML3758.I53S86 2013
　780.9598'2—dc23

2013011376

A catalogue record for this title is available from the British Library.

This publication is printed on acid-free paper.
Printed in the United States of America

"What we need to question, then, is not so much hybridity as such, which would be a futile enterprise, but the depoliticization involved in the reduction of hybridity to happy fusion and synthesis. I would argue that it is the *ambivalence* which is immanent to hybridity that needs to be highlighted, as we also need to examine the *specific contexts and conditions* in which hybridity operates."

—Ien Ang, *On Not Speaking Chinese*

"But was the public's interest in the kampong really anthropological at all? What did the visitors actually see, when they entered the kampong at the exhibition's lessons on the evolution of civilization and colonial superiority? Did they actually connect the explanations in the exposition halls to the world exhibited in the kampong?"

—Marieke Bloembergen, *Colonial Spectacle: The Netherlands and the Dutch East Indies at the World Exhibitions, 1880–1931*

Contents

	List of Illustrations	ix
	Preface	xi
	Acknowledgments	xv
	Note on Orthography	xvii
	Introduction	1

Part One: Hybridity in Javanese Performing Arts

1	Performing Colonialism	11
2	Performing the Nation-State	26
3	*Opera Diponegoro*	54

Part Two: Gamelan as Intercultural Object

4	Deterritorializing and Appropriating Gamelan	77
5	Cross-Cultural Perspectives on Gamelan Theory: Metaphorical Readings of Gamelan	115
	Conclusion	139
	Notes	143
	Glossary	169
	Selected Discography	177
	Bibliography	179
	Index	193

Illustrations

Examples

4.1	Comparison of Julien Tiersot's transcription of Vani-Vani (excerpt) and Koesoemadinata's Wani-Wani	100
5.1	The Ngelik section of Puspa Warna	131

Figures

1.1	Javanese musicians playing trumpets and snare drum in gendhing mares	20
2.1	Electric keyboards in a wayang spektakular	36
3.1	A scene in the *Opera Diponegoro*	55
4.1	Gamelan at the 1883 Amsterdam Exhibition	91
4.2	Mangkunegaran dancers at the 1889 Paris Exposition	97
4.3	Mantle Hood and his international students	114

Preface

I have been a student, teacher, and performer of gamelan in Indonesia and the United States for most of my life. In the United States, I teach mostly American students, but also those from other countries. I have also been very fortunate to study ethnomusicology at two American universities: Wesleyan in the mid-1970s and Cornell from the mid-1980s to the early 1990s. This cross-pollination of performer-teacher and academic might be the most ideal pursuit in the study of music, but the task has been demanding. Maintaining a balance of time and energy between the two aspects has been a challenge, and at times it has been necessary to prioritize one at the expense of the other.

I came to significantly engage in the world of scholarship quite late, although the seed of my interest can be traced to my years as a student and teacher of gamelan in Indonesia. In 1964, I started teaching at the gamelan conservatory (KOKAR, Konservatori Karawitan Indonesia, now SMK, Sekolah Menengah Kejuruan), a high school of Javanese performing arts. I taught an ensemble, a class on *kendhang* (drum), and a course on the theory of gamelan playing (*Teori Menabuh*) for first-year students. Conservatory classes were held in the morning, and in the afternoons I was a student at the gamelan academy (ASKI, Akademi Seni Karawitan Indonesia, now ISI, Institut Seni Indonesia). In 1969, I was appointed a part-time assistant to R. L. Martopangrawit, a gamelan teacher and the only gamelan theorist at the academy, work which allowed me to continue my interest in gamelan theory. I published a book on kendhang, containing notations of kendhang with brief commentary.[1] I also published a booklet on *gendèr*, containing a list of gendèr patterns named according to Martopangrawit's way of naming them.[2] I graduated from the academy in 1968, and subsequently enrolled in a degree equivalent to an MM in the United States, which I never completed; in 1970, I was assigned to join a government performing-arts group performing at the 1970 World Exposition in Osaka, Japan for seven months. After returning to Indonesia for one year, I was assigned to teach gamelan at the Indonesian Embassy in Canberra, Australia. From there, I went to the United States to teach gamelan at Wesleyan University.

After being exposed to the intellectual life at Wesleyan, I was bothered by my failure to complete my degree in Indonesia. In 1974, I enrolled in the MA program in world music at Wesleyan, while continuing to teach gamelan. I completed the degree in 1976, and my continuing interest in academic work led me to embark on a doctoral program at Cornell University in 1983, during my sabbatical leave from Wesleyan. I was already in my late forties when I completed my doctorate in 1992. I feel now that I still have a lot of catching up to do, and writing in a language not my own presents another challenge.

I should mention that in the graduate musicology program at Cornell, students can work with an advisor to design a specific program to suit their interest. Whatever the student's area of focus, he or she must take courses in theory, musicology, ethnomusicology, performance, and composition, or courses from other disciplines. I took advantage of this flexibility by designating ethnomusicology as the field of my study, focusing on Indonesian music. Instead of taking classes in musicology or music theory, I took classes in Southeast Asian studies, including a seminar on Indonesian politics and culture and a number of classes on the history of Southeast Asia. This fusion of Southeast Asian studies and ethnomusicology has led me to focus on the study of gamelan in its historical and cultural context. However, I continue to be fascinated with theoretical issues of music as sound structure thanks to my upbringing as a gamelan musician and my early interest in gamelan theory. I devoted the final chapter of my last book to gamelan theory,[3] and readers of the present work will find that again I address gamelan theory in the last chapter, examining the particular way that scholars formulate gamelan theory epistemologically, and seeking to expand this discussion in ways I feel necessary.

I thought it important to share the above reflections so that the reader may better understand my perspective, and where my limitations lie. I have often been favored with encouraging comments from American colleagues about how special my status is, since I am Javanese and a gamelan musician; according to them, this status allows me to be an arbiter between Javanese and Western ideas. I of course very much appreciate such positive comments, but I hope that readers do not approach this work with the expectation that I possess a full-fledged insider's or "emic" perspective. This seems to have been the response to my early work about melody in Javanese gamelan,[4] a hypothesis that was subsequently examined critically by Marc Perlman.[5]

In that early work, I was responding to a misconception among Western scholars in identifying the melodic skeleton (*balungan*) of gamelan composition, especially regarding the octave ranges of such melodic skeletons. I described a melodic complexity which emerges during performance, when musicians treat the melody of their instruments as they interact with each other. Central to this musical process is the musicians' knowledge and competence in understanding the nature of the composition's melody. In my subsequent work, I expanded the discussion of this topic by tracing the melodic precedents of several gamelan compositions.[6] I also pointed out the imposition of Western concepts on the development of gamelan theory.[7]

Perlman sees this as a kind of anticolonialism, arising from what I perceived as a need to indigenize gamelan theory after I found myself "surrounded by an entrenched conceptual framework built over a period of decades under heavy Western influence."[8]

Setting aside the colonial context for the moment, I wonder whether my opinion should fall solely on the side of the "inside" or "emic" perspective. Indeed, the issue of "emic" and "etic" understanding of non-Western music (sometimes encapsulated by the term "ethnotheory") has occupied the work of some ethnomusicologists for several decades. Perlman traces the ethnomusicological use of these terms and concepts to the writings of Hugo Zemp in the late 1970s.[9] Although the search for emic musical understanding has produced rich and well-conceived literature, its pros and cons are still being discussed. Perlman rightly asserts that early ethnotheory "seemed to assume a greater degree of homogeneity and integration of culture than actually exists," hence focusing "on concepts assumed to represent a cultural consensus, ignoring issues of intracultural variability, historical change, and individual intellectual creativity."[10] Accordingly, ethnotheory oversimplified the discourse by assuming that "musical knowledge is a single type of thing, thereby underestimating the internal heterogeneity of cognitive processes."[11]

Marc Benamou approaches this issue as follows: "The goal of being true to the insiders' perspectives is even more elusive, however, in the *presenting* of the material gathered, and it may not be entirely desirable. I do not mean by this that in constructing my narrative I should have been free to choose any interpretation that came to mind; rather, that another force besides the musicians' perspective was at work in shaping the material."[12] Following Kenneth Pike's work, Benamou goes on to say that emic analysis is not simply about reporting insiders' speech; instead, it is an attempt by the researcher to come up with a model built up from principles derived from, rather than based upon, the data.[13]

For Perlman, the central question is not limited to what an emic perspective is; it is also how this perspective comes into being—both the process and the product should be understood. In this sense, sorting out musicians' statements as emic or etic presents a challenge.[14] For example, I would think that a statement from a conservatory-trained musician is more likely to be considered an "etic" perspective than a statement from a traditional musician. However, since nowadays traditional musicians work closely with conservatory-trained musicians, the statements of both sides could be influenced by one another's perspectives.

It goes without saying that the colonial legacy has brought about a complex society in which individuals' and institutions' viewpoints cannot be sorted in terms of a simple inside-outside dichotomy. Because the study of any music should not be only about "outside looking in," but also "inside looking in and out," or even "inside and outside looking in and out," I employ any line of thought that I consider relevant and useful regardless of who has produced the knowledge in question. If anything, I take seriously the perspective of Western thinkers for their critical examination of culture and cultural performances. In addition to the works of ethnomusicologists, my reference tends to include the works of Southeast Asianists and recent works on contemporary cultural theory and criticism. I have also drawn on Javanese sources, from past centuries and contemporary writing, from the nineteenth-century *Serat Centhini* to Supanggah's work in the twenty-first century. Unless otherwise noted, all translations are my own.

Acknowledgments

Parts of chapter 5 were previously published as "Iconic Reading of Gamelan Revisited," in *A Search in Asia for a New Theory of Music*, ed. José S. Buenconsejo (Manila: University of the Philippines Center for Ethnomusicology, 2003); and "Binary Division of Javanese *Gamelan* and Socio-Cosmological Order," in *Hybridity in the Performing Arts of Southeast Asia*, ed. Mohd Anis Md Nor, Patricia Matusky, Tan Sooi Beng, Jacqueline-Pugh Kitingan, and Felicidad Prudente (Kuala Lumpur: International Council for Traditional Music Study Group on Performing Arts in Southeast Asia, 2011). Both articles are revised and extended in this volume. I would like to thank the University of the Philippines Center for Ethnomusicology and the International Council for Traditional Music Study Group on Performing Arts in Southeast Asia, respectively, for permission to reproduce them here.

This book is the result of many years of research and writing. I am indebted to colleagues and students who have read early drafts of different parts of the chapters and have given their invaluable comments: Emily Ferrigno, Maho Ishiguro, Mark Nelson, Margaret Sarkissian, Mark Slobin, Rachel Thompson, Chris Miller, Sarah-Jane Ripa, and Jonathan Jucker.

I am grateful to my own institution, Wesleyan University, for several Grants in Support of Scholarship for researching and writing this book, and for its generous contribution toward the production of the book. I wish to thank colleagues and administrative assistants in my department for their intellectual and moral support during my forty years of teaching at Wesleyan. To Pak Harjito, thank you for many years of collaboration in teaching and performing gamelan at Wesleyan and elsewhere.

Special thanks are due to Tony Day, who was my professor at Cornell and who has continued to be a close colleague since then, for allowing me to read his unpublished manuscript, "Sound, Feeling, Knowledge." In chapter 4, I adapt and expand a number of his points. Thanks to Jean-Pierre Chazal, who has done significant research and publication on the presence of gamelan at the Paris Exposition, and Bambang Suryono (a dancer of the Mangkunegaran court), who via e-mail and in person have shared with me their thoughts about some aspects of the presence of Javanese performing arts at the 1889 Paris Exposition.

I also would like to extend my deeper appreciation to two readers (originally anonymous, both of them have revealed to me who they are), Sarah

Weiss of Yale University and Henry Spiller of the University of California–Davis, for their thorough, positive, encouraging, and helpful comments. Without their meticulous reading and constructive criticism in the full spirit of academic integrity and collegiality, I would not have been able to complete the book in the form that you are reading it. Of course, I am responsible for any infelicities that remain.

I am very grateful to the editorial staff at the University of Rochester Press: Julia Cook, Ryan Peterson, Tracey Engel, and others have been very patient in guiding me through the process of editing and publishing this book. Special thanks to the copyeditor, who did an excellent job of shepherding me, going beyond smoothing out my grammar to strengthen my arguments, make better connections between chapters and paragraphs, and much more.

This book project has demanded a lot of my time and energy for research, reading, writing, and rewriting. I am grateful to my wife, my son, and my daughter and her family for their support, tolerance, and understanding. It is especially encouraging to be frequently asked by my grandchildren, Tristan and Bella: "Are you still writing your book? When will you be done?"

Note on Orthography

With the exception of personal names, the spelling of Javanese and Indonesian words cited in this study follows the orthographic convention officially adopted by the Indonesian government since 1972, but citations from material written in Indonesian are written in their original spelling. The difference between the old and modern transliteration lies mainly in the following spellings: dj represents modern j, tj represents c, and oe represent u.

In Javanese, *e* can take certain diacritical marks. The following is a list of vowels and consonants in Javanese that require particular notice.

	English equivalent	Javanese example
a	1. in a closed syllable (ending with a consonant), as in f<u>a</u>ther	lek<u>a</u>s
	2. in an open syllable (ending with vowel, like aw in law)	buk<u>a</u>
c	<u>ch</u>urch	<u>c</u>elempung
d	pronounced with tongue-tip touching inside upper teeth	<u>d</u>emung
dh	pronounced with tongue-tip touching palate (i.e., palatal), e.g., <u>d</u>ay	<u>dh</u>alang
e	<u>a</u>bout	<u>e</u>mbat
è	l<u>e</u>t	g<u>è</u>nder
é	<u>a</u>te	p<u>é</u>log
i	1. a closed syllable ends in vowel-plus-consonant., e.g., b<u>i</u>t	al<u>i</u>t
	2. an open syllable ends in vowel, e.g., pol<u>i</u>ce	kinanth<u>i</u>
ny	ca<u>ny</u>on	<u>ny</u>ela

o	1. a closed syllable ends in vowel-plus-consonant., e.g., b<u>o</u>re	pél<u>o</u>g
	2. an open syllable ends in vowel, e.g., zer<u>o</u>	b<u>o</u>nang
r	rolled r	salisi<u>r</u>
t	pronounced with tongue-tip touching inside upper teeth (i.e., dental), e.g., <u>t</u>ry	ke<u>t</u>ipung
th	pronounced with tongue-tip touch palate (i.e., palatal), e.g., la<u>t</u>er	pa<u>th</u>et
u	1. a closed syllable ends in vowel-plus-consonant., e.g., p<u>u</u>t	w<u>u</u>s
	2. an open syllable ends in vowel, e.g., tr<u>ue</u>	mlak<u>u</u>

Introduction

Encountering foreign cultures has been an inescapable part of life in Asia for many centuries. Indonesians have come into contact with many cultures, three of which—Hindu, Islamic, and Western—have had significant effects on the development of their own. Each encounter has had a different character, and a hybrid culture eventually formed.

I use the term "hybrid" or "hybridity" to denote contact between cultures that bring about a wide register of multiple identity experiences and intensive cultural communication.[1] Hybridity is concerned with intercultural encounters in which people from different traditions or worldviews come into contact with one another, followed by the changing hands of cultural artifacts.[2] These artifacts are not only observed and handled by the recipient, but also reproduced in a variety of ways.[3] Such an intercultural exchange brings about both change to and continuity of cultural tradition, as people in the home culture adopt, adapt, reject, or negotiate the ideology of the impinging culture. Such change and continuity will lead the tradition not only to a happy fusion and synthesis, but also to ambiguity and ambivalence;[4] hence, the dynamic of hybridity.

When people in what is now Indonesia made contact with Hinduism and Islam, they generally expressed flexibility and tolerance toward these foreign religions and cultures; the means by which they came to Java—via trade, instead of conquest—made this possible.[5] Indonesians' acceptance of Hinduism and Islam occurred through gradual localization and assimilation, allowing these religions to play important roles in Indonesian cultural development. "Localization" happens when foreign "materials tended to be fractured and restated and therefore drained of their original significance . . . The materials, be they words, sounds of words, books, or artifacts, had to be localized in different ways before they could fit into various local complexes or religious, social, and political systems and belong to new cultural 'wholes.'"[6] I would suggest that such significant transformations of religious and socio-political conventions must have carried with them a certain amount of uncertainty and delicate negotiation. For example, the Hindu caste system, with its emphasis on endogamy and heredity, has never been fully accepted by the Javanese. For another example, after the Islamization of Java the tradition of reenacting stories based on Hindu epics (*Mahabharata* and *Ramayana*) had to go through a long process of negotiation.[7]

The Westernization of Indonesia played out differently than its Hinduization and Islamization, since religion played a very small role. Christianity was first introduced to Indonesia by the Portuguese in the sixteenth century, on the island of Maluku in the Eastern part of the archipelago.[8] In spite of its early introduction, Christianity never gained a stronghold in Indonesia. The presence of the Dutch in the late seventeenth century, taking over the area's trade from the Portuguese, did not foster the spread of Christianity. Both the Portuguese and the Dutch focused on trade, with interference in the political life of local states. The interference reached its peak in the nineteenth century, with the formal colonization of Indonesia by the Dutch.

The prolonged presence of Europeans in the archipelago has made the localization and hybridization of Western ideas and elements unavoidable. By the early twentieth century, exposure to European history and politics, combined with longstanding colonial exploitation, inspired the Indonesians to unite in a revolution, bringing about the nation's independence from European colonialism in the late 1940s. With sovereignty achieved, Indonesians were challenged by the task of nation-building and uniting a diverse population. In the search for national identity, debates emerged centering "around the question of the content, relative weight, and proper relationship of two rather towering abstractions: 'The Indigenous Way of Life' and 'The Spirit of the Age.'"[9] The latter is a notion of the creation of culture from different influences (particularly Western), and the former is based on the continuing cultivation of indigenous cultures. The creative tension between these two impulses provides the key to understanding the growth of contemporary Indonesian culture.

In the 1980s, questions of identity resurfaced as Indonesia experienced another phase of interaction with the West through a process commonly known as "globalization." Globalization is the result of cultural encounter and communication, and the emergence of multiple centers of economic power. The impetus for modern globalization has been Western economic superiority, and it has provided Indonesians with resources and advanced communications technology. The wealth, power, and economic expertise underlying Western capitalism persuaded Indonesia and other Asian nations to throw open their doors to Western investors. Aided by Indonesia's booming oil production, Western investment significantly improved Indonesia's economic position and purchasing power.

As globalization has allowed Indonesia greater and more rapid access to Western goods, technology, mass media, and information, has it threatened local knowledge? What cultural hybrids have emerged from globalization, and how are they different from previous hybrids? On what level can a hybrid form be seen as cohesive or not? To what extent do local cultural values resist the globalization juggernaut? These questions are certainly relevant to a careful consideration of contemporary Indonesia, a country whose sudden economic plunge during the Asian financial crisis of 1997 caused a worldwide ripple of economic trouble (and further demonstrated globalization's reach).

The globalization process in general leads us to a broader issue affecting the study of regional culture. A regional culture should not be seen as a set of permanent geographical and cultural facts; but rather, we need to study regional culture "that is based on process geographies and sees significant areas of human organization as precipitates of various kinds of action, interaction, and motion—trade, travel, pilgrimage, warfare, proselytisation, colonisation, exile, and the like."[10] Interaction between Indonesia and foreign cultures has occurred over many centuries. However, because Indonesia is an archipelago of several thousand islands, home to more than 300 ethnic groups, contact between different Indonesian regions and foreign cultures has been uneven, and the impact of these encounters on the development of regional cultures is heterogeneous.

The present study centers on Java, especially Central Java, though in certain cases it is necessary to contextualize it in a broader discussion of Indonesian culture. Java has long been the center of attention for scholars studying Indonesia. This is because, as Holt observes, not only has Java "been through much of history the principal locus both of power and of converging insular and international commerce, but it has also provided the bulk of historical records."[11]

I feel it is necessary, with this book, to revisit discourses about Javanese cultural performances in the context of contemporary global or transcultural encounters. New evidence and a fresh theoretical approach might lead us to a new perspective and better understanding of past and present Javanese culture. In addition, recent cultural developments in Java and their impact on the performing arts has made the study of contemporary Javanese culture a worthwhile effort.

The processes of hybridization shape the formation of the *nation-state, culture, and cultural performance*—an interdependent trilogy that can loosely be applied to any period and socio-political structure, whether "traditional," "colonial," or "modern" Java.[12] This trilogy informs us that cultural performances are more than just entertainment, but also "occasions in which as a culture or society we reflect upon and define ourselves, dramatize our collective myths and history, present ourselves with alternatives, and eventually change in some ways while remaining the same in others."[13] Cultural performance as a dramatization of culture is one of the themes of the present study.

Java in Focus

This book focuses on traditional Javanese performing arts, especially gamelan and its related arts. I was born in east Java, and after elementary and junior high school I continued my education at the secondary and tertiary schools of Javanese performing arts in Surakarta, central Java. Although the schools also teach Balinese and Sundanese gamelan, their curriculum focuses on central Javanese gamelan, especially the Surakarta and Yogyakarta court styles. In my studies in the United States, at Wesleyan and Cornell, I have continued to focus on the theory, history, and practice of Javanese gamelan.

From the early centuries of the common era to the present time, Javanese people have had intensive contacts with foreign cultures, encounters which have played a part in developing their own culture, and which caused Javanese performing arts to flourish. The encounter with Europeans in the context of trading and colonialism made Javanese culture the most important Indonesian culture for European officials, scholars, and people. In governing their colony, European authorities had to maintain close relationships with native power brokers, especially the courtiers of Surakarta and Yogyakarta, and this exposure to Javanese court cultures prompted Europeans to begin studying them.

In the late nineteenth century, Javanese performing art was introduced to Europeans and Americans through World's Fairs and other exhibitions. Continuing into the twentieth century, there were more gamelan performances and performing ensembles in Europe, North America, and elsewhere. Academia also played an important role in the expansion of gamelan outside of Indonesia. With the spread of ethnomusicology programs, gamelan, along with other non-Western music, has become part of many universities' music departments, either as part of the curriculum or as an extra-curricular activity.

Early independence movements against the Dutch in the nineteenth century were essentially regional in nature; the movement in Java, for example, had barely any connection with the movement in Sumatra. In the twentieth century, a large-scale Indonesian national awakening took place; nationalists and national awakenings from different regions were connected to each other. The 1928 declaration of the *Sumpah Pemuda* (Youth pledge) by organizations of young nationalists marked the peak of this larger national movement. The pledge's phrase, "one nation, one people, and one language of Indonesia," was a powerful mantra for those seeking national unity and Indonesia's new identity. Indonesia's national anthem, composed in a Western musical idiom (with lyrics in the Indonesian language), was also created during the period of this large-scale nationalism.

This new political phase generated discussion and debates among nationalists from different ethnic groups as they sought to define Indonesia's new cultural identity. In what way should one consider the role of regional performing arts in forming a new national culture? One segment of Javanese nationalists considered court performing arts as national arts, while another considered them irrelevant to modern Indonesia.[14] The latter group proposed to search for a new national entity (including music) that could represent all Indonesians, regardless of their ethnic background. However, defining a single Indonesian cultural identity continued to be a hotly debated issue.

Amidst this debate, Javanese court cultures continued their preeminence. New cultural policy is typically first implemented in Java: for example, secondary and tertiary performing arts education was first established in central Java, in the court cities of Surakarta and Yogyakarta. Although one of the aims of the schools was to create a new Indonesian music by amalgamating regional musical forms, this aspiration was never realized; instead, the curriculum focused on Javanese court-style performing arts.[15] There was even a period in which "Karawitan," a Javanese courtly term for gamelan music as fine art, was used to name government-sponsored music schools and academies in all regions of Indonesia.

Indonesian history has been written from a Javanese perspective.[16] The state motto "Bhineka Tunggal Ika" (unity in diversity) was adapted from a fourteenth-century Javanese literary work, *Sutasoma*, although its original meaning is quite different from its modern use. The majority of early Indonesian intellectuals and literary scholars were Javanese educated in the Dutch system. Written in the Indonesian language, many of their works are translations, adaptations, or analyses of old Javanese literature; examples include the translation of *Bharatayuda* by Sutjipto Wirjosuparto, and the study of the East Javanese story *Panji* by Poerbotjaroko. Even a Sumatran-born literary scholar, Sanusi Pane, was also fascinated with the depth of old Javanese literary works, and rewrote the twelfth-century East Javanese literary work *Arjunawiwaha*. He also established red and white as the colors of the Indonesian flag, which according to him referred to a thirteenth-century Javanese tradition. It was also Pane who adopted the above-mentioned motto. All things considered, it is not farfetched to say that in the process of formulating the Indonesian nation-state, we witnessed the "Indonesianization" of the Javanese cultural tradition.[17]

Performing arts activities in the presidential palaces in Jakarta and Bogor contributed to the fascination with Javanese cultural performances.[18] Although the first president of the Republic of Indonesia, Sukarno, had no royal blood, he was known for his keen admiration for the court's performing arts. The presidential Javanese palace has quite an extensive collection of Javanese gamelan and *wayang* puppets, and performances of these—and Javanese dance—were staged more frequently than cultural performances from other Indonesian regions. Periodically, Sukarno invited his favorite *dhalang* (puppeteer), Ki Pudjosumarto from Klaten, to perform in the presidential palace. His favorite dancer, Rusman from the Sriwedari *wayang wong* dance-drama troupe in Surakarta, was often invited to dance his favorite heroic wayang figure, Gathutkaca,[19] for his presidential guests.[20] On one occasion where I participated as a gamelan performer at the Bogor presidential palace, I witnessed President Sukarno watching Rusman dance. As Rusman, portraying Gathutkaca, was preparing to fly overhead, President Sukarno stood up and positioned himself closer to the *bedhug*, a large hanging drum which was to be struck, punctuating certain movements when Gathutkaca was preparing himself to fly and during his imagined ascending and flying overhead.

I do not mean to say that Javanese performing art was Sukarno's only favorite type, though he had a profound appreciation for it. Dancers and musicians from other Indonesian regions, including those from Sunda, Sumatra, Sulawesi, and Bali, were also invited to dance in the Presidential palace. In fact, having a Balinese mother made Sukarno very conscious of the worthiness of Balinese culture. To him, Bali was a kind of mother culture, while Javanese was a father culture.[21] He always had dances performed for him when he visited his Tampak Siring palace in Bali, and his important guests were welcomed with Balinese dance when they landed at the airport.

Featuring the well-known artistic production of Bali and Java locally and internationally was one of the ways Sukarno carried out his policy of *mercu suar* (lighthouse): to promote the visibility of Indonesia, its glory, its development, and its beautiful traditional performing arts in order to reach faraway places. To this end, Balinese, along with Javanese and Sundanese gamelan and dance, were the prime attractions of the government's cultural missions abroad.

The fascination with gamelan and its related arts continued during President Suharto's regime, although the depth of his personal involvement didn't reach that of President Sukarno. Javanese and Balinese performing arts continued to welcome presidential guests; in the early 1970s I performed gamelan at the presidential palace in Bogor. Accompanying a dance drama enacting a story drawn from the Ramayana epic, the performance was to welcome President Nixon.

I was also one of the musicians at a performing group dispatched by the government to perform Javanese and Balinese gamelan at the 1970 Osaka World Exposition. Although music and dances from other islands were also performed, Javanese and Balinese gamelan and dance tended to be featured in the program. In the first place, the gamelan group demanded many resources, as two sets of gamelan had to be transported to Osaka, and the Javanese and Balinese musicians and dancers outnumbered the artists from other regions.

Suharto's regime continued to see Indonesian traditional performing arts as having an important role as a distinct marker of Indonesia's artistic expression. The regime paid special attention, culturally and politically, to preserving and fostering traditional Indonesian performing arts. *Pengembangan* (developing), *pelestarian* (preserving), and *pembinaan* (fostering) became ubiquitous terms used by Indonesian administrators and artists working at the Cultural Office and at art institutions to promote and maintain traditional performing arts.[22]

In spite of Indonesia's commitment to preserving its traditional culture, Western popular culture has continued to influence Indonesian music. Western forms of popular music have a long history in Indonesia, which can be traced to the sixteenth-century arrival of Portuguese sailors, who introduced songs which developed into a popular music genre called *kroncong*.[23] Subsequently, the Dutch introduced European secular and military music, and in the twentieth century American music added significantly to the Indonesian popular culture scene.[24]

Under Sukarno's regime, known for its opposition to Western capitalism, Western popular culture's influence was curtailed; but in the late 1960s this was relaxed and eventually lifted by Suharto's regime. The booming Indonesian economy contributed to the spread of all sorts of Western popular culture. Indonesianized Western popular music became an important mode of entertainment and social interaction among young Indonesians. By the 1980s, in step with modernity (as the younger generation saw it), the repertoire of the traditional performing arts entered into popular music genres—and vice versa.

Overview

The present study discusses localization and hybridization portrayed in Javanese cultural performances as Western cultures were encountered, from nineteenth-century colonial Java to contemporary Indonesia. The book consists of two parts: the first addresses the impact that the encounter with Western culture made on Javanese cultural performances. Entitled "Performing Colonialism," chapter 1 presents three case studies: (1) *kroncong*, a musical hybrid the development of which can be traced back to Indonesia's encounter with Portuguese music in the sixteenth century; (2) European brass bands in the *tanjidor* music of west Java; and (3) *gendhing mares* of the court of Yogyakarta. Because the last two musical hybrids incorporate the same types of European instruments, they are discussed at length, both musically and culturally. "Performing the Nation State," chapter 2, consists of two case studies: (1) the presence of Western styles of popular music in contemporary *wayang* performance; and (2) experimental music in an Indonesian music festival. Chapter 3 discusses the influence of Western theatrical idioms on contemporary Javanese production, focusing on the production of *Opera Diponegoro*, composed by contemporary choreographer Sardono W. Kusumo. Because the play employs several traditional theatrical genres, a background for each is presented before the discussion of the main topic.

As gamelan became a transnational object, in what ways had the West been in contact with Javanese cultural performances? What has been the significance and consequence of this contact, in the West and in Java? How do people in the West represent gamelan and gamelan culture? These are among the key questions addressed in the second part of the book. Chapter 4 examines the history of the introduction of gamelan to the West, illuminating the first and second questions mentioned above. With regard to the third, I will discuss the differences and similarities surrounding the adaptation of gamelan in different institutional contexts in the United States and Europe.

Chapter 5 presents an example of discourse on gamelan theory: that linked to the development of ethnomusicology. It is well known that the study of Indonesian music contributed to the initial development of ethnomusicology during the post–World War II period. My aim in this chapter is to articulate one of the definitions of ethnomusicology that gained currency a few decades ago, namely "the study of music *as* culture"; or the most recent version, proposed by Monson: "the interdisciplinary study of music as cultural practice."[25] Here the emphasis is on music processes as a reflection of cultural practice.

Part One

Hybridity in Javanese Performing Arts

Chapter One

Performing Colonialism

In the introduction, I laid out a general premise of cultural hybridity: cultural contact that brings about a wide register of multiple identities and intensive cultural communication. In this chapter, I will begin my discussion with musical hybridity. But before I do so, it is useful to make note of a few key points about hybridity. One can think of hybridity either "as a space of liminality between two worlds (neither here nor there but in between) that can just as easily be emancipatory or tragic or as a source of potential strength since cultural hybrids can free themselves from the chains of tradition by adding on successive of layers of strategic identity."[1] The receiver of hybrid production is expected, Weiss writes, "to adjust his or her internal expectations about appropriation, agency, and authenticity."[2] Weiss goes on to say that "the highlighting of cultural mixture... situates issues of authenticity, ownership, purity, difference, and power, as unavoidable filters through which people of any cultures process the aesthetic impact of the production."[3] It is thus highly relevant that Ang, as quoted in the epigraph above, emphasize the presence of ambiguities and ambivalences in hybridity.

There are a few key questions to be considered: first, how is a particular hybrid music cultivated and developed in reaction to, and as a manifestation of, certain historical, socio-cultural, and regional phenomena? Secondly, what kinds of musical considerations might have taken place in the hybridization process?

To illustrate musical hybridity in Java during the colonial period, this chapter discusses three early hybrid musical forms: (1) kroncong, which has developed in the vicinity of Batavia (now Jakarta); (2) tanjidor, a genre that can be found in the Sundanese cultural area in villages on the outskirts of Jakarta; and (3) gendhing mares, a creation of musicians in the court of Yogyakarta.

As mentioned in the introduction, the localization and hybridization of foreign elements have brought about the development of Indonesian culture; music and musical culture have also followed this general scheme. The genres of Indonesian musical hybrids have been broadly categorized by Philip Yampolsky as follows: (1) the European music complex; (2) the Muslim music complex; and (3) the Melayu (the world of Malay) complex.[4] The Chinese music complex can also be added to these categories. The categories often overlap. The musical hybrids I will discuss in chapters 1 and 2 fall in the first category.

In the sixteenth and seventeenth centuries, the Portuguese and Dutch brought religious, secular, and military music to Java. The first encounter with church music, introduced by Portuguese missionaries, took place in the Eastern Indonesian islands in the sixteenth century, and its influence later spread to the other islands. In spite of the continuous presence of church music in Indonesia (even though Christianity never gained a strong foothold in the archipelago), it was only in the late nineteenth century that localized forms of church worship began to develop, as a handful of European and Javanese Christian priests began to incorporate Javanese cultural symbols in their services.[5] In the twentieth century, a number of localized-hybridized forms of church rituals sprang up involving gamelan, Javanese dance,[6] and the creation of new wayang (*wayang wahyu*) that present stories from the Bible.[7]

Kroncong

In the seventeenth and eighteenth centuries, Indonesians encountered secular European music in the homes of rich Portuguese (and later Dutch) traders in Batavia and its vicinity.[8] A rich trader would typically own hundreds of slaves from India, Africa, and Southeast Asia; besides their main jobs as gardeners, cooks, and stable-boys, many of the slaves were also skilled musicians. They played music for their own enjoyment, and more significantly, to entertain their masters at mealtimes, social dances, and processions. They sang Portuguese folk songs, accompanying themselves on plucked string instruments similar to ukuleles, and played in string or brass ensembles. As I will discuss below, it is likely that the first Javanese-European hybrid music began in these traders' houses. Kroncong is one of these musical hybrids that can trace its early development to this kind of cultural context.

Kroncong is an Indonesianized form of European popular music, dominated by string instruments: violin, guitar, cello, string bass, and ukulele; flute and vocals complete the ensemble. Yampolsky nicely summarizes the function of the instruments in the modern kroncong ensemble: "At different points in the piece, the singer, violin, or flute may carry a rhythmically loose, often quite florid main melody, while an instrument that is not soloing will decorate and support the main line. The rest of the instruments provide a steady, driving background of rapid figuration."[9] Kroncong songs have *pantun* (quatrain) text, expressing feelings of nostalgia, romantic sentiment, the beauty of nature, and so forth, sung to a predictable harmonic progression.

It should be mentioned that both the style of kroncong and the genre's position in Indonesian society have changed over time. In 1511, the Portuguese conquered Malacca and established a trade headquarters there. From

Malacca, the Portuguese continued trading with a number of islands in eastern Indonesia (the "Spice Islands"), establishing a headquarters in Maluku. Small Portuguese settlements were started in the trading towns around harbors, such as the town now called Jakarta, but their sojourn in Southeast Asia was short-lived; by 1602 the Dutch had seized trading control of the area. The Portuguese were marginalized and had to assimilate themselves into the Dutch (later Indo-Dutch) and Indonesian population. In 1661 the Dutch East Indies Company granted a group of freed, Christianized, mestizo slaves (*mardijkers* or "black Portuguese") some land on the outskirts of Batavia (Jakarta), an area called Tugu; it has been suggested that it was here that kroncong developed.[10] Yampolsky has debunked this assertion, arguing instead that the genre consists of divergent branches of Mardijker music that existed around the capital city of Batavia; music in Tugu represents one of these branches.[11]

In the late nineteenth century, kroncong became associated with the lower strata of the Indo community, the mixed-blood offspring of European fathers and Indonesian mothers. Matthew Cohen asserts that "many of the accomplished players were Indos who wandered the streets in gangs of three or five, committing petty crimes, wooing women with their romantic songs."[12] Its popularity soared when it became an integral part of *komedie stambul*, an urban folk theater developed in Surabaya at the end of the nineteenth century. As komedie stambul traveled from one city to another, kroncong went with it, and was adapted by local musicians. A new style called *langgam Jawa* emerged when kroncong was adapted by central Javanese musicians, influenced by and incorporating the musical idioms of Javanese gamelan. For example, a piece may be preceded by *bawa* (a long vocal introduction to a gamelan piece); the cello is played in the manner of *kendhang ciblon* drumming; and the guitar performs interlocking patterns in the *imbal-imbalan* style of the *bonang*.

So penetrating was the spread of kroncong throughout Java that even the Surakarta court allowed kroncong to be performed as part of court events. *Serat Srikarongron*, written in the early part of the twentieth century, reports the playing of kroncong during rests in the king's hunt in the time of King Paku Buwana X (r. 1893–1939). It is most likely that the kroncong was performed in a boat, as it is related that after the king shot a deer in the water from a boat, he, his family, and his servants were served food and drink.

[They ate] while listening to
the enjoyable sound of violin,

guitar, flute, terbang, and mandolin
[The music] was played softly
by blind and handicapped musicians.
They began to play [a piece] Kembang Kacang,
Preceded by a solo vocal introduction,
The song Megatruh.

Next the song Pinggir Kali [was played],
Then the sound of a kroncong
Song Bintang Surabaya. They rested
briefly; then played again.
Sambul began,
[Sambul] one, two, and three.

The players [while playing their instruments] also sang.
Two of them moved to the front.
Their hands and mouths were working together.
In this way, they had a good time.[13]

How was it possible that kroncong could join the musical repertoire in the court of Surakarta? A partial answer can be found in the history of the incorporation of Western music in Central Javanese courts.

As mentioned earlier, besides church and secular music, military music was another European genre introduced to Indonesia. Music played an integral part in seaborne trading voyages, and the trumpet was one of the most important shipboard instruments, followed by strings and drums, for military and ceremonial purposes.[14] This music was important for the purpose of "ornament and delight" during long-distance voyages: for example, when in 1577 the Drake expedition arrived at Ternate in the Malucas (Maluku), the local ruler was received with the sounds of "our ordinance thundred, which wee mixed with great store of small shot, among which sounding our trumpets and other instruments of musick, both of still and loud noise."[15] Most likely the "still" music came from the sound of string instruments.

As European traders began to settle in Indonesia, European secular and military music became an integral part of Portuguese and Dutch traders' households, mostly performed by their slave musicians (a topic discussed below in the section on tanjidor). As the Dutch collaborated with Javanese rulers in their trading, European music was incorporated in the music of the court.

According to the admittedly scant references from this period, an early Javanese-European musical hybrid emerged in the Mataram court of central Java. A hint of such hybrids can be seen in the late eighteenth-century text *Babad Giyanti*, which describes the accompanying music during a royal procession at the removal of the court capital from Kartasura to Surakarta:

Upon the appearance of the King,
the [Dutch] Company and the Javanese troops
saluted with a loud salvo,
and were answered by the great cannon's
shattering thunder.
The music of trumpets, the drums
suling (flute), *bendhé* (a small hand-gong) together

with the incessant sound of *monggang, kodhok ngorèk,
carabalèn* gamelan, beautifully sounded.
Tumultuous were the people of the capital.[16]

It is most likely that this music was a Javanese-European hybrid form. Other passages confirm it; there is mention of the *musikan kumpeni* (the Dutch Company's military music troop) playing trumpets, drums, flutes, bendhé, and kendhang. Such marching bands, called *music prajuritan* (military music), still exist in the courts of Yogyakarta and Surakarta. One such ensemble consists of European drums, fifes, a pair of Javanese bendhé, and a wind instrument called *puwi-puwi*.[17]

The point here is that by the mid-eighteenth century European music (and European gunfire salutes) had been fully integrated into Javanese court ceremonies.[18] Social events which included Javanese aristocrats and European officials required European tunes to accompany their dances. Waltzes, polkas, quadrilles, and other popular dance tunes were part of the repertoire in the nineteenth- and early twentieth-century courts of central Java.[19] In addition, European clubs were built in the vicinity of the courts; light European music was played at social gatherings of Dutch officials, company managers, and members of the Javanese aristocracy. I have previously discussed the ceremonial role of European music in the life of Central Javanese courts, including the performance of the Dutch national anthem when the king of Surakarta would appear in the court chambers, and the playing of a string ensemble in the court towers every Thursday evening (a religiously auspicious time for the Javanese, an appropriate evening for acquiring blessings from ancestors and gods).[20]

By the early part of the twentieth century kroncong became popular among urban dwellers throughout Indonesia. The language in which the song-texts are sung—bahasa Indonesia, the national language—contributed to this popularity. Kroncong's position in society had changed from its initial association with people of low status in colonial Java to a music admired by all strata of society across Indonesia. Kroncong music captured the hearts of Indonesians regardless of ethnic group, so much so that in the search for national cultural identity it was promoted as a national music form, competing with gamelan.[21] However, as other popular genres like *dangdut* and *campursari* emerged in the 1970s (see chapter 2), the popularity of kroncong began to decline, and is now mostly of historic interest.

Tanjidor and Gendhing Mares

European brass bands were introduced to Java just as they were across the world: as part of European colonization, and they can be seen to represent "the brightly polished expression of a Western sense of beauty and order, and the resounding proof of Western military, religious and cultural superiority."[22] Under the tutelage of European bandmasters, native musicians were taught European musical idioms, scales, tunes, and hymns; however, it was not long before native musicians began to infuse the bands' music with their local musical idioms and meaning.

What did this transformation of brass bands mean to native populations? How did Europeans feel listening to localized forms of their music? John Furnivall, in his study of a pluralistic society in the colonial period, describes how Europeans and natives responded to music that was not their own: "To most Europeans oriental music is unmeaning, and to Orientals, a band of fife and drum is just a noise."[23] But evidence suggests a different, more complex picture than Furnivall's clear polarity.[24] We learn from a court manuscript of *Babad Nitik Mangkunegara* that the court of Mangkunegaran proudly adapted European marching band music, calling it *srageni*.[25] Male and female bands routinely marched to celebrate important court events such as the *tingalan ageng* ("big" or annual birthday celebration) of Mangkunegara I. As the passage below testifies, Javanese spectators admired a procession featuring this European military band.

> Then male *srageni* (marching army)
> followed by female *srageni*
> fired their rifles in the *paringgitan* hall.
> The prince gave them commands.
> In uniform was the female *srageni*, more impressive than the male *srageni*.
> Most astonished were the spectators.
> The drummers and flutist were all female . . .[26]

The admiration of European music by elites was not uncommon in colonial societies. Nepal is a case in point: in line with King Rana and his dynasty's strong admiration of Western culture and its achievements, the court committed itself to forming full-fledged army bands—with great attention paid to uniforms—and eventually boasted seven different bands.[27] In the same spirit, such bands have also been successful in India, Thailand, the Philippines, and throughout Africa. Observing East African *beni ngoma*, competitive dance associations accompanied by European brass bands, Terence Ranger writes: "Beni dancers copied European military and ceremonial uniforms; took pride in their skill at drill; and often put on lavish displays of loyalty to the British Crown . . . both the missionaries and the freed slaves regarded European-style drill and uniforms and above all European-style military music as important symbols of progress towards the desired new life."[28] He is quick to point out, however, that the band in beni ngoma is successful in part because of the compatibility of aspects of band tradition with East Africans' long tradition of competitive dance, manifested in dance associations which possessed "an elaborate hierarchy of ranks, which specialized in dances displaying military skills, and which were vehicles for musical and other innovations."[29] Ranger's discussion of the localization-hybridization process of brass bands in East Africa gives us a useful perspective on the process as it happened in Java.

It is to be expected that the dynamic of hybridity develops differently, in accordance with the socio-political and cultural environment in which it occurs. However, feelings of anxiety and ambivalence are always present. What follows is the discussion of two musical genres that developed in Java during the colonial period, namely tanjidor in the cultural area of Sunda in the vicinity of what is now the capital city of Jakarta, West Java, and gendhing mares in the court of Yogyakarta.[30] In the case of tanjidor, in Sundanizing European music Sundanese musicians produced a very elaborate, lively musical repertoire. In gendhing mares, however, while the incorporation of brass bands resulted in less elaborate music, it had a powerful symbolism that evoked the nuances of power domestication and contestation by the Javanese.

Tanjidor is an Indonesian version of the European brass ensemble. The term tanjidor is said to derive from the Portuguese word *tangedor*, which according to Paramita Abdurachman is derived from the root *tanger*, which means to play on musical instruments.[31] Tangedor itself refers to a musician who plays a string instrument, usually outdoors: it can also refer to a brass band used to accompany military and religious processions. The early form of the tangedor ensemble in Indonesia is not well documented; nor is when, and in what context, tanjidor as we know it today was created. The assumption is that tanjidor traces its origin to the eighteenth century, when leading European households in and around Batavia (now Jakarta) maintained civilian wind ensembles staffed by house-slaves or soldiers.[32] Several authors have mentioned these slave orchestras in their writings.[33] These musicians performed European marches and dance tunes for their masters.

The lifestyle of Augustijn Michiels, who owned a large estate in Citeureup (near Bogor) in the early nineteenth century, gives us evidence of the place of music in the homes of wealthy European landlords.[34] As reported by Doren, who visited Citeureup in 1822, Michiels liked to entertain his guests with lavish parties and performances in a number of different music genres.[35] He had four ensembles in his household, for European music, army marching music, Chinese music, and gamelan.[36] Wall notes that when Michiels died in 1833, his family had to auction thirty slave musicians and their instruments: clarinet players, viola players, trumpeters, harpists, bass horn players, bassoon players, bass players, trombonists, and drummers. These instruments (minus viola and harp) are pretty much the same as those used in contemporary tanjidor, although we do not know if the term tanjidor was already in use at the time.

Evidence from the court of Surakarta testifies that by the 1860s the term "tanjidor" (spelled "tanjidhur") was in use as a generic term for European brass bands. This evidence is mentioned in a piece of sung poetry from the court,

Babad Krama Dalem. Describing the wedding celebration for Paku Buwana IX (r. 1861–93) and the daughter of the Sultan of Yogyakarta, the poet relates that the Dutch offered a toast for the safety of the marriage of the king, followed by repeated boisterous "hurrahs" from the guests: then they all drank, accompanied by the sound of tanjidhur. It remains unknown, however, when this name came into use.

We know that after slavery was abolished in the mid-nineteenth century, native Batavian musicians continued the tanjidor tradition. By the turn of the twentieth century, these bands functioned as street ensembles (*ngamèn*), playing in well-to-do neighborhoods of Jakarta, especially during the Chinese and European New Year celebrations. In the course of its development, tanjidor was employed to accompany various functions in villages on the outskirts of Jakarta, and the repertoires of Sundanese (including *jaipongan*) and Batavian music genres (*lenong, melayu*, dangdut, and *gambang kromong*) became the standard repertoire of the bands. The cultural space in which tanjidor is performed determines which repertoire is expected by the audience.[37] In the eastern part of Jakarta—the border between Sundanese and Betawi culture—the repertoire includes traditional Sundanese songs, while in the western part of the island Betawi song is featured. Interestingly, tanjidor musicians considered European marches and waltzes to be the signature pieces of the genre; they are played as overtures, regardless of the context of the performance.[38]

In the 1950s, tanjidor experienced a setback. Ngamèn were banned by the local government because the mayor of Jakarta was displeased to see native Betawi musicians perceived as beggars by wealthy Chinese (usually the owner of stores and restaurants) to whom they performed.[39] Abdurachman argues that the ban was imposed because the loud music disturbed people from their afternoon rest.[40] Eventually, the ban was relaxed, although musicians had to seek a letter of permission from the government. This rule caused the continuing marginalization of tanjidor.

The main instruments of tanjidor are clarinet, trumpet, trombone, helicon (tuba) or bass horn, snare and bass drum, and cymbals.[41] According to the demands of the repertoire, traditional Indonesian or Chinese instruments are also added to the band. To perform Sundanese repertoire, *kulantèr, kethuk, kecrèk, angkok*, and gong are added. *Tehian* is added when performing Chinese-influenced *gambang kromong* music.

When a tanjidor performs Sundanese music, the clarinet plays the main melody in the style of Sundanese vocals, *rebab*, or *terompèt*, while the brass instruments (trombone, bass horn or helicon) play material with no definite correlation to idiomatic Sundanese music. The snare and bass drums are played with bare hands in the manner of Sundanese drumming, and the *kenong* (a small hanging gong), *gong angkog* (a low-pitched keyed gong), and kecrèk (two metal plates played with a mallet) have traditional Sundanese functions, marking and accentuating the musical cycle. Tanjidor musicians have created a European brass ensemble that plays in the flamboyant and lively style of Sundanese music.

Unlike tanjidor, gendhing mares was cultivated in the highest social circles at the court of Yogyakarta. Before discussing gendhing mares in detail, it is useful to remember the extent to which European culture penetrated the musical life of eighteenth- and nineteenth-century Javanese courts. European brass bands were introduced to symbolize European military power, and subsequently became an integral part of musical life in the Javanese courts, accompanying many types of ceremonies. Like tanjidor, the bands accompanied European social dances in addition to their military functions. For this reason, Javanese courts had to maintain ensembles, which consisted of Javanese musicians under the tutelage of European bandmasters. Although Javanese gamelan and European bands were often housed under the same roof, and played in juxtaposition or simultaneously, the two musical systems seemed reluctant to hybridize, except in notable cases such as gendhing mares.[42]

The term "gendhing mares" refers to a group of gamelan compositions (*gendhing*), the performance of which requires the incorporation of European brass instruments, side drums, and cymbals into the gamelan ensemble. "*Mares*" is derived from the Dutch "*mars*" (march): during the Japanese occupation (1942–45), perhaps because the use of Dutch was suppressed, the Javanese word "*gati*" (hasty) replaced "mares."[43] The thirty or so gendhing mares all use the *pélog* tuning system, presumably because it is closest to the Western diatonic system.[44]

The origin of gendhing mares is not well documented. Court musicians and dancers have different opinions regarding its creation: a court dancer and musician, Pustakamardawa, told Roger Vetter that the tradition of playing gendhing mares started during the reign of Hamengku Buwana (HB) V, who reigned from 1825–55.[45] Musicians interviewed by Subuh identified HB VII (r. 1877–1921) or HB VIII (r. 1921–39) as the creator of gendhing mares. The same musicians also point out that the term "mares" was used only during the reign of HB VIII, replacing the previous term "*sabrangan*" (foreign) which referred to the same type of pieces.[46]

The most compelling evidence for the origins of gendhing mares can be found in a court manuscript called *Serat Pakem Wirama* (henceforth, *Pakem Wirama*), begun in 1889, and completed in 1921. It lists thirty-some pieces, and the term gendhing mares is used. However, *Pakem Wirama* was written over the span of several decades as a kind of anthology of gendhing, wherein each manuscript is rewritten and new gendhing added. In other words, each subsequent copy is not meant to be a reproduction of the original manuscript.[47] The manuscript does not specify the year when gendhing mares were composed. In any event, it is safe to say that the genre emerged in the late nineteenth or early twentieth century.

Figure 1.1. Javanese musicians playing trumpets and snare drum in the performance of gendhing mares. Photograph by Alex Dea.

One of the reasons for the creation of gendhing mares was for the Yogyakarta court to establish a distinctive musical style and identity from that of its competitor at Surakarta. It is true that in the court of Surakarta, like in Yogyakarta, European music also became an integral part of court ceremonial events, but the Surakarta court never went beyond the custom of having European music and gamelan in separate spaces, each ensemble playing their own pieces.

The function of gendhing mares is to accompany the entrance and exit of refined female *bedhaya* and *serimpi* dancers. These two ceremonial dance genres epitomize the concept of refinement (*alus*), a hallmark of Javanese behavior contained and revealed in the inner realm (*batin*) and external action (*lahir*) of human experience.[48] Besides symbolizing the concept of alus, the bedhaya dances were also considered an emblem of the ruler's power.

If we believe that the gamelan ensemble is "endowed with a special aura that forged the link to figures of authority,"[49] and that bedhaya and serimpi represent the concept of alus (a hallmark of the Javanese world view), how do we explain the incorporation of European sound into the gamelan ensemble? Is this a kind of European-Javanese intercultural sonic dialogue, a subversive act of European authority, or a domestication of exotic sound? The following section attempts to address these questions.

Some incompatible musical elements (linear versus horizontal orientation, a cyclic versus a through-composed structure, and the particularities of the *sléndro-pélog* tuning system) seem to keep gamelan and European music apart. However, the evidence provided by tanjidor and gendhing mares reveals that the compatibility (or incompatibility) of musical systems should be discussed in conjunction with their socio-political and cultural circumstances.

Tanjidor has passed through many different socio-historical contexts, from the eighteenth-century slave orchestra to Betawi music of the early twentieth century; from entertainment for wealthy masters to military music, street music, and finally music accompanying rites of passage; and from colonial to postcolonial times. Throughout these evolutions, tanjidor was cultivated and developed by members of the lower class (slaves and native Betawi folk musicians). It is not known what the slaves playing European music for their masters felt, but the fact that slaves were known for their musical accomplishment suggests that the music helped serve the emotional needs of their difficult lives, in addition to providing for their masters' need for entertainment. However, the band in this context did not symbolize progress toward a better life for the slaves, as it did in the case of the aforementioned beni ngoma in East Africa. Rather tanjidor fulfilled the needs of both the slaves and their masters. Perhaps the slave musicians were well taken care of because of their special ability to provide private musical pleasures; yet the band and its musicians were still the master's personal property. The music was performed only in the closed world of traders and landowners, comparable to that of King Rana's band in Nepal.[50] When the genre evolved into urban folk music in the twentieth century, the musicians lost this patronage.

The suppleness of tanjidor is commensurate with the character of folk music generally. Folk musicians are both executive and creative artists in the true sense of the words—they have the flexibility to execute a piece of music in any way possible, limited by their creativity. By looking at two repeated cycles of a piece, we see the different ways in which the clarinet, helicon, and bass horn render the same melodic phrase by adding passing notes, lengthening principal notes, and altering rhythms. In addition, the singer and solo melodic instrument (rebab, trumpet, or clarinet) help to define this lively genre by shifting from one tuning system to another (from sléndro to a pélog-like system). Elaborate drumming, which accompanies animated dance movements, adds to the musical liveliness of tanjidor. The clarinet, drum, and even at times the kecrèk, interact, exchanging and imitating each others' rhythms. Tanjidor often accompanies male dance parties, in which male guests take turns dancing with professional female dancers.

In gendhing mares, we find a more limited contribution to the gamelan from European brass instruments and drums. The reason for this lies in the choice of the treatment (*garap*) of the piece. Sundanese and Javanese court gamelan compositions comprise several layers of melodic lines within a fixed formal structure (a *gongan* cycle). What is distinctive about Javanese court gamelan is the prominent presentation of a steady, pulsed melodic skeleton (*balungan*) of the gendhing by a group of several *saron* (metallophones of various octaves). The presentation of the balungan is very strong indeed, as the melodic skeleton is performed in unison by at least seven, and as many as sixteen, saron (a typical court gamelan ensemble has one *slenthem*, two *demung*, and four *saron barung*).

Another factor determining whether a piece (or sections of a piece) should be performed in a soft or loud style is the concept of *irama*. The irama involves the shifting of both temporal flow (fast, medium, and slow) and temporal space (the expanding and contracting of the gongan cycle). A change in irama involves the slowing down or speeding up of the basic pulse (played by all of the saron), accompanied by an increase or decrease in the density of certain instruments in relation to the basic pulse.[51] There are four irama: *tanggung*, *dadi*, *wilet*, and *rangkep*, representing gong cycles from small to large, respectively. Each irama determines both the playing style and the treatment of the melody for elaborating instruments, namely whether a piece should be played in the soft or loud style.[52] Gendhing mares is played in irama tanggung, in a loud playing style, featuring the balungan instruments and without the participation of soft-sounding, elaborating instruments. One consequence of irama tanggung is that it constrains the melodic treatment of a gendhing: the absence of instruments playing elaborated forms of melodies does not allow the ensemble to project musical complexity.

It is intriguing that gendhing mares was born at a time when conflict between Javanese courts and the European colonial government reached its peak, in the mid nineteenth to early twentieth century. This is the period when, after much European interference in the state affairs of Javanese courts, and especially after the Javanese revolt in 1825–30, true colonialism was established: "For the first time the Dutch were in a position to exploit and control the whole island, and there was not to be any serious challenge to their dominance until the twentieth century."[53] During this period, the dependence of Javanese rulers on the Dutch government was so unbearable that Ronggowarsito, the well-known *pujangga* (court poet), felt compelled to write a poem called "Kalatidha" (A Time of Darkness), describing the feelings of hopelessness caused by the impotence of his court.[54]

What was the reaction of Javanese royal culture toward the consolidation of colonial control? One interpretation is that, faced with political impotency, members of the royal family focused their energies inward, cultivating and refining art and culture. In the words of Merle Calvin Ricklefs, the central Javanese courts "became ritual establishments and generally docile clients of the Dutch."[55] This position, however, ignores evidence of the dynamics of court culture during the domestication of non-Javanese elements. In my previous study of this topic I concluded that

> nineteenth-century Javanese court culture should be viewed not only as the consequence of an "inward focus" of court activity, but also as an "outward

expression" of court attempts to accommodate the diversity of society. More importantly, the development of Javanese culture should be understood as the result of complex interactions in the multi-class and multi-ethnic population of Java: Javanese (aristocrats and common folk), Dutch, Indos, and Chinese. Such interactions involved competing and conflicting models of culture, religion, and ideology. The heterogenous court culture was the result of a cultural consensus between the colonizers and their Javanese subjects.[56]

The reaction of Javanese courtiers to the penetration of colonial culture was to reestablish a well-ordered cultural landscape by ritually situating the Dutch not as intruders, but as respected guests in the country's domicile.[57] Gendhing mares and other Javanese-European cultural hybrids were the products of this domestication. The fact that gendhing mares was created to accompany one of the most important royal cultural practices, the serimpi dance, proves its powerful symbolic significance.

What has emerged from the discussion of these two hybrid musical forms is the heterogeneous nature of the localization and hybridization process. The process involves regional history, power relationships, and the attitudes of the musicians as shaped by historical and cultural circumstances. Often, this locally and historically constructed hybrid music persists as a marker of a regional identity. Even during the period of the Indonesian independence movement, the music lived on as a legacy and marker of distinctive features of a particular locale. Today, tanjidor is still performed, albeit rarely. The marginalization of the bands mentioned earlier caused the loss of their stable patronage, and competition with other forms of urban folk and popular music, with appeal reaching beyond the city of Jakarta, contributed to the decline. In spite of this marginalization, however, tanjidor is considered a distinctive musical form of Jakartan music, a historic Indonesian-European hybrid that was created and developed in the vicinity of the city. The local government is trying to revitalize the life of the bands by holding symposia and workshops and presenting awards to older tanjidor musicians. It remains to be seen in what way tanjidor will survive.

Today's royal family of the Yogyakarta court only occasionally sponsors the performance of serimpi dance to the accompaniment of gendhing mares. Recently, a notable use of gendhing mares emerged in a project to reconstruct the most sacred ceremonial dance of a long-defunct, four-hour *bedhaya Semang*. This dance and its counterpart, the *bedhaya Ketawang* in the court of Surakarta, are considered the most sacred dances in their respective courts, the ruler's emblem of power. Its connection with the story of the most powerful spiritual entity, the goddess of the southern ocean (Ratu Kidul), gives this bedhaya its special status.[58] The story goes that in preparation for becoming a king, Sultan Agung had to familiarize himself with the true scope of his realm, including Ratu Kidul, the goddess of spiritual beings, dangerous and powerful.[59] The young Agung accompanied the goddess to her beautiful palace beneath the southern ocean, where bedhaya Semang was created for him.

Bedhaya Semang has not been performed since the second half of the reign of Hamengku Buwana VII (1877–1921). In 1972 the court wanted to reconstruct the dance, but this failed to materialize because the necessary resources were not available. Theresia Suharti, then a student at the Indonesian Art Institution (ISI) in Yogyakarta and also a court dancer, used this reconstruction attempt as material for her thesis. Suharti became a faculty member of ISI and a senior teacher and dancer of the court, and in 2002 she decided to continue the reconstruction. Under the supervision of an older court dancer and teacher, Bandara Raden Ayu Yudanegara, she led the project, gathering old documents about the dance and its music, organizing and leading rehearsals, and securing financial support from different agencies and individuals. She also wrote an article about the reconstruction process.[60] The reconstruction was completed in 2006, and performed before the present Sultan HB XII and his families, fully documented in audio and video format. As far as I know, there have not been any further performances of this dance since then.

In the course of the reconstruction, questions about musical accompaniment for the entrance and exit of the dancers surfaced.[61] Should they be accompanied by a refined *ladrang* piece or by gendhing mares? The refined ladrang piece was suggested by the musicians and dance teachers; gendhing mares was the preference of a high-ranking courtier. Eventually the dance teachers and musicians had to accept the decision made by the courtier, so gendhing mares accompanied the entrance and exit of the dancers in the performance for the Sultan. However, during the rehearsals a refined ladrang piece was often used. The high-ranking courtier in question was a young prince who preferred gendhing mares because of its *sigrak* (lively) character. Aside from the distinctive feature of gendhing mares as a historic Javanese-European hybrid music, the assumption here is that the choice of gendhing mares to accompany bedhaya Semang can be linked to contemporary trends of gamelan in Yogyakarta and Indonesia. As I discuss in chapter 2, the assumption here is that this ideology of hybridizing traditional music with Western music in contemporary Indonesia influenced the decision to use gendhing mares in the reconstructed bedhaya Semang.

To recapitulate: in discussing the Hinduization of Southeast Asia, O. W. Wolters states that "Indian materials tended to be fractured and restated and therefore drained of their original significance ... The materials ... had to be localized in different ways before they could fit into various local complexes or religious, social, and political systems and belong to [a] new cultural 'whole.' Only when this happened would the fragments make sense in their new ambiences."[62] The localization process referred to by Wolters can be found in any historical period, but in each region (or even within a region) the process bears quite different results. In the case of tanjidor, a Western brass ensemble was localized to the extent to which the European music became Sundanese music. Gendhing mares played out differently: the Javanese did not substantively localize European music, but the end result is symbolically very rich. The development of these cultural performances was interdependent with the life of European traders (for tanjidor), central Javanese courtiers (for gendhing mares), and colonialism.

Tanjidor and kroncong (less so gendhing mares) are forms of what Sarah Weiss (following Mikhail Bhaktin's work) calls "natural" hybrid production.[63] This process involves a long period of coexistence of two or more genres before a new genre emerges, performed by more than one person or group.[64] A hybrid genre can be said to have become "natural" in this way when listeners no longer think about the elements that compose it.[65]

It is always important to take note of the feelings of anxiety and ambivalence associated with hybridization. As the discussion in the following chapter will show, localizing and hybridizing Western elements in twentieth-century Javanese performing arts are no exception.

Chapter Two

Performing the Nation-State

A 1996 newspaper headline in Surabaya proudly proclaimed the unveiling of a new statue in the Javanese city's harbor: "Monjaya, the second largest after [the statue of Liberty]."[1] The inauguration ceremony for the monument—a thirty-meter-high figure of a navy colonel in dress uniform posed atop a twenty-nine-meter-high base—was marked by the sounding of the world's largest gong, named *Kyai Tentrem* (The venerable sir tranquility). Five meters in diameter, with a one-meter-wide center knob, and weighing 2.4 tons, the gong had to be cut into three pieces for transport and welded back together upon arrival at its permanent location. In fact, the gong was so large that the Indonesian president did not actually strike it during the ceremony (perhaps for the president to pick up such a large mallet to strike the gong would be ceremoniously unsuitable); instead, he struck a smaller replica, leaving the original to be struck later by a navy commander.

This account of the Statue of Liberty-like Monjaya statue and the five-meter gong inspired in me further thought about the cultural interaction between Indonesia (particularly Java) and the West. Current East-West interactions tend to bring about the production of spectacular cultural expression: the Monjaya monument is but one example. The seventy-meter-high Garuda statue in Bali, which has been compared to the Eiffel Tower in terms of height and visual impact, is another. Spectacular cultural expressions—be they monuments, gigantic gongs, or skyscrapers—are obvious representations of Asian-Western cultural hybridity. But what has this phenomenon to do with music? I would like to suggest that—the symbolically powerful *Kyai Tentrem* gong aside—there are examples of hybrid musical presentations whose formulations, forms, and contexts are comparable to the above-mentioned cultural expressions. Like these monuments, the performing arts are metaphorical or allegorical representations of society, and it is therefore imperative to view music or musical events in terms of their performance contexts, their sociopolitical and technological character, and their historical backgrounds.[2]

We learned in the previous chapter that in nineteenth-century colonial Java, exposure to European popular music was limited to the circles of aristocratic families and European communities of officials and traders. By the early part of the twentieth century the circumstances had changed: films, radio, and the phonograph widened the dissemination of Western popular genres. In the mid-twentieth century, the world was flooded with American popular culture, expedited by the development of the cassette tape in the 1970s. Subsequently, new forms of Western-based Indonesian popular music emerged.

The spread of Western popular music was temporarily halted during the Sukarno regime, which was known for its anti-Western cultural sentiment. Imported Western popular music and its Indonesianized versions were officially banned, and members of the pop music group Koes Bersaudara were even detained.[3]

In spite of this development, other genres of Indonesianized Western music, such as patriotic songs, continued to be fostered. These songs, including the national anthem (composed in 1928), were created as an expression of national fervor in the spirit of revolution and independence. With lyrics in the Indonesian language, the songs evoke a sense of unity, a sense of "one place, one nation, and one language," a powerful aspiration born during the period of the rise of nationalism. Even if not all Indonesians speak the Indonesian language, singing these songs creates an experience of simultaneity, providing occasions for the physical realization of the imagined national unity.[4]

The banning of Western popular culture changed after the Sukarno government was toppled in 1967 by a new regime under the command of army general Suharto. Sukarno's downfall was allegedly caused by a thwarted communist coup d'état.[5] The abortive coup began with the killing of six army generals by a group of military officers from the airforce, who were later was linked to members of the Communist Party by a certain faction of army led by general Suharto. This series of events led to bloody conflicts throughout Indonesia aimed at exterminating the communists and their allies.

In place of Sukarno's left-wing ideology arose Suharto's "New Order" (Orde Baru), referring to Sukarno's era as the "Old Order" (Orde Lama). During the 1970s, the New Order relaxed and eventually lifted the ban on Western popular culture, which consequently flooded Indonesia. Indonesian popular music was reinvigorated, and new and varied popular genres emerged, sharing the use of the Indonesian language in their lyrics. Only occasionally did regional genres of *musik pop* arise with lyrics in a local language.

Dangdut and Campursari

The penetration of Western popular music in the late 1960s and early 1970s brought about the development of new hybrid musical forms. One of them, *dangdut*, is a fusion of Western rock and Indian film music. The latter was introduced to Indonesia through Indian movies and live performances by local ensembles, such as the *orkes melayu* in north Sumatra.[6] First developed in the late nineteenth century, orkes melayu is itself a form of hybrid popular music. Its instrumentation consists of voice, violin, a large circular drum (*gendang melayu*), and gong. In the 1930s, the gong was dropped and the harmonium was added, later replaced by the accordion. After the penetration of Western music, the ensemble expanded to include (optionally) guitars, saxophone, piano, etc.

In his recent work, Andrew Weintraub provides a thorough account of the Melayu connection with the development of dangdut.[7] He contextualizes dangdut in terms of a dialogue among the Melayu, Indian, Arab, and European cultures, which began in the late nineteenth century in the cities of Jakarta (Batavia) and Surabaya. Traveling orchestras accompanying theatrical productions of *stambul, bangsawan,* and *opera* made this dialogue possible, as all sorts of music genres presented in the productions—Melayu, Chinese, Indian, Middle Eastern, and European music—intermingled. The dialogue continued throughout the twentieth century, resulting in the emergence of the hybrid music of dangdut in the 1970s.

The instrumentation of dangdut is electric lead guitar, electric keyboard, and rhythm and bass guitars, but also includes the flute, tambourine, and north Indian *tabla* (which is sometimes substituted for by a bongo-like drum). The name dangdut is the onomatopoetic realization of the drum rhythm: a repetitive "*dang-doot*" sound, with "*dang*" falling on the off-beats and "*doot*" on the beats. Peter Manuel identifies this rhythm with the north Indian *kaherva*, the most popular rhythm in Indian film music.[8]

The lyrics of dangdut songs are usually concerned with love and dancing, but in the 1970s lyrics concerning Islamic religious precepts also became popular. The chief proponent of this trend was singer Rhoma Irama, known as the "king of dangdut." In addition to being a popular music genre, the Islamic message of dangdut lyrics has allowed it to reach all levels of Indonesian society, and the production of dangdut films starring Rhoma Irama has only increased its popularity. Writing in 1988, Manuel states:

> Dangdut, then, represents much more than a musical style; it is a major sociocultural phenomenon, involving cinema, fashion, youth culture, Islamic resurgence, and populism as well as the capitalist entertainment industry. As such it has been the subject of much controversy in Indonesia. Articulate supporters assert that its egalitarianism and inherent vitality impart to it a unique ability to respond to mass tastes and needs, and that its didacticism constitutes a healthy moral influence. Meanwhile, progressive critics denounce its commercialism, and elitist detractors dismiss it as *kampung* trash.[9]

The conflict and controversy he describes persist. The popularity of an East Javanese dangdut singer, Inul Daratista in 2003, famous for her highly eroticized movements called *ngebor* ("drilling," conjuring a sexual image) and performance of "pole dances," in imitation of dancers' movements in strip clubs, heightened the controversy.[10] Conservative Muslims and other

Indonesian traditionalists see eroticized movements as highly inappropriate, but some (including former President Abdulrachman Wahid) argue that—in an Indonesia trying to strengthen its democracy—Inul has the right to use ngebor in her performances. Politics, religion, and culture all enter into the debate.

The context and place of dangdut in society has evolved through different stages, as Weintraub explains: "Denigrated as a debased form of popular culture in the early 1970s, dangdut was commercialized in the 1980s, resignified as a form of national and global pop in the 1990s, and localized within ethnic communities in the 2000s.[11] Dangdut is often incorporated in contemporary wayang performance, which I will discuss later.

In the context of the popularity of dangdut, a new Java-Western musical hybrid called campursari (a mix of essences) was born. A mixture of gamelan and Western instruments, a campursari ensemble performs pieces from the kroncong and dangdut, and light pieces from gamelan repertoires. Like kroncong, a solo singer is the feature of campursari, with electronic keyboard as the lead and obligatory instrument, providing melodic and harmonic accompaniment. A variable assortment of Western instruments (such as violin, flute, bass guitar, and drum set) and gamelan instruments (such as kendhang, gendèr, demung, saron, and gong) complete the campursari ensemble.

There has been a great deal of discussion about campursari, seeking to understand the genre's domination of Javanese musical life. The debate often intensifies in light of noticeable musical conflicts in the genre, especially an incompatibility between a Western diatonic-based pentatonic scale and a pentatonic gamelan tuning system. Although a few campursari groups tune their gamelan to match a diatonic Western scale, others are not concerned with this tuning incompatibility, which results in instruments and singers not being in tune with each other. Jan Mrázek suggests that this incompatibility, together with other factors, is a kind of metaphor for conflict in the world, especially central Java.[12] Concurring with this line of thought, Rahayu Supanggah sees the "clashes" in campursari as reflecting larger socio-cultural problems caused by modernization, a clash between humanitarian and cultural values, and more significantly a crisis of values resulting from diminished adherence to norms, rules, and laws.[13]

It is interesting that, unlike gamelan theorists and traditional-minded gamelan musicians, fans of campursari do not mind this musical conflict—they listen to the music in a peculiar way. In the words of Mrázek, many people "listen to gamelan instruments and techniques, and they listen to the keyboard and other non-gamelan instruments at the same time, but not to their not-being-in-tune. They try to ignore the wholeness of the whole, because the whole lacks wholeness. The result is a kind of selective listening, listening that separates and often does not put things together, but rather keeps them separate, and enjoys them separately, though at the same time."[14]

Marc Perlman has a different interpretation: "Campursari may prove to have little to do with tuning systems. Campursari may be more interesting as a symptom of the emergence of a broad musical borderland, where the lightest parts of the gamelan repertory mingle with kroncong, *langgam Jawa*, dangdut, and even Indonesian pop songs."[15]

Certainly this focus on light, popular pieces is the primary reason for the widespread popularity of campursari, so much so that the conflict in tuning systems is largely ignored by its fans. Sutton observes that to younger musicians, campursari is a means of preserving Javanese gamelan tradition, since by incorporating gamelan into modern or popular styles, younger audiences will enjoy this music. "Better a compromised Javanese music than none at all, perhaps."[16] But Sutton's older gamelan teachers and acquaintances disagree. Campursari "is as great a threat to the gamelan tradition they know as is Western-style pop music, for campusari emphasizes a pop, commercial ethos and takes the place of more traditional gamelan playing (of much higher artistic value, they would say) in village and family rituals, not to mention in the regional cassette industry. Thus ... *campursari* does popularize some aspects of the indigenous, but at the same time severely compromises the indigenous tradition on which it draws."[17]

As related above, Supanggah sees the problem of campursari in terms of "clashes" or "collisions" of all musical elements, including audience behavior, musicians' costumes, instrumentation, tuning, composition, genre, playing style, musical concepts, and language usage. He wonders why campursari artists, audience, listeners, and sponsors have no problem with the "clashes." "The *campur sari* community accepts the music openly, and with pleasure and sincerity. They consider that everything happens naturally. Some people recognize that *campur sari* is a work of art, product of creativity of a group of artists. *Campur sari* can also be considered as a collective attempt to save one or more musical genres. Without (the help of) *campur sari*, it is believed that one of the above musical genres could die out."[18]

Elsewhere, Supanggah explains that the long history of Java has been responsible for the production of highly developed Javanese arts, such as gamelan, which have over time passed through natural and strict selection.[19] Consequently, "these arts have crystallized, and therefore carry socio-cultural and historic values and possess a high esthetic quality."[20]

Members of the younger generation, especially urban dwellers, do not necessarily share Supanggah's perspective: they think that gamelan is old-fashioned, irrelevant to the modern world. What is clear is that the mixture of traditional gamelan and non-gamelan music (in particular Western music) has been popular among this younger generation. By mixing with "international" music, gamelan no longer is outdated—it becomes modern. Campursari, some repertoires presented at the Yogyakarta Gamelan Festival and contemporary wayang performance (discussed below) are all popular genres which mix gamelan and Western music.

In the last two decades, campursari has experienced astonishing development, earning fame from live performances in a wide variety of contexts. Campursari is also a mass-mediated music, widely disseminated on cassette, CD, and DVD. There have been many campursari festivals and competitions at the regional and national levels, and regional television programs periodically broadcast campursari in the form of a *manasuka*, a musical program that takes musical requests from audience members and home viewers. These all generate wealth for its producers, success which has created resentment among traditional gamelan players, who complain that with investment in only a few instruments and a repertoire of light pieces, campursari leads to easy wealth and fame. Once I heard a traditional gamelan musician asked whether he liked campursari. Pretending to not quite hear the question, he replied: "What did you say, *campur tahi?*" ("tahi" means "excrement").

One factor in the success of campursari involves the notion of "modernization." The mixing of gamelan with electric keyboards and other modern Western instruments may, in reality or symbolically, be seen as a way to modernize gamelan and make it part of "international" (Western) music. The people of Gunung Kidul (a village in the southern province of Yogyakarta considered the birthplace of campursari) sum it up, as related by Nancy Cooper, by asserting that "'we [the people in Gunung Kidul] may not be urban, but we have the best of both worlds' [Indonesia and the West]."[21] It is this fleshing out of modernity that has made campursari such a success.

Contemporary Wayang Performance

Western instruments have not just been used in campursari; for decades now, they—notably drums and cymbals—have been incorporated into wayang performance. Musically, these instruments have been an insignificant addition to the gamelan: the drum and cymbals do little more than help the kendhang and *kepyak* (a set of metal plates beaten by the dhalang's foot) to accentuate puppet movements. In some recent performances, however, other non-wayang and non-gamelan elements have been added into certain scenes, especially the humorous scene in the first plot division (*Limbukan*) and the midnight clown scene. As a point of departure, it is necessary to provide a brief background of wayang plot structure (*lakon*) and to explain a few points about wayang aesthetics.[22]

Wayang, specifically *wayang kulit* (kulit means leather), refers to a shadow puppet play. An all-night wayang performance is divided into three major sections. Each section is named after one of the three musical modes (*pathet*) of the gamelan: (1) Nem, (2) Sanga, and (3) Manyura. The Javanese believe that the three plot divisions represent the three stages of human life: youth, middle age, and old age. Each division consists of several scenes: below is the sequence of scenes in the first plot division.

Jejer (the first scene). Commonly, this setting is a formal court audience, but it can be a heavenly kingdom. Accompanied by a *gendhing* (gamelan composition), the scene begins with the removal of the *kayon* (a puppet representing the tree of life),[23] signaling the beginning of the play, followed by the entrance and arrangement of puppets on the screen, a narration, *sulukan* songs, and a dialogue.

Tamu (guest), the scene of the arriving guest. The scene begins with a sulukan song and narration, followed by the entrance of a puppet, a narration, another sulukan song, and a dialogue.

Bedholan (from *bedhol*, to pull out) ends the *Jejer*, and consists of the removal of puppets, accompanied by a gendhing.

Gapuran (from *gapura*, gate). Following the *bedholan*, the *gapuran* shows a king admiring the beauty of a palace-gate (an entrance to the inner palace). It consists of the king, accompanied by ladies-in-waiting, pausing in front of the gate (represented by the kayon), a narration, and the king's exit.

Kedhatonan (inner-palace scene). This portrays the queen waiting for and greeting the king. Accompanied by a gendhing, this scene consists of the entrance of the queen and ladies-in-waiting, a narration, the queen greeting the king, a sulukan song, a dialogue between the king and queen, and another sulukan song accompanying their exit.

Paseban Jawi (outer hall). This scene takes place in the palace's outer hall, where an army leader or leaders and soldiers assemble. It consists of the entrance and arrangement of puppets, a narration, a sulukan song, a dialogue, and a series of sulukan.

Budhalan (from *budhal*, departure). The departure of the army. Soldiers on horseback, dancing to various rhythmic patterns, are featured in this scene.

Sabrangan (overseas kingdom). This scene portrays an antagonistic overseas kingdom, typically ruled by giants. Accompanied by a gendhing, it begins with the removal of the kayon, the entrance of puppets, a narration, a sulukan song, and a dialogue.

Paseban Jawi, the scene of the outer hall. Accompanied by a *srepegan*, a piece composed in a compact rhythmic structure, for the entrance and exit of the puppet(s), it consists of the entrance, a sulukan song, a dialogue, and a dispersal of the assembly.

Budhalan, another scene showing the army's departure.

Perang Gagal (skirmishes). An inconclusive battle between two armies.

If a dhalang must adjust the length of his performance,[24] he might expand, shorten, or eliminate one or more scenes, *janturan* (narration), or dialogue. In the first plot division, for example, the guest scene, gate scene, or inner-palace scene can be eliminated. The guest scene is presented only when required by the story, and can also be integrated into the first scene. While adjusting to time constraints, the dhalang can perform or eliminate the gate scene, and can eliminate or expand the inner-palace scene.

As I have mentioned elsewhere, wayang is a form of dramatic art. However, other arts—music, dance, literature, and visual arts—are essential parts of a wayang performance.[25] The presence of these other arts produces effects that are peripheral to the story, but essential to wayang; I call these "ornamentations of the dramatic action." These ornamentations often draw the listeners' attention away from the story; the key to understanding and appreciating wayang performance lies in the interplay between the drama and its ornamentations.

To illustrate, let us consider the gate scene. After departing from the palace assembly, the king pauses in front of the palace gate. Accompanied by the soft-sounding (*sirepan*) *Ayak-Ayakan Panjang Mas*,[26] the dhalang delivers a narration in stylized prose describing the beauty of the palace gate, the king's attire, and the landscape of the palace. On the screen, spectators see the puppets in *tanceban* (stationary position)[27]—the king stands with ladies-in-waiting behind him, and the kayon (a tree figure) in front of him represents the palace gate. Because the puppets remain stationary, the gate scene offers spectators the opportunity to appreciate the craftsmanship of the puppets; the composition of the puppets arranged on the screen is even admired as visual art.[28] The juxtaposition of visual presentation, soft music, and the stylized language of the dhalang's narration emphasize pure aesthetics while the story itself recedes into the background. The sequential clarity of the plot becomes ambiguous as the relation between one scene and another is often "disturbed" by ornamentation.

A traditional dhalang tries to maintain balance among the scenes, in terms of both duration and content, and in so doing fosters the performance's inherent wholeness.[29] Evidence from performances in the 1960s supports this point, notably a recording I studied of a well-known dhalang, the late Ki Poedjosoemarto (as I mentioned in the Introduction, he was President Sukarno's favorite dhalang). In this recording, sponsored and broadcast by Radio of the Republic of Indonesia (RRI) in Jakarta, he distributed the duration of each of the scenes as follows: *Jejer* is one hour, with a five-minute gapuran scene; *Kedhatonan* is thirty-two minutes; *Paseban Jawi* is thirty-five minutes; and *Sabrangan* is thirty-four minutes.

It would be considered out of the norm for a traditional dhalang to present one scene much longer than the others, but in contemporary wayang this does occur. In the first place, the gapuran scene is rarely performed in contemporary wayang. Instead, an optional subscene in the inner-palace scene, commonly called Limbukan, is featured; not all traditional dhalang during the time of Poedjosoemarto delivered this scene, and Poedjosoemarto does not present it in his above-mentioned performance. But in contemporary wayang, the Limbukan is a must. This scene and a midnight subscene called *gara-gara* involve the appearance of clowns: humorous dialogue and light musical pieces distinguish these scenes from the others. Limbukan and gara-gara are presented for a much longer duration than the other scenes.[30]

The inner-palace scene is the second in the first plot division, and depicts the queen and her entourage in the inner court, awaiting the arrival of the king. Upon his arrival, the king has a conversation with the queen about the main purpose of his court assembly, after which they enter the inner palace. A narration by the dhalang follows, describing the king at a feast with his family, and then entering a chamber to meditate. In the meantime, two female clowns, a slender Cangik and her fat daughter Limbuk, have a lengthy and humorous conversation on topics that relate only minimally, if at all, to the story at hand. It is this conversation that dominates the inner-palace scene. In addition, requests from the audience to the musicians and singers, through letters that have been given to the dhalang, expand the length of this subscene to two or even three times the duration of other scenes.

Other humorous dialogue and requests for light pieces appear in garagara, the scene at the beginning of the second plot division, which portrays the world in turmoil. The turmoil is conveyed only through narration, and is represented by the dhalang's animated shaking of the tree of life. To stifle the turmoil, the clowns entertain themselves with jokes and songs. The narration of gara-gara is delivered to the accompaniment of the steady beat of *dhodhogan* (the sound of the wooden chest which holds the puppets as it is tapped with a mallet by the dhalang) or kepyakan (the sound of hung metal plates as they are kicked by the dhalang's foot) and soft musical accompaniment on gendèr. Here is an excerpt of a gara-gara narration that I translated, and sometimes use it when I, as dhalang, perform wayang performance at Wesleyan and elsewhere in the United States:

> The world erupts! The earth shakes; volcanoes spew out fire. The oceans' waters boil, and tidal waves engulf the land. Earthquakes and volcanoes rumble like the breaking news of the day. The world is as dark as a dust-clouded night. Lightning streaks; dragons roar. The violence reaches up to the gods themselves, breaking the horn of the sacred cow Andini, snapping Anantaboga's dragon-tail, cracking open the gates of heaven. Boiling mud and molten lava are vomited from the cauldron of hell. The world is out of joint, thrown out of balance by the force of a mighty prince in search of enlightenment (my translation, with the help of Prof. Ron Jenkin of Wesleyan University).

Humorous presentations by a set of clowns (the prince's companion Semar and his sons Gareng, Pétruk, and Bagong) dominate this scene. Like Limbukan in the inner-palace scene, the clowns converse about current and local topics, and musical interludes are featured; these sections function as "intermezzi." Many dhalang and cultural commentators debate the extent to which local issues and musical interludes should be incorporated into wayang, but in any event the expanded versions of the two scenes described above have become common in contemporary wayang performance.

Because of the expansion of these scenes, the dhalang must condense others. There is a revealing anecdote that my Javanese colleagues told me: a dhalang spent hours presenting the clown scene in gara-gara without realizing that dawn was breaking (wayang performances typically end at daybreak). The dhalang's narration stated that the prince had not yet received his *wahyu* (divine boon)—the main theme of the story—which he has to achieve by practicing self-denial and physical and spiritual practices with other princes. These elements typically take another couple of hours to portray, but the dhalang had to end the story shortly. How could he do it? When the dhalang realized that he had only ten minutes or so to end the performance, he presented a brief dialogue between a clown-servant and his prince. The clown asks whether the prince will continue his journey to search for divine boon, and the prince replies: "I have received the *wahyu* while you all were clowning around and singing songs." A couple of minutes later the usual final battle ensued, marking the end of the performance. This anecdote gives a good indication of the dhalang's preoccupation with lengthening the clown scene.

It is these expanded versions of the inner-palace and gara-gara scenes into which Western and other nontraditional wayang elements are incorporated. These elements may even include a rock band or campursari. In a wayang I saw in 1997, the dhalang, speaking for either Limbuk or Cangik, engaged in conversation with some rock singers, asking them to stand up, sing, and dance on a specially built and lit stage.[31] The musical accompaniment consisted of an electric keyboard and drum kit, and some gamelan instruments joined in the interlude. There was no question that rock music dominated this scene, and the result was a spectacular presentation of gamelan-rock hybrid music. While Western rock music was presented in conjunction (or perhaps disjunction?) with gamelan, it was understood not as a part of gamelan, but instead as foreign.

Stand-up comedy is also a common feature of contemporary wayang; one or more comedians (sitting down or sometimes standing up in the gamelan area) engage in humorous conversations with the dhalang on various topics. One subject, a discussion about the *pesindhèn* (a female vocal soloist), is never absent from this conversation. In traditional wayang, one to three pesindhèn sit down among the musicians, usually behind the *rebab* player. There was a period when pesindhèn sat on the right side of the dhalang, facing him, though the dhalang and pesindhèn singer(s) did not engage in conversation. In contemporary wayang, the presence of several pesindhèn—sometimes more than a half dozen—has become the norm. With heavy make-up and sensuous attire, they are "displayed" on an elevated stage in front of the right *simpingan* (puppets placed for decoration on the left and right sides of the screen). These pesindhèn sit down in line with the simpingan puppets, facing spectators located behind or within the perimeter of the gamelan.[32] The pesindhèn are discussed and joked about by the dhalang and the comedian(s), and it is now not uncommon for one or more pesindhèn to engage in this humorous conversation.

Figure 2.1. Electric keyboards as part of musical accompaniment for certain scenes of wayang spektakuler. Courtesy of Jan Mrázek.

It is also common for traditional dhalang to ask pesindhèn to sing certain songs, such as pieces from the *jineman* and *gendhing dolanan* genres, thus offering a demonstration of skill and melodic treatment by the singer. In the 1960s, dhalang began asking pesindhèn to sing more light songs, solo or in chorus. According to Sumanto,[33] the dhalang and composer Nartosabdo started this practice in the late 1960s: as a composer, he wanted to incorporate his own pieces into his wayang performance, and always included at least four of his own compositions. Other dhalang followed in his footsteps, and interaction between dhalang and pesindhèn increased.

In contemporary wayang, this interaction often includes comments and innuendo by the dhalang or comedian about the pesindhèn's physical features and background. It is also not uncommon for a dhalang to act as a "DJ": during the inner-palace or gara-gara scene, the dhalang reads request letters from the audience or the sponsor, asking the musicians to play favorite pieces. These requests often include dedications to a friend, organization, or influential person in the audience.

The boundary between the world of wayang (the dhalang's world) and the world surrounding it has become less clear. The title of Umar Kayam's book, *Kelir Tanpa Batas* (Screen without boundary), conveys the character of contemporary wayang. He describes the diversion from traditional practice as a "dimming of order" (*tatanan yang memudar*) in the wayang performance.[34]

"Breaking the rules of wayang performance" (*merusak pakem*) is another common characterization of contemporary wayang by its critics. First, the role of the dhalang is compromised: traditionally, the dhalang plays the central role of ordering time; he must be able to "shepherd" or "guide" time (*angon waktu*), dividing scenes with a sense of balance. Kayam elaborates: "The dhalang is the 'Sang Nata' (the Supreme-being of Order), or at least representative of a force that is responsible for ordering time, [but he is] not to be carried away by time. He is not to force himself toward time, toward life; he will not leave time outside his control, but he does not control time. He is floating (*ngeli*) but not adrift on a current (*keli*)."[35]

There is an organic bond between the dhalang and his puppets, as Mrázek explains: "It is in the context of this organic bond that the union of the voice and the puppet has to be understood: the speech belongs both to the puppeteer and the puppet, and this ambiguity, or rather collaboration, participates in giving meaning and feeling to what is said; this twinness allows the dhalang to speak in the puppet's voice. Both the dhalang and the puppet participate."[36] The presence of comedians and guest singers requires that the dhalang share his role, his speaking voice, with them.[37] Consequently, the organic relationship between the dhalang and his puppets is broken; the dhalang becomes just one of many performers who are interacting with, listening to, and competing with each other, at least in the the inner-palace and gara-gara scenes.

Contemporary wayang incorporates many more non-Javanese elements outside of music. The best example of this is the use of very elaborate sound systems, incorporating multiple large speakers and microphones. Some dhalang even incorporate special sound effects to accompany fight scenes (e.g., the sound of weapons clashing). To optimize presentation, a well-known dhalang might even have his own sound amplification system and specialized technical crew.

Another modernization incorporated into wayang performance is the light source used. Wayang is commonly understood as a shadow play, and the *bléncong*, an oil lamp with illuminated wick, is traditionally used to project shadows behind the screen. The continuous flickering light of the bléncong helps make the shadow figures seem alive, and the spectators can watch a performance from either the shadow or puppet side. Typically, in a performance for a rite-of-passage celebration, the wayang screen is set up between the front hall and the inner part of a house. Most invited male guests sit on the puppet-musician side, while uninvited guests sit on the floor or stand behind the musicians. Most spectators occupying the space behind the wayang screen are female guests.

Since the mid-twentieth century, spectators have increasingly preferred to watch wayang from the puppet-musician side, not from the shadow side. This change had partly to do with the replacement of the bléncong with an electric light. The strong and sharp light of the electric bulb (nowadays, halogen is preferred) allows spectators to clearly view the puppets and their shadows.[38] The electric light's very clear shadow has encouraged many dhalang to create elaborate and complex techniques of puppet movements. The only moveable parts of a wayang puppet are its two arms (for most giant puppets, only the front arm is moveable), but even within this constraint a good dhalang can manipulate puppets in many remarkable ways. For example, the somersault has become a standard movement for any puppet of strong character. Some puppeteers can make giant puppets do double, even triple, somersaults. Usually, the puppeteer demonstrates his dexterity during fight scenes such as *perang kembang*, the midnight battle between the prince and a group of ogres; the puppeteer flips the prince's arms (one followed by the other) by snapping them with his fingers while holding the main rod, and the prince's arms catch or hit the giants as they move about in menacing ways, with occasional somersault stunts.

Our discussions have addressed the use of modern technology (such as keyboards, electric guitar, and elaborate sound systems), the expansion of humorous scenes, and the incorporation of non-wayang elements into the performance. In addition, there has been a tendency to expand the size of certain components of the performance to achieve a spectacular presentation. This visual spectacularization includes the presence of many pesindhèn singers in heavy make-up, the use of an elaborate sound system, the presence of stand-up comedians, the use of electric light, and the development of complex puppet movements.

Spectacular wayang originated with government-affiliated wayang organizations, the Ganasidi, created to promote the ruling political party (Golongan Karya or Golkar).[39] The committee responsible for this *wayang kolosal* project was called Pantap, an acronym of Panitya Tetap Apresiasi dan Pengembangan Seni Pewayangan Jawa Tengah (The Permanent Committee for the Appreciation and Development of Central Javanese Wayang). Kuwato wrote a dissertation on wayang Pantap, and the following section is drawn from his work.[40]

According to Sudjadi, the head of Ganasidi, the aim of Pantap was to attract the interest of Indonesian youth to wayang in the face of the dominance of Western popular culture. This was to be achieved by promoting younger dhalang and improving their skills, and by making wayang performances more attractive to youth. Performing wayang with two or more dhalang made it possible for them to learn from each other and to develop complementary skills. Pantap wayang performances were held once a month in the courtyard of the office of the central Javanese government (Setwilda Propinsi Jawa Tingkat I Jawa Tengah): each performance was broadcast by government-sponsored television and radio. In this way the Pantap committee hoped that the assigned dhalang would become well-known and be hired to perform more often.

To make the performance more attractive, the Pantap wayang appended new elements to the traditional wayang format, including the appearance of stand-up comedians and guest stars, a new stage setup with two or three screens, and the addition of another stage with its own lighting for the comedians and guest stars (including rock or dangdut singers). The wayang was performed on an elevated wooden stage, 20 meters wide by 10 meters deep; a yellow carpet covered the stage floor. One thousand folding chairs were placed to the front, left, and right of the stage, and a camera for the live television broadcast was front and center. A small (12 by 3.5 meters) stage was set up and connected to the main stage, to be used by comedians, pesindhèn singers, guest singers and dancers, and any other attractions incorporated in the Limbukan and gara-gara scenes. In front of this small stage, inside the terrace, fifty chairs and several tables were placed on a yellow carpet to accommodate government officials.

Clearly wayang Pantap was meant to promote Golkar. The extensive use of the color yellow (the symbol of Golkar) and the conspicuous presence of government officials (with their specially assigned seating area) were meant to boost Golkar's political reputation among the masses: Golkar was "eager to see wayang become popular wayang, mass wayang, eager to see it attract people."[41] Mrázek adds: "Golkar's wayang performances are trying to attract people in the same way that the various performers at a *pasar malam* (fair) do, and this is another way in which the wayang performance is like a market. [Contemporary] Wayang is, first of all, an attraction; and it is an attraction that brings together many attractions."[42]

Many government-sponsored wayang were modeled after the wayang Pantap; the terms *spektakular* and kolosal were used to describe these productions. Wayang kolosal may have been somewhat smaller productions than the original wayang Pantap, but in some cases they were even more "spektakular" and "kolosal." For example, Mrázek reports that a performance in the summer of 1996, celebrating the fiftieth "birthday" (Hari Ulang Tahun) of the town of Sukohardjo, involved fifty pesindhèns (to symbolize the fifty years), in addition to pop singers, comedians, and other guest stars. Mrázek goes on to say that "many smaller events imitate the large ones, and many a village wayang, with only one screen and one dhalang, involves standing pop and rock singers, colored lights, and other attractions, and generally there is an attempt to make even small and medium-size performances *spektakular*."[43] Bambang Murtiyoso sees the effect of these kolosal productions on the commercialization and entertainment of the art, and their influence on the dhalang's perspective.[44]

> As entertainment, this wayang [kolosal] has widened gradually, altering the other functions of wayang performance. As commercially-packaged media of entertainment, wayang kolosal gives financial fortune to dhalang and their crews. . . . This large financial award encourages a dhalang to compete with other dhalang [by incorporating] various forms of entertainment in his performance, so that he could maximally serve the desire of wayang lovers. It seems that the relatively large amount of financial reward then becomes one of the factors for a dhalang to comply with the wishes of the spectators. . . . Today's dhalang considers his wayang performance as a commercial commodity.[45]

The "other functions" to which Murtiyoso refers are those of wayang beyond entertainment—its spiritual and educational functions. He feels that the audience of contemporary wayang does not benefit from these, as their taste (*selera*) stresses wayang as entertainment.

Contemporary wayang can be seen as an example of the spectacle genre in the modern world, a public form of thinking out and telling stories in which ambiguities and ambivalences are part of our shared experience—a line of thought proposed by John MacAloon.[46] This ambiguity and ambivalence was most transparent in the New Order period. The New Order brought about material prosperity that had a significant impact on the lives of Indonesians, but this positive economic development was accompanied by pollution, deforestation, the destruction of marine life, and so on.[47] Virginia Hooker and Howard Dick say that this kind of conflict can also be observed in the cultural environment. On the one hand, wealth has brought about an unprecedented efflorescence of cultural pursuits and creativity, including increased publication of newspapers, books, and magazines, and the transmission of cultural performances and spoken words through radio and television. The mass media has also made Indonesia open to foreign influences and ideas. On the other hand, there are also cultural losses. For example, as Bahasa Indonesia becomes the national language of the country, the literary vitality of regional languages has faded away. Hooker and Dick also observe that "*gamelan* music is no longer much heard outside of the foyers of international hotels. Young people, especially boys, can now pursue so many other activities that, even in Yogyakarta and Solo, they are reluctant to submit to the rigorous discipline of mastering traditional dances."[48]

It is an exaggeration to say that traditional gamelan can only be heard in hotel foyers.[49] One should take into account the almost daily broadcasting of gamelan by private and government-sponsored radio stations; there are also periodic gamelan rehearsals at the four Javanese courts in Surakarta and Yogyakarta. But Hooker and Dick's point is well taken: in my experience, the frequency of gamelan performance has generally been declining, especially at rite-of-passage events.

Traditional artists have become apprehensive about contextualizing their art in this unfamiliar environment.[50] Are gamelan and wayang confronting a world that is threatening them, or a world that offers them security? This is a dilemma that the worlds of gamelan and wayang have had to face since the New Order era, one answer to which is the emergence of the controversial contemporary wayang I have described above.

Contemporary wayang fits James Siegel's description of another genre of Javanese theater, Srimulat, which is built "on the notion of 'odd' (*anèh*), on what does not fit the rest of one's thoughts or what is not recognizable."[51] The incorporation of stand-up comedians, with their often self-deprecating jokes, the dhalang, the pesindhèn singers, the sponsor, and sometimes the guests, is funny (*lucu*), but it is "odd" (anèh), since it is out of place from the plot structure of wayang performance. At this "odd" moment, no attempt is made by the performers, including the dhalang, to connect their jokes with the story, but because they are funny, heavily situational, and take up a large portion of the performance, the audience forgets this oddness, and the humorous scene becomes the feature of the performance.

Kayam expands Siegel's discussion of anèh in a provocative way: he points to wayang devotees' nicknaming of their favorite dhalang as a way to explain the oddness in wayang during the New Order era.[52] One of the most popular dhalang, Manteb Soedharsono, has been given the nickname "*sétan*" (spiritual being), since he is very skilful and remarkably creative in making the puppets come alive, especially in fight scenes. The connotation is that it is as if a spiritual being enters into Manteb's body, which can make him move the puppets in a lifelike and creative manner.

The nickname *Dhalang édan* (crazy dhalang) is given to a well-known dhalang from Salatiga, Ki Djoko Hadiwidjojo, referring to the daring, risk-taking, and dangerous moves in his performances. Djoko is known for not following the rules (*pakem*) of the wayang performance, but rather assigning himself, as dhalang, the same status as other performers, the guest stars such as rock, dangdut, or campursari singers, and comedians.

Another young dhalang, Warseno, is nicknamed "*Slenk*," a nickname that sounds like it could be an English word, connoting a modern, international, and youthful spirit. Like Djoko, Warseno incorporates many nontraditional wayang elements, even including computer-generated lighting. In so doing, he seeks to attract a younger audience, who in his opinion have ignored wayang, preferring Western forms of popular culture.

About these three nicknames, Kayam concludes:

> During the peak of the New Order period, wayang connoisseurs were offered a heavily mixed (*campur aduk*) experience, bringing them all kinds of directions, as if led by the three nicknames mentioned above: édan [crazy], sétan [spiritual being], slenk [modern, youth spirit]. Confronting the new world of anèh [odd] delivered by these dhalang at the time, they were caught in the middle of two worldviews: the traditional world of the past and the foreign world. As all of the *anèh* elements become part of their world, they are being positioned in two possible worlds: the world similar to édan or the world similar to sétan. As they appreciate wayang for its foreign element, they are confronted with a feeling of amazement and the urge to enter into it, but at the same time they hesitate to enter and leave their own world.[53]

The New Order's objective of fostering and developing traditional culture did not revitalize gamelan performance in the community, but instead brought about the combination of Western music and wayang, which is full of sétan, édan, and slenk. In this sense, wayang (and campursari and dangdut, for that matter) developed as a consequence of the interplay between economic and cultural progress.

Musik Kontemporer and Gamelan Festivals

Before addressing specific cases of *musik kontemporer*, I will provide a brief background. After the ban on Western popular music in the 1960s by the Old Order government, the 1970s witnessed the rapid dissemination of Western music genres. New, cheap cassette technology and transistor radios were responsible for this development.[54] Beginning in the 1970s the New Order government, through its cultural offices (under the Department of Education and Culture) and state-sponsored music institutions, was very active in fostering and developing Indonesian regional arts by sponsoring art competitions, commissioning performances for dignitaries, and organizing festivals.[55] This sort of government-guided control of regional arts has made them conform to a standard aesthetic of respectability "in step with the times."[56] Philip Yampolsky writes:

> What the times demand, evidently, is art that is neat and orderly, disciplined, inoffensive, attractive or impressive to look at, pleasant to listen to. And indeed, some of the Indonesian performing arts best known and most respected both in Indonesia and abroad (the dance and gamelan music of Central Javanese courts and Balinese temples, for instance) fit the requirements without difficulty. Other Indonesian arts, however, may not care what they look like: they are concerned with their music and their dance, but not with glamour and costumes.[57]

In most cases, these guided performances were directed toward nonlocal (nonregional) audiences, taking the form of festivals, competitions, or television programs. Yampolsky observes further that when an art form is redesigned for external consumption, whether for tourists, television viewers, or festival audiences, all local meaning and resonance are lost.[58] According to Greg Acciaioli, this guided artistic development has resulted in the "aestheticization" of ritual arts for display or entertainment, thus "emasculating" local traditions.[59] Yampolsky doubts, however, whether the government was capable of directly shaping the development of all traditional performing arts and replacing original regional forms. He refers to the guided performing arts as "*official art*, parallel to but divorced from the true artistic life of Indonesians."[60] In what way do these views apply to contemporary Indonesian hybrid music as presented at festivals? My assumption is that the recent hybrid musical forms fall between "official" and "unofficial" (even "resistant") art.

One genre which falls into this scheme of development is *musik kontemporer*, or "experimental music." The term musik kontemporer has been debated by Indonesian musicians, composers, and scholars, centering on the following questions: what is new Indonesian music? Why is the term musik kontemporer preferred? In what cultural contexts has the term emerged?

The term *musik* (from the Dutch *muziek*) was introduced to Java in the eighteenth century and refers specifically to Western music, while the word *kontemporer* is from the English "contemporary." Why was it necessary for Indonesians to coin this foreign term? Andy McGraw explains that the term represents a new Indonesian geopolitical or regional perspective that transcends ethnically specific terms such as "gamelan." He writes: "The incorporation of the Indonesian state into a global system of politics and culture lead to the effort to create expressions that could be intelligible and competitive in a global setting. This in turn leads to the development of terms which incorporated the Western concept of 'music' (as in '*musik kontemporer*'), and oftentimes Western musical languages directly."[61] McGraw adds: "During the New Order, there was a perceived need to reify or bind so-called great traditions. By categorizing contemporary composition under a different terminology preexisting works were de facto defined as old, static, traditional, and worthy of preservation. New works were not necessarily extensions of tradition; they drew upon the richness of an imagined golden age but involved different forms of patronage and performance contexts."[62]

I can find no evidence to place the earliest use of the term "kontemporer," but it seems that by the mid-1970s the term was commonly being used interchangeably with "modern" and "*kreasi baru*" (new creation). A few speakers in the 1974 Pertemuan Musik, a conference held at the Jakarta Arts Center, used the term in their papers and panel discussion.[63] In her opening remarks to the conference, a representative of the Jakarta Arts Council mentions three previous festivals sponsored by the Center: the Festival of *Seni Rakyat* (folk arts), the Festival of *Seni Tradisional* (traditional arts), and the Festival of *Seni Kontemporer* (contemporary arts). In his essay entitled "Membina musik kritik" (Fostering Music Criticism), presented at the same conference, Gendon Humardani uses the term kontemporer, although only in passing. He points out that at that time people had access to a wide range of musical genres, and lists a number of them as categorical opposites: *hiburan* (light entertainment)—*seriosa* (art songs); regional—pan-Indonesian; and traditional karawitan—musik kontemporer.[64] He does not explain beyond this categorical term, however, but subsequently uses kontemporer interchangeably with "modern" in reference to the process of "modernizing" or "contemporizing" traditional arts.[65] In the same context, referring to new works for gamelan, he uses the term *baru* (new), such as in "*komposisi karawitan baru*" (new gamelan composition).[66] The point here is that the term "kontemporer" was frequently used in the late 1970s, but its usage was limited to categorical and general terms.

In his "Sketsa Kehidupan Musik Kontemporer di Indonesia" (A Sketch for the Life of Contemporary Music in Indonesia), Franki Raden proposes a broad definition of the term musik kontemporer: music that has emerged as a consequence of the encounter between Western and Indonesian traditional culture, cultivated in urban environments like Jakarta.[67] He traces the embryo of musik kontemporer to the sixteenth century, when the Portuguese entered Indonesia. As I mentioned earlier, the meeting between Portuguese music and traditional Indonesian music brought about the creation of kroncong and tanjidor.

According to Raden, another factor from which musik kontemporer developed was the introduction of Western music education to Indonesia. In 1920, before the Indonesian independence, the first music school was founded in Muntilan, Central Java; after the independence, a music academy was founded in Yogyakarta, in 1950.[68] These two schools produced several composers known for their Indonesian patriotic songs. Subsequently, a number of European-trained composers entered the musik kontemporer scene, such as the German-trained Suka Hardjana and the French-trained Slamet Abdul Sjukur. Raden suggests that the crystallization of musik kontemporer occurred in the 1970s, with the founding of the Jakarta Art Center, whose educational division (Lembaga Pendidikan Kesenian Jakarta, LPKJ, now Institut Kesenian Jakarta, IKJ) offered the study of music. The IKJ produced some composers of new Indonesian music, including Raden himself.

In a 1994 paper, Raden emphasizes the birth of musik kontemporer as a consequence of the encounter between Indonesian cultural tradition and European culture.[69] He identifies three composers—Soerjo Poetro (who lived mostly in Holland), Atmadarsana, and Rahardja—as the originators of musik kontemporer: these composers converted traditional Javanese songs into Western musical forms; for example, a new arrangement of a traditional Javanese song, performed with the accompaniment of a violin. Raden then goes on to explain the development of musik kontemporer during the Old Order period (1942–65). He points out that the Old Order period produced two different types of musical work: (1) works by composers with traditional backgrounds and orientations (i.e., pentatonic music); and (2) musical works by composers with Western diatonic backgrounds. The first type of work emerged with the support of court-educated intellectuals and artists; government-sponsored gamelan conservatories and academies in the 1950s and 1960s subsequently revitalized these works. The second type emerged from composers who traced their influences to church music and a Western musical education. These composers felt that Indonesian national music must not be represented by a work based on traditional music, but by a classical Western music idiom.

Raden asserts that during the New Order, Indonesian-Western musical interplay entered a new phase. Leaving behind the pentatonic-diatonic conflict, some composers conceived of musical instruments solely as sound sources.

However, most composers could not totally abandon the concepts and elements of traditional music; Raden states that this inevitable fusion proves that musik kontemporer straddles two cultural systems: Western and traditional Indonesian. In spite of Raden's persistent use of "musik kontemporer" in his writing up to 1998, he abandoned the term altogether in his dissertation, preferring to use the term "Indonesian art music" as a substitute.[70]

Raden offers us a useful chronology of new music in Indonesia. Nonetheless, his critics point out—at times harshly—that Raden makes too many generalizations and sometimes treats his topic haphazardly.[71] These critics charge Raden with holding a simplistic, outdated view of new Indonesian music as being a consequence of a Western-Indonesian and pentatonic-diatonic encounter.[72] However, Raden's critics offer neither detailed explanation for nor any elaboration of their position. For example, Sjukur considers East-West musical encounters in a general sense to be the result of world history, not a local or historical accident. He thus implies that the localizing process of Western music has meaning beyond the impact of Western culture alone, but fails to elaborate this point.

As mentioned, Raden asserts that some Western-educated Indonesian musicians preferred Western classical music, instead of traditional Indonesian music, to express Indonesian national culture. He refers to Western music as *musik klasik-akademis* (academic classical music), a term strongly criticized by Sjukur, who feels that Raden does not fully understand Western music. Sjukur explains that to understand Western music, one must go beyond the use of notation, tonality, formal technique, academic music, specialized concert halls, and marketing, as discussed by Raden in his essay. Sjukur goes on to say: "There is no single composer in the West who is proud of the fact that his music is being called academic music. These composers are like pioneering market-sellers (*asongan*). Whether their [musical] 'discoveries' are later studied in schools of music is a different issue. Beethoven would reject the inference that he is an academic composer."[73]

Another criticism addresses the musical competency of the composers whose works are endorsed by Raden as musik kontemporer. Let us consider the work of Soerjo Poetro, whom Raden considers one of the founders of the movement. Born to a royal family of the Paku Alam court in Yogyakarta, his parents sent him to the Netherlands to study engineering. Unfortunately, there is not much information available about his background as a musician or composer. Did he compose when he lived at the Paku Alam? Did he play gamelan there? Raden does not present any evidence. During this time, according to Raden, the Paku Alam court was the center of experimentation for gamelan music: important figures in Javanese gamelan met with progressive Western musicians such as Walter Spies, Linda Bandara, and Colin McPhee. Spies was a pianist and director of the Yogyakarta court's European orchestra.[74] He was also learning to play gamelan, transcribing gamelan compositions, and had written and performed a piece for gamelan, singers, and pianos.[75] Spies ultimately moved to Bali, where he became a well-known painter, leaving behind the musical profession. Linda Bandara (a pseudonym) was perhaps the most active musician among the three. Born in Java of Austrian-Dutch parentage, Linda Bandara's real name was Sieglinde Hofland. She was a pianist and composer and worked with Spies on his above-mentioned pieces. Returning to Europe, she settled in Austria, where she continued to perform and compose. Colin McPhee, a Canadian-born composer who lived in New York, never lived in Java or had any serious interaction with Javanese musicians. Instead, he settled in Bali, studying Balinese music, making just a few side trips to Java. All in all, there is not enough evidence to conclude that the Paku Alam court became the center of gamelan experimentation.

For examples of early contemporary Indonesian music, Raden points to the works of a number of Indonesian musicians in the early twentieth century. In the 1920s, while living in Holland, Soerjo Poetro (see above) composed "Rarjwo Sarojo" for vocal and violin. Raden suggests that the material of the piece is "taken" from Javanese children's songs; in fact, the piece is an exact transcription of the following children's songs: Langen Gita, Jamuran, and [Em]Prit Peking.[76] Raden describes the violin as similar to the vocal part, but with some ornamentation executed in the manner that a rebab player or Javanese vocalist treats his or her melodies.[77] This observation is inaccurate, since there is no rebab involved in performing or singing children's songs.

Raden's point is that the works of Soerjo Poetro and his contemporaries (Soehardjo and Atmadarsana) represent an early attempt to Westernize traditional Javanese music, such as playing rebab melodies on violin, standardizing rebab patterns in Western notation, and trying to rationalize rhythm through frequent changes in meter. Regarding Soehardjo's work, Raden says: "Soehardjo presents his work in a polyphonic texture [characteristic of gamelan] to be interweaved using a contrapuntal technique, which is a characteristic of Western music."[78] General statements like these about the characters of Western and gamelan music, along with his inaccurate observation, has led to sharp criticism.

The general meaning of musik kontemporer proposed by Raden has made it possible for the term to be applied to a wide range of genres, but Raden's critics demand precision in his use of the term. Sjukur asks: is musik kontemporer a contemporary musical genre with a specific character, or is it any music assumed to be an Indonesian-European hybrid? He implies that musik kontemporer (he does not particularly like this term) should refer to a contemporary music genre with a unique character.

The development of new Indonesian music and the coining of and debate about the term musik kontemporer occurred in the late 1970s, during the New Order. In this period the term "globalization" became commonly used to describe the encounter between non-Western regions and the West.

Globalization has meant more access to Western goods, technology, mass media, and information, and has also given Indonesian cultural institutions the ability to communicate and organize more effectively. Access to the resources and Indonesia's economic progress have also made it possible for the Jakarta Arts Center to sponsor performing arts from various Indonesian regions and abroad. Certain musical events sponsored by the Center since the late 1970s have had a direct effect on the development of new music in Indonesia, the most important being the 1979 Young Composers' Week (Pekan Komponis Muda, PKM).

Founded in 1968, the Jakarta Arts Center is the most important venue for a wide range of performing arts: traditional, modern, classical, and folk. Since the mid-1970s, the Center has sponsored all sorts of musical events, including concerts of new music and an annual competition for new music composition. The 1974 Pertemuan Musik (music conference) was another Center event. With regard to traditional music, the meeting concluded:

> The variety of genres and styles of traditional music in this country should be seen as a fact that will have an important role in the development of musical life. Admittedly, the development of traditional music is rather slow because of the sociological attachment to its communities.
>
> To enliven the creation of new traditional music, firstly, it is necessary to have new perspectives in studying tradition and its future. Furthermore, training to create new work must be intensified. In addition, orientation in new compositional techniques (which can be drawn from today's musical styles) should be widened especially to include young musicians.[79]

I would add that the notion of exploring traditional music as the basis for creating new music set the tone for the development of Indonesian music.

In 1976, as a follow-up to the 1974 music gathering, the Center held a competition for composers to create music for chorus, chamber music, and kroncong. In 1979, the Center launched the first PKM, held annually except in 1980 (due to an Indonesian economic crisis). The Center's financial problems caused the suspension of the festival in 1985.[80] The festival hoped to increase the number of Indonesian composers and to give opportunities to young composers to perform their new works. Barring a few exceptions, the composers invited to perform at the festival represented their respective institutions: ASKI (now ISI) Surakarta; ASTI (now ISI) Bali; ASTI (now part of ISI) Yogyakarta; AMI (now part of ISI) Yogyakarta; SMKI Bandung; SMKI Surabaya; and LPKJ (now IKJ).

The prominent presence of composers from the art institutes, whose programs focus on regional gamelan, resulted in the dominance of the festival by gamelan-based new music.[81] In fact, more than half of the works presented during the six years of the festival were gamelan-based, and composers from the STSI Surakarta and STSI Denpasar were well represented.[82] The tone set at the 1974 music gathering—the notion of developing new music based on traditional music—was crystallized at the 1979 PKM festival. Suka Hardjana rightly points out that the majority of new works for the gamelan consist of idiomatic expansions of traditional music.

As mentioned earlier, economic wealth has fostered artistic creativity and increased access to and interactions with composers from abroad. Funded by the Indonesian government and private institutions, or in collaboration with institutions in composers' home countries, workshops and lectures by foreign guest artists have been held. Sjukur's report of one of these encounters gives us a glance at its dynamics. The invited composer was Ton de Leeuw, a prominent Dutch composer, who led a month of workshops at the Jakarta Arts Center. Participants came from Medan, Jakarta, Bandung, Surakarta, Yogyakarta, and Ambon. First, de Leeuw asked participants "to find for themselves a way of working and interpreting [*menggarap*] composition," and offered his own response and some suggestions. It happened that Roestopo and Suwardi were playing gendèr, collaborating with a pianist from Surabaya. Throughout the morning, they had tried to work on a piece, but had a hard time deciding how to proceed. Ton de Leeuw came by, suggesting that the two instruments (gendèr and piano) should be considered as one body in creating an atmosphere, and not to think about the instruments' tuning systems as independent entities. Rather, they should think of the instruments as if they were in dialogue. According to de Leeuw, this very practical advice could have a significant impact.[83]

In the 1979 edition of the PKM, Supanggah of ASKI (now ISI) Surakarta presented "Gambuh," his first new composition. His gamelan set consisted of three *bonang* (*klénang*) from the *carabalèn* gamelan, four *suling* (flute), two *siter* (plucked string), a *pencon* (horizontal gong), *keprak* (wooden block), dhalang, and *gangsingan* (bamboo top), as well as several vocalists. Supanggah reveals the purpose of new music as an idiomatic expansion of traditional gamelan.

> My composition is a new work that originates from the material of traditional karawitan [instrumental and vocal music of gamelan]. The basic ideas rest on the fact that traditional karawitan has a strong potential for musical [development]. Facts indicate, however, that [in karawitan] there are weak elements: such as, among others, lacking in treatment of volume, timbre, tempo, dynamics, and so forth. But there are also positive aspects, such as the freedom of each musician [to interpret] within the structure of gendhing and the [rich] sound quality of each gamelan instrument. My work departs from these elements.[84]

At the 1984 PKM, A. L. Suwardi presented "Gendèr," a composition featuring a gendèr metallophone modeled after a vibraphone, along with five regular gendèr. Other instruments—three *slenthem*, rebab, two *kecapi*, and *saluang* (Sumatranese flute)—and the vocalist are all treated as supporting elements. Suwardi explains that a gendèr modeled after a vibraphone was needed to satisfy a special sound effect. In composing his new piece, Suwardi was surprised to learn that the committee had limited the number of instruments he could use in presenting his composition. Consequently, he became very careful in choosing his instruments:

> The most important thing is that we are not losing freedom in the treatment of a composition. . . . initially, we explore all possibilities [to produce new sounds] by altering the instrument (by taking apart its slabs), or striking, dampening the slabs unconventionally or conventionally (according to old conventions), and to mix *slendro* and *pelog* tunings. These techniques represent an accumulative exploration, finding as many different sound textures and characters as possible . . . It turns out, however, that the most important compositional technique is to manipulate each of the sounds that I discover, to coherently treat them. Here a problem arises, namely, the hurdle and challenge concerning rasa (inner feeling).[85]

Suwardi was given full freedom for his composition. However, he says he sometimes felt compelled to find "texture, technique, and idiomatic expression which are closer to traditional patterns. This should be expected because I have a background in traditional music." Music critic Suka Hardjana confirms the traditional character of "Gendèr."

> In spite of the technical freedom applied by Suwardi and his group, and however non-orderly is the sound of his composition, because Suwardi is a gentleman from Solo, I feel his music has rules. This is conveyed in spontaneous improvisation whose responses are always guarded. *Tenggang rasa* (feeling of going along) is felt. The composition is enjoyable because it is still *laras* (harmonious), not departing from the essential life of a Solo man: [the importance of] rasa.[86]

There were also composers who tried to break away from traditional idioms, but were doubtful whether this was achievable. For example, discussing their piece for the 1983 PKM, Santoso and Subono say:

> In composing 'Sworo Pencon' we agreed to try to break away from conventional gamelan idioms such as structure, pleasant endings, interpretation of *irama*, volume, sound texture, and so on. Deliberately we do this because we both want to diverge from what has been done by previous gamelan musicians. However, this seems somewhat difficult because we have long lived in depth with traditional *karawitan* and it has strongly rooted in us.[87]

I have discussed PKM as a national music festival held in the capital, and it is worth discussing regional music festivals by way of comparison.

Since 1995, there has been an annual gamelan festival in Yogyakarta, which has become an important venue for performances of new Indonesian music. The seed of the festival can be traced to gamelan concerts in 1993 and 1994 at the annual Yogyakarta Art Festival (Festival Kesenian Yogyakarta, FKY). One part of the festival featured new compositions for gamelan by Cokrowasito, Wasisto Surjodiningrat, and Sapto Raharjo. In the following year, the festival presented the works of Ben Pasaribu, Slamet Abdul Sjukur, Jaduk Ferianto, and Sapto Raharjo. In 1995, the gamelan section of FKY was named the Yogyakarta Gamelan Festival (YGF), which—in spite of its name—includes non-gamelan music. The organizer of YGF, Sapto Rahardjo[88] explains this philosophically: "gamelan is a spirit, not an object. The instruments are just the medium." This statement became a motto that appeared on the 1995 YGF website. In addition to performances, the festival includes related events such as lectures, panel discussions, radio talk shows, and gamelan broadcasting.

YGF concerts tended to consist of "spectacular" presentations of various music genres: traditional gamelan, hybrid Western-traditional music, and new music for gamelan or other ensembles. Besides an elaborate sound system, two large screens for video projections were installed on the left and right sides of the stage (in the Gayam productions, the screens were installed at either end of the street). At the 1996 festival, the stage backdrops were very elaborate, employing smoke machines, colorful lighting, and sometimes projections, which added to the excitement.

The festival attracted a primarily young, urban, educated audience, interested in musical performances that feature traditional and Western elements in modern, hybrid synthesis. Traditional gamelan was not excluded from the festival, but typically presented only if of a special nature: examples include performances by groups of very young children, traditional gamelan groups from abroad, and a group from Singapore consisting of Javanese who have settled there over the past century.

Earlier I mentioned four composers—Djaduk Ferianto, Slamet Abdul Sjukur, Cokrowasito, and Sapto Rahardjo—who planted the seed of YGF. The repertoire presented by these composers set the tone for subsequent festivals: traditional music, secular genres, kreasi baru (a new creation for gamelan which is drawn from traditional instrumentation and idioms), and experimental music. It would be useful here to describe these composers and their works.

Djaduk Ferianto's hybrid ensemble, Kua Etnika, consists of a mixture of traditional instruments (including Balinese and Javanese gamelan), Western instruments, and sometimes certain "nonmusical" objects. Kua Etnika's repertoire is sometimes playful, and often contains social commentary and criticism. A statement from the liner notes of one of its recordings helps us grasp their sensibility:

A self-taught musician very familiar with ethnic music, Djaduk created music that is based on a discipline called "*ngeng*": a traditional musical concept (i.e., sensitivity toward sound, pitch and rhythm) which is innate to any person. *Ngeng* is also used as "conditional mood" of the music. For Djaduk and his community, the potentiality of *ngeng* is an important factor in their treatment of the music. *Ngeng* also becomes an "abstract score" to be used for the basis of creating music.

The discipline of *ngeng* is then fused with the discipline of *Nang Ning Nong*, which is drawn from Balinese traditional music. *Nang Ning Nong* is a key word (i.e., sound or symbol) for the Balinese to teach and communicate melody. It is through Nang Ning Nong that the exploration of sound, tone, and rhythm evolves. Each musical instrument has the potential to form a structure of tones, rhythm and meaning. Nang Ning Nong is used for orientation, because in their musical exploration Djaduk and his friends use Balinese gamelan, along with Western music instruments, percussion and other objects.

The timbres of various musical and percussion instruments are combined to form new musical meaning. This is a process that provides wide interpretive possibilities for the treatment of sound material, and that should be understood as containing qualitative nuances. As a creator living in the dynamics of the life of a community, Djaduk is obsessed about reflecting various tendencies and the reality of the complexity of social life. Without being caught in corporeal or verbal expression, the music of Nang Ning Nong Orkes Sumpek is an attempt to be in close contact with the reality of society.[89]

Some of Sapto Rahardjo's pieces involve the use of computers to manipulate samples of gamelan sounds.[90] In the 1996 festival, he performed standing up and hopping around on stage, playing an electric keyboard connected to a computer in front of him. Behind him was a complete set of gamelan: while Sapto played, musicians entered the stage one by one, each sitting down at his assigned instrument. Playing on kendhang, *demung*, *kenong*, and *kempul*, each musician responded "freely" to Sapto's melodies. Western elements in the composition—computer-generated gamelan sounds—were the reason this music was featured.

Cokrowasito is a well-known musician, gamelan teacher, and composer in Yogyakarta, leading a gamelan group at the Paku Alam palace and the Radio Republik Indonesia.[91] His work falls into the category of kreasi baru (new creation). Using traditional instrumentation (with minimal modification), the repertoire of kreasi baru is drawn largely from traditional musical idioms. His Jaya Manggala Gita (Song of Triumph) is an important topic in Judith Becker's work: she emphasizes his role as a modern *pujangga* (poet and chronicler) of Java.[92] The song is a history of Java, from the twelfth-century King Erlangga through Indonesian independence in the 1940s. The whole ensemble consists of a complete gamelan, along with archaic monggang and kodhok ngorèk ensembles, and includes more than one rebab and gendèr. Each period of history is portrayed with different pieces or different ensembles. Jaya Manggala Gita is narrative music, with song-texts describing each period of history. It includes new pieces composed by Cokrowasito, but several traditional gendhing are also integral parts of the composition; the new pieces use traditional gamelan structure and idioms. Two elements in Jaya Manggala Gita are nontraditional: (1) a Western style of chorus with multiple parts, and (2) a conductor directing the ensemble in the manner of a Western orchestra conductor (in the 1970 performance that I saw, Cokrowasito himself conducted the ensemble).

Slamet Abdul Sjukur is one of the most prominent Indonesian composers. In the 1950s he studied at the Indonesian Music School (Sekolah Music Indonesia, SMI) in Yogyakarta, and in the 1960s he continued his musical training in Paris, where his teachers included Messiaen and Dutilleux.[93] In 1972 he returned to Indonesia, composing, teaching, and directing a music program at the IKJ. In 1982, he moved to Surabaya to become an independent composer. Some of his works are in the style of Western minimalism, often using material drawn from Indonesian sources. He defines his music as "Minimax," implying that it has minimalist sources, but makes maximum use of them.[94] He states: "It seems that not too many people in the musical circle are interested in this kind of approach. They have become accustomed to searching for a highly complex [musical] goal; therefore, it is not anymore possible for them to perceive a thing as it is, let alone to have an interest to cultivate carefully the potentials inside the plainness."[95]

As exemplified by the works of these four composers, hybrid music of various genres typifies the YGF program. The performance of hybrid music helps attract an audience that is primarily youthful, a point on which YGF differs from PKM. PKM was designed as a special project to promote new, experimental music and encourage the emergence of more composers. This is not the emphasis of YGF, although it is one of its goals: the YGF is mainly aimed at A younger audience, which thinks of traditional music as old, conservative, and "out of step with the world," considers it to be "in step with the world" if it is mixed with Western music.[96]

The presence of groups from abroad raises the profile of YGF. The foreign groups also offer a variety of hybrid genres. The Australian GengGong group, led by the Indonesian former rock guitarist Sawo Jabung, incorporates musical idioms from Java, Sumatra, Madura, the Middle East, and Bulgaria, reflecting the diverse backgrounds of its members. The use of bonang, Javanese folk melodies, and Sundanese drumming performed by Ron Reeves are especially popular with the audience.

Alvin Lucier and his group from Wesleyan University in the United States represent the American experimental music genre. Lucier is a well-known composer of electronic music. At Wesleyan since the late 1960s, he has had long contact with non-Western music, including the gamelan, but it has taken long and careful consideration for him to incorporate non-Western music into his work, as he was searching for music that reflects his musical style and structure.

One of the fundamental concepts of Lucier's music is the acoustical resonance of a space. He uses the gamelan as a resonant chamber in which the instruments' acoustical physicality is explored. In his *Music for Gamelan Instruments, Microphones, Amplifiers and Loudspeakers*, he makes each of the several bonang pots produce audible beats as they resonate with the acoustic characteristics of the room. In the meantime, the gendèr players strike the bars, searching for pitches that can produce feedback.

To recapitulate, one could see the issue of the growth of performing arts in Geertzian terms: state ritual theater is a manifestation of state power in the making. "The state ceremonials of classical Bali were metaphysical theater: theater designed to express a view of the ultimate nature of reality and, at the same time, to shape the existing conditions of life to be consonant with that reality; that is, theater to present an ontology and, by presenting it, to make it happen—make it actual."[97] One could approach these gamelan festivals in a Geertzian manner, but it is more appropriate to see performing arts and bureaucratic practices as interacting, instead of one performing the other. Music in twentieth-century Indonesia (such as campursari and dangdut), music in contemporary wayang, and the music presented in festivals, can all be seen in this light.

One of the central issues in the discussion of Javanese-Western hybrid cultural performances is their reception by Indonesians. Is the Western element in cultural performances enjoyed on Javanese terms, or because of its inherent Western-ness? There is no doubt that, the more foreign elements are acknowledged and featured, the more spectacular is the presentation. The next chapter will further discuss this point by focusing on a dramatic production by the well-known choreographer Sardono W. Kusumo.

Chapter Three

Opera Diponegoro

A very large reproduction of nineteenth-century painter Raden Saleh's depiction of the arrest of Diponegoro (one of the most prominent Javanese heroes of the nineteenth century) by the Dutch extended across the back of the proscenium stage; contemporary painters added new figures on the right side to maintain the proportions. The play began with a monologue (in Indonesian) by narrator and choreographer Sardono W. Kusumo, introducing himself as Raden Saleh. Sardono addressed the audience: "In the era of democracy, it is important that I ask the opinion of many people... As Raden Saleh, should I wear a mustache or not?" Many audience members answered "yes" to the question, while a few responded in the negative. Sardono replied: "Thank you for your opinion, because all opinions should be respected. I value your opinions, but I must insist that I will carry out my own opinion alone—Raden Saleh does not wear a mustache." The audience laughed; at a time when Suharto's New Order regime was widely considered to be losing its sense of democracy, the relevance of such a comment was quite apparent.[1] Sardono then explained the historical context of Saleh and his painting, sketching a background of Diponegoro as a nineteenth-century heroic figure rebelling against Dutch colonialism.

After the monologue, Mozart's Requiem began to sound on the darkened stage, accompanied by the appearance of a dancer wrapped in ropes and wearing only a loincloth. He danced in slow and anguished movements, in the style of Western modern dance, surrounded by dancers representing Islamic saints (*wali*), wearing white robes and turbans, and sitting cross-legged on the floor. A few European figures stood behind the dancer, and occasionally the crack of a whip could be heard as one of them struck the dancers.[2]

In another scene, Diponegoro performed a refined solo in Javanese style, accompanied by gamelan. He then went into the sleeping chamber and slept; his wife did not dare wake him, but simply kept watch. Entering the chamber, she performed a female style of Javanese dance while singing a couple of verses of *macapat* sung poetry. Then Mount Merapi exploded. The thunderous sound and fire in the sky caused a commotion: maids and servants were screaming, running around the house. The commotion awakened Diponegoro, who stood up, looked at the sky and sang verses in macapat describing the explosion. After the eruption ended, Diponegoro carried his wife back to the sleeping chamber. A love scene followed, portraying an intense sexual union of the couple.

Figure 3.1. A scene from the *Opera Diponegoro*. Courtesy of Fabianus Koesoemadinata.

Entitled *Opera Diponegoro*, it is a play about the nineteenth-century Javanese prince who fought for five years against the presence of the Dutch in Java. Staged at the proscenium theater of the Jakarta Arts Center, the play was commissioned by the Committee of the 1995 Art Summit Indonesia, a month-long festival consisting of nightly performances of contemporary music and dance from Indonesia and abroad, and a two-day symposium on "The Challenge of Multiculturalism: Frontiers for Composers and Choreographers."[3]

Using the history of Diponegoro as a theme, the play represents an ethnographic interpretation of past and present Javanese cultural significances. *Opera Diponegoro* can be thought of as representing what Clifford Geertz called (following Gilbert Ryle's line of thought) "thick description."[4] It is an ethnographic venture that addresses two general issues of what the ethnographer is doing: "Thinking and Reflecting" and "The Thinking of Thoughts." *Opera Diponegoro* can be interpreted in this ethnographic scheme: the play does not limit itself to the events involving Diponegoro in nineteenth-century Java; it also incorporates the perspectives of modern Indonesia perspectives on human conflict generally.

In the beginning of the play, the audience is forcibly exposed to the modality of a Western production. The stage is a European proscenium; the lighting is based on Western models; the music is Mozart's Requiem; the solo dance is in the idiom of Western modern dance. Implicitly, the meeting of Java and the West is also represented by the story behind the painter, Raden Saleh, and his paintings.

As Denys Lombard observes, Raden Saleh's life and painting are early examples of the meeting between the Javanese intellectual class and European culture.[5] He was born and grew up in a North Coast-urban milieu, in an elite family. In 1829 he received a scholarship to study painting with Schelfhout and Kruseman in the Netherlands (a rare opportunity for anyone at the time), remaining for eight years. After his scholarship he decided to stay in Europe to further his experience. He lived in Dresden, Germany and in Paris until he returned to Java in 1851. In Java, he lived in the Cikini area in Batavia, in a Gothic house of his own design. In 1875 he went back to Europe, visiting several cities. Again returning to Java from his travels in 1879, he passed away a year later in Buitenzorg (now Bogor). It is generally held that his painting of the capture of Diponegoro shows a spirit of nationalism, although there is disagreement on this point. In any event, he is recognized as the "father" of Indonesian visual art.

Who was Diponegoro? Born around 1787, Diponegoro (1785–1855) was a grandson of the first Sultan of Yogyakarta, the eldest son of Hamengku Buwana III. He grew up as the Dutch consolidated their control of Java. During his childhood and adolescence he was under the care of his grandmother in Tegalrejo, a village quite distant from the court capital. In his view, the court of Yogyakarta was full of intrigues, decadence, immorality, and corrupting European influence.[6] He therefore distanced himself from the court, devoting much of his time to spiritual and religious practices, including meditation, the study of Islamic religious texts, and time spent at an Islamic boarding school (*pesantrèn*). While devoting himself to the study of Islam, Diponegoro also maintained pre-Islamic, Javanese beliefs. For example, he took time for pilgrimages to holy sites associated with the ancient Hindu-Javanese Mataram dynasty, and claimed to have had a meeting with the mythic goddess of the South Seas, Ratu Kidul, who confirmed his status as the future king of Java.

Diponegoro was charismatic, and had an aptitude for mixing with and caring for common people; so much so that the commoners viewed him messianically as the coming Ratu Adil or "Just King."[7] As the Dutch stepped up their exploitation of Java's resources and the Javanese people in the 1830s, Diponegoro and his followers rebelled, asking the Dutch to revert to their original position as traders. The rebellion sparked five years of warfare (1825–30), and is reported to have caused the death of 200,000 Javanese people and 15000 soldiers of the Dutch government, consisting of 8000 Europeans and 7000 Indonesians.[8] The war ended with the Dutch detaining Diponegoro at a meeting to supposedly discuss a truce. They sent Diponegoro and his entourage to exile in Makasar (Sulawesi), where he died in 1855. During exile, he wrote his own chronicle in a form of sung poetry, the *Babad Diponegoro*.

From school textbooks to traditional theatrical productions such as *kethoprak*, Indonesians learn about Diponegoro as one of the most prominent national heroes. Sardono's monologue and commentary throughout also unified the play's content. However, *Opera Diponegoro* is a stylized human story. Even if the audience could correlate the play with the history of the character, the play contains many variables that the audience must take on. This makes any attempt to discuss the audience's response difficult, though still worthwhile.

Richard Schechner, drawing on Brecht and others, asserts that acting is an incomplete transformation of consciousness, which is responded to in the same way by the audience.[9] This means that the actor will never be able to fully transform himself into the character he represents. The idea can also be applied to the dialectic existing between the play's essential content and its realization on stage. In *Opera Diponegoro*, the play's essential story is the nineteenth-century history of the title character. However, what was shown on stage also included perspectives and elements of contemporary Java. The tension between the play's essential content and its onstage manifestation is an unresolved dialectic of consciousness, which forms the basis of the audience's delight.

It is useful to understand the difference between Javanese and Western systems of theater. James Brandon gives us a helpful general description:

> In the West, the play is the measure of all things. Each play is thought of as a unique creation, an artistic entity complete unto itself. It is especially created by a writer—the playwright—and it may be totally unlike any other play ever written. In both of the main systems of production in use in the West—repertory and the producer system—the play is the unit of production. In the producer system, the system we have on Broadway, theater artists are brought together to produce a single play; after that play is finished the group disbands, perhaps never to work together again. In repertory, though actors work together on a series of plays and a play may be revived, still each play is prepared and mounted as a separate work of art. The focus of Western dramatic art, that is, is on the uniqueness of each play. And our production systems are geared to provide just that: they are systems for "hand-crafting" each production.
>
> In Southeast Asia the aim of production is not to produce one play, or even ten or a hundred separate plays, but to stage examples of a specific genre. The genre, not the play, is the unit of production. Production is organized around permanent troupes of between ten to a hundred and fifty actors, writers, producers, musicians, singers, technicians, and administrative staff. It is not at all unusual for actors to have performed together in the same troupes several thousand times. Since a troupe performs in a single genre (with few and minor exceptions), dancers are expert in the dance patterns of the genre, musicians and singers know its traditional melodies and songs, actors know the stories on which plays are based, the standard dialogue patterns, and the style of performance. As a rule a troupe performs a different play every night. Actors play the same type of role night after night, and in some cases they play the same character all their lives (for example, the clown). A few standard types of scenery, costumes, and make-up satisfy the

production needs of any play that might be given. If theatre productions are "hand-crafted" in the West, they are "prefabricated" in Southeast Asia. In successive performances the standard parts of the genre are shifted, rearranged, put into different combinations. Each of these particular combinations is, of course, a "play." Like the patterns of a kaleidoscope, all the combinations or plays are regroupings of the same basic elements. No two patterns are exactly alike; none are totally different.[10]

Wayang wong is not a unique production created by the playwright, but an example of a specific genre. I should mention that wayang wong incorporates idioms from other genres. For example, it is not uncommon for wayang wong to include a palace scene in which the king performs a five-minute introductory dance before he has any dialogue with his entourage. The king's dance is to be enjoyed purely as dance; it has little bearing on the story, except to show the general temperament of the king. It is also a common practice in wayang wong for two actors to exchange tense words in songs, an idiom from a genre of operatic play, *langendriyan* (see below). Hence, I see wayang wong as a play that consists of more than one genre. In his *Opera*, Sardono expands the number of genres, incorporating Western modern dance, kethoprak, wayang wong, langendriyan, Islamic *zapin*-like dance, and others.

On the other hand, *Opera Diponegoro* shares some of the systems of Western production. Individual creativity is featured—in this case Sardono W. Kusumo, and the composer Waluyo Sastro Sukarno. The play brings together dancers and musicians especially for the production, thus embodying the Western sense of a special "hand-crafted" show. In addition, written documents were provided to the performers, including an essay on the history of Diponegoro and a detailed script and a synopsis of the story.[11]

The availability of a detailed script for the performers is an uncommon practice in traditional Javanese theater, where performers traditionally use only a synopsis of the story: before the play starts, the director helps the performers prepare by explaining in detail the scene in which they will appear. Thus, "the actor is a top man. . . . The playwright does not as a rule write dialogue for the actors. Actors improvise dialogue around the story line, using certain patterns of dialogue and in some cases set speeches."[12]

It is worth commenting on the use of the term "opera." *Opera Diponegoro* is somewhat like a European opera, especially a Baroque one (in its use of dance); however, singing is not employed for the whole play, and dialogue and narration in prose are featured in some scenes. Calling the play "opera" blurs the distinction between Western and Javanese. The play as a whole is not necessarily a full-fledged hybrid form; rather, different theatrical and musical idioms are presented side-by-side, a reflection of an "anxiety in aesthetic" that Lombard observes regarding the artistic development at the Jakarta Arts Center during Sardono's tenure there (see below).

As a member of the audience during the play's premiere, I came away with two questions: what inspired Sardono to come up with that particular format for his sunject? And in what way could members of the audience be giving meaning to the play?

Before answering these questions, I should mention that much of the theatrical idiom employed in the opera is drawn from Javanese genres, especially wayang, langendriyan, and kethoprak, the genres in which Sardono has been trained since his teenage years. The next sections provide a background for these genres.

Wayang, Langendriyan, Kethoprak, and Réyog

It is usually held that wayang—specifically wayang kulit—represents the pinnacle of Javanese performing arts. A single dhalang (puppet master) controls the entire performance, which traditionally lasts all night. He (very rarely she) delivers the dialogue of all the characters, sings *sulukan* songs to heighten the mood of the scenes, and leads the musicians in starting or stopping the musical accompaniment. The dhalang also punctuates the movements of the puppets by using a mallet to rap on the wooden chest which holds them, or by kicking hung metal plates with his foot; all movements are executed while the dhalang is sitting cross-legged.

The Javanese refer to wayang kulit as wayang *purwa*—"beginning" (of time)—because of their belief in its antiquity.[13] The origin of wayang is not well documented, however. In fact, the term itself has a double meaning: wayang can refer to any dramatic performance, not just shadow plays. There is a possibility that shadow wayang originated from nonshadow plays, or vice versa.

The stories portrayed in wayang are based mostly on the Hindu epics the *Mahabharata* and the *Ramayana*. These two epics were introduced to Java in the eighteenth century, in the period when Hindu culture spread throughout Indonesia and Southeast Asia beginning in the early Christian era.[14] The *Mahabharata* concerns a tragic conflict between a set of cousins descended from the Bharata family: the five Pandhawa brothers and the ninety-nine brothers and one sister of the Kurawa family.[15] The *Ramayana* tells the adventure of Rama, his wife Sinta, and his brother Laksmana.[16]

There are a number of dance dramas interconnected with wayang kulit shadow plays. One of the most important genres in this category is wayang wong. Based on its performance practice, it is clear that contemporary wayang wong is modeled after wayang purwa performance. Whereas in wayang purwa the dhalang speaks the dialogue for all the characters, in wayang wong all dialogue is spoken by the actors themselves. The function of the dhalang, who sits with the musicians, is limited to providing narration, punctuating the movements of the dancer-actors by tapping with a mallet on a wooden box, and singing sulukan songs to accentuate the mood of a scene. Wayang wong tells the same stories (based on the *Mahabharata* and *Ramayana*) and shares its three-part plot structure with wayang purwa. However, contemporary wayang wong only lasts about three hours, whereas wayang wong in the nineteenth-century court of Yogyakarta was commonly held over many days and nights.[17]

There are two kinds of wayang wong: wayang wong *pendhapa* and wayang wong *panggung*. Wayang wong pendhapa is performed in a wall-less room (pendhapa), the main hall of a house, prince's residency, or palace.[18] In this setting, the middle of the hall is the "stage," the gamelan is set up on one side of this stage, and the audience (sitting on chairs, squatting on the floor, or standing) forms a semicircle around the stage. There is no clear demarcation between stage and audience; analogous to a Western arena theater, this setting creates an intimate relationship between spectators and actors. The court style of wayang wong was born in the minor court of Mangkunegaran in Surakarta and the major court of Kasultanan in Yogyakarta during the period of relative tranquility after the permanent division of the Mataram court into two major and two minor courts between the mid-eighteenth and early nineteenth centuries.

Wayang wong panggung (panggung means "stage") was born in the late nineteenth century at a time when the courts' political and economic power had sharply declined, hence the weakening of the courts' support for wayang wong performance. This is also the period when the European proscenium stage was introduced to the Indonesians by the Indian Parsi theater on their tours to Southeast Asian cities. The combination of lack of court support, and the new idea of the proscenium stage, created a commercial form of wayang wong in the last decade of the century. Typically, this commercial wayang wong travels from town to town, performing in temporary theaters complete with seating. The main structure of these theaters is bamboo, and the roof is made of palm thatch. In a few cities, wayang wong panggung have established permanent concert halls.

Although a great war occurred in the 1830s between the Javanese (under the leadership of Diponegoro) and the Dutch, its consequences did not halt the flowering of Javanese literature and performing arts. In the Mangkunegaran minor court, under the reign of Mangkunegara IV, a genre of dance drama called langendriyan was created. It is a dance opera in which dialogue is sung in the poetic form by dancers accompanied by the gamelan. What is distinctive about langendriyan is that both female and male character roles—strong, refined, demonic, and clown—are performed exclusively by women.

The reason behind exclusively casting women in the langendriyan can be found in its origin. A European or Indo named Godlieb Kilian (or Tuwan Godlieb) was known for his interest in Javanese dance.[19] According to an oral account, Godlieb was the owner of a batik factory in Surakarta which employed dozens of women. While working, the women often sang macapat (nonmetrical unaccompanied song). Godlieb enjoyed listening to these songs, and thought they would be enhanced if the women danced as well as sang. He invited Raden Harya Tondhakusuma, a master dancer and musician in the minor court of the Mangkunegaran, to create a dance-opera for them. After a number of experimental performances of this new genre, Tondhakusuma asked Godlieb to finance the first performance of langendriyan.[20] When Prince Mangkunegara IV saw the play for the first time, he admired the new work; consequently, the genre has remained closely associated with the minor court of the Mangkunegaran.

Like the court style of wayang wong, langendriyan was performed indoors in a wall-less pendhapa. The story material is drawn from an east Javanese legend. Damar Wulan, a handsome and charismatic young man, is the main figure in the story. He is the nephew of the prime minister of Majapahit, but grew up in the hermitage of his grandfather. He seeks employment from his uncle, but the prime minister—worried that Damar Wulan may become a rival to his own sons—gives him a lowly position as a stable boy and grass cutter. Damar Wulan is often mistreated by the prime minister's sons, but he is helped by the prime minister's daughter, Anjasmara. The pair fall in love and secretly marry. One day, the Queen of Majapahit announces that her kingdom is threatened by Ménak Jingga (the king of Balambangan), who also seeks to marry her. According to a divine revelation, the only person who can defeat Ménak Jingga is a village boy by the name of Damar Wulan. Reluctantly, the prime minister presents Damar Wulan to the Queen, and the hero sets out on the dangerous mission to kill Ménak Jingga. At first, he is in danger of losing the battle, but two princesses held captive by Ménak Jingga steal the tyrant's yellow iron club (*gada wesi kuning*) while he is sleeping and give it to Damar Wulan. The young man returns to the battleground and beheads the king with his own secret weapon. On his way to present Ménak Jingga's head to the Queen, Damar Wulan is attacked by the prime minister's sons, who try to take Ménak Jingga's head from him, but he defeats them. To reward his success, the Queen makes Damar Wulan her husband (even as he continues to be the husband of Anjasmara).

The primary musical feature of langendriyan is the interactive singing of poetic forms by the singer-dancers, accompanied by the gamelan. The gamelan also accompanies fight scenes in the piece called Srepegan. When the singer-dancer is about to sing the poem, the player of the *keprak* (a wooden box, sounded to guide the dancers in their movements) cues the drummer, who then cues the ensemble for *sirep* (a quiet moment); in this moment, most of the instruments drop out, except a few instruments that are needed to accompany the song. Besides Srepegan, there are also other gamelan compositions accompanying various scenes, such as romantic scenes, or the exchange of tense words before a battle scene. The music of langendriyan is quite complex, involving a high degree of interactity among the singer-dancers, keprak player, drummer, and other musicians; it is a combination of singing, dancing, choreography, and drama.

Evidence of music and dance for langendriyan from the mid nineteenth century is hard to find. There is a treatise called *Pakem Mondraswara: Lampahan Damarwulan Ngarit* (written in 1881), containing vocal lyrics for an episode of the langendriyan.[21] The treatise suggests that at this time, the play already took the musical form that I described above. A report from the first decade of the twentieth century provides further evidence for langendriyan practice in the mid to late nineteenth century: one of the leaders of the gamelan group at the court of Surakarta, Warsodiningrat, explains that the piece called Pangkur (one of the feature song of langendriyan) was recomposed in the style of langendriyan by the creator of the play himself, Tondhakusuma.[22] Warsodiningrat gathered his information from his father, also one of the leaders of the Surakartan court gamelan before him, who lived during the creation and development of the langendriyan. The real proof of the music and performance of langendriyan appears in the 1920s and 1930s, from the phonograph recordings produced by Columbia and Beka recording company.[23] As the duration of each phonograph was limited to only three minute long, the recording contains only the selections or excerpts of the scene of the play.[24] More often the recording contains srepegan with sirepan (the quite moment during which the dancer sings poetry)—the musical feature of langendriyan.

As mentioned above, the decline of the court's political and economic power weakened support for performing arts. Kethoprak is one of the arts developed, as a result, outside the courts. It is a dance drama developed in the early twentieth century. Originally, kethoprak was staged in an arena-type stage. As kethoprak developed, the staging format became inspired by wayang wong panggung. It also incorporates the langendriyan idiom much like wayang wong does. Unlike wayang wong, however, there is almost no dancing in kethoprak; dancing is reserved for only a few characters and for fight scenes. There is also no dhalang. Dialogue is less elaborate than in wayang wong or wayang purwa, and the musical repertoire accompanying kethoprak is simpler.

As popular entertainment for *wong cilik* (commoners), kethoprak is more like social drama. The stories presented in kethoprak are drawn from indigenous Javanese stories and history, including the history of the Mataram dynasty. As Budi Susanto notes, for the most part these stories are inspired not by literary work or written documents, but by "peoples' collective memories (their recollection of images), Precisely because of this, *ketoprak* is vulnerable to ideologies introduced in the course of its society's history."[25] Susanto goes on to say: "There are certain conventional patterns which define *ketoprak* as a theater form that resonates with key areas of the actors' experience and thoughts, as well as with the spectator's participation. As these patterns are reproduced in invidual performances, their shaping by the circumstances of production of the show gives rise to specific kinds of social reference."[26]

Beside kethoprak, *réyog* is another theatrical genre popular with commoners. It is a dance that involves trance, given different names from region to region. *Jathilan* and réyog are two of the most common names for these folk dances in central Java. The genres have two things in common: (1) they use a two-dimensional horse without legs, made of pleated bamboo, as a prop; and (2) by the end of the performance at least one dancer is in a state of trance.

Usually the theme of the dance is a story drawn from one of the indigenous Javanese myths, such as the story of Panji. One or two clowns and other figures might also take part, and a dance by a group of horsemen is the feature of the performance. The most significant event happens when one of the horsemen reaches a state of trance toward the end of the performance, until the leader of the troupe brings him out of it with his magic powers. The dancer-in-trance exhibits his strength by eating grass, rice chaff, or broken glass. The performance "can be both a fascinating, enjoyable diversion and an agitating, even terrifying experience."[27]

Sardono's Background

Returning to *Opera Diponegoro*, let me begin by introducing the choreographer, Sardono W. Kusumo.[28] He was born in 1945: his father was a middle-ranking officer of the *kraton* (court) of Surakarta, but his main occupation was as owner of a pharmacy. Sardono's mother was also a hard-working businesswoman. From an early age, Sardono was trained as a Javanese dancer, and began to earn his fame when he was selected to dance two of the main characters from the Ramayana story, the white monkey General Anoman and King Rahwana of Alengka, in a spectacular dance drama production at the amphitheater in front of the Prambanan temple in central Java.[29]

It was his early training in dance that piqued his interest in creative and syncretistic exploration. He recounts having two teachers who conducted their lives and taught dance in different ways. One teacher insisted on him learning the *alusan*, the style of dance portraying refined characters from the *Ramayana* or *Mahabharata* stories. He was of the opinion that such refined dancing movements taught students an ability to control fluctuating emotions—the ideal behavior of a Javanese man, which inspired the teacher, living as he did in the kraton (court) environment.[30] But the other teacher was known to be of "explosive character . . . full of surprises and socially disorderly." He started "a lesson with a discussion on various topics while drinking Jenewer and Bolsch or Bekonang rice wine. Needless to say, the atmosphere was warm, full of life and often the discussion touched upon pornographic subjects."[31]

Sardono encountered a similar experience when he was assigned to dance at the amphitheater in front of the Prambanan temple as mentioned above. After years of learning the refined alusan style, his teacher assigned him to dance a robust and lively character, the white monkey Anoman. Not knowing the dance vocabulary for this monkey character—as his previous training focused on the refined style—he was at a loss. But, remembering a *Tarzan* comic book, for months he imitated the poses of Tarzan in front of a mirror. As a result he became the best dancer of the monkey commander Anoman; he was able to fuse robust, refined, Tarzan-style movements, as well as self-defense movements that he had previously studied.

In 1964, Sardono was chosen as one of the dancers to perform at the New York World's Fair. At the close of the fair, he remained in New York to see performances and observe classes taught by modern choreographers, especially Martha Graham and Jean Erdman.[32] Returning to Indonesia in 1965, he eventually committed himself to revitalizing Javanese dance.[33] To experience the traditional way of learning to dance, occasionally he, sometimes with his group, dances outdoors, for example at the ocean shore. He might carry out "fieldwork" in a particular village or region in Indonesia, living in the community, observing and learning their performing arts; he has done this in Tengger in east Java, Nias in Sumatra, Dayak in Kalimantan, and Teges in Bali. He formed the opinion that Javanese dance is an aesthetic endeavor and form of self-expression that tries to resolve various human problems.[34] This concept became the basis of many of his works, especially during his tenure in the Jakarta Art Center (Taman Ismail Marzuki, TIM) starting in 1968.

The program at TIM and Sardono's works are encounters in which old, traditional, and modern (Western) values meet. Since its inception, TIM has been known for staging traditional performances from many regions of Indonesia, as well as Western productions. The program makes it possible for artists from different social classes, ethnic groups, and nationalities to present their works side by side. Lombard asserts that, in spite of the presence of different value systems in the arts at TIM, there is no real confrontation.[35] Instead, different systems of the arts are placed side by side. There is rarely an attempt to synthesize them, which is a difficult thing to do. "On the one hand, there are young poets who just returned from the West, teachers of modern ballet, painters producing an abstract style of painting . . . On the other hand, there is dalang (puppeteer of shadow plays), young gamelan musicians, actors of wayang wong, hobby horse dance, coming almost nameless, performing many nights to show their works, which still have a ritual connotation."[36]

I would say that Sardono is one of the few who have taken advantage of the trans-cultural nature of the TIM program as a platform to expand his creative expression beyond traditional Javanese dance. In this sense, he is creatively responding to what Lombard characterizes as a period of "an anxiety in aesthetic," as the West penetrates into the heart of Indonesian culture.

In his works, Sardono emphasizes an idiom that incorporates dancing, dialogue, acting, music, and drama. This criss-crossing of different art forms is not alien to the traditional Javanese dance and theater in which Sardono's seminal works are grounded, but he infuses them with non-Javanese and non-Indonesian cultural references.

More on Diponegoro's Background

Diponegoro is one of Java's most highly documented historical figures. A substantial number of written documents about him were produced during his lifetime: in addition to reports by Dutch officials, a number of *babad* (traditional Javanese chronicles) were also written about him. Considered to have great value as historical sources, babad are literary works usually consisting of verses in the macapat genre of sung poetry. Macapat is written according to certain prosodic rules: a fixed number of lines per stanza, a fixed number of syllables per line, and fixed end-vowels at the end of each line. A macapat is meant to be sung, not read: the Javanese consider babad "a symbol of the legitimization or authorization of power in the Javanese context, for a ruling dynasty or even for a family, and particular babads often had the status of *pusaka* (sacred family heirlooms)."[37]

Diponegoro is a subject of four babad: that written by Diponegoro himself with the assistance of his family, that written under the order of the Bupati Purwareja (an opponent of Diponegoro), and those written at the courts of Surakarta and Yogyakarta.[38] In writing his piece, Sardono consulted those written by Diponegoro and at the court of Surakarta.

Diponegoro also had a deep knowledge of wayang performance and its significance for the lives of Javanese people. Evidence shows that wayang symbolism and mythology were already embedded in the psyche of Javanese society in the early nineteenth century.[39] By then, members of the Javanese royal family were important patrons of wayang and gamelan, and Diponegoro was no exception. He had a large gamelan set in his residence, and most likely held frequent wayang performances.[40] In addition, Diponegoro was well acquainted with wayang literature. His babad depicts him reading a number of wayang stories with his circle at his residence, including the *Arjuna Wijaya*, *Serat Rama*, *Arjuna Wiwaha*, and *Bhoma Kawya*. Peter Carey provides us with evidence from the babad about Diponegoro's great interest in wayang literature and the educational and symbolic significance of wayang.

> He [Diponegoro] recommended such texts [literary works on wayang] to his younger brother, the fourth Sultan, for his education when he was still a minor. In his autobiographical Babad Dipanagara described how, in December 1822, when he was appointed guardian to his nephew the fifth Sultan, without his advice being asked and without even being invited to the coronation ceremony in Yogyakarta, he instructed his *abdi-dalem* (retainer) at Tegalreja, Sastrawinangun, to read *Arjuna Wijaya* and begin with Arjuna's anger and penance; a suitable passage given the circumstances.[41]

Diponegoro represents a highly syncretistic way of life, in which pre-Islamic and Islamic cultural practices and ideals complemented one another. In addition, European colonial culture began to exert its influence upon the Javanese elite. For Diponegoro, knowledge of European colonial politics and methods of warfare was an integral part of his way of life.

Javanese Ecology and Wayang

After the introductory scene described in the opening of this chapter, the remaining scenes can be divided into two parts. The first depicts Diponegoro's struggle to find his identity, his meeting with four wali (Islamic saints) who assign him the task of freeing Java from colonialism, and his surrender to history and nature to carry out that task. The second part consists of the confrontation between the Javanese and the Dutch army, Diponegoro's actions in the battle, and his capture and exile. I would like to discuss three scenes that capture the essence of the first part of the play: (1) the eruption of Mount Merapi; (2) the love scene between Diponegoro and his wife; and (3) his encounter with Ratu Kidul.

Perhaps the most unexpected scene for the audience was the love scene between Diponegoro and his wife, which took place right after Merapi's explosion (which occurred in 1822). Many people were enraptured by this scene because of its rather graphic representation of the couple's amorous relationship (I will say more below). The program notes give the audience a hint of why Diponegoro makes love to his wife after the eruption of Merapi: the scene is subtitled "Penyatuan Dengan Alam (Union with Nature)."[42] A brief description of the scene states: "Mount Merapi's eruption was a sign that a new epoch was approaching that demanded the emergence of a chosen person who has received a calling. Diponegoro surrendered himself to the will of history by making himself one with the power of nature. He dedicated his entire life to the struggle, to sacrifice himself in order to carry out his holy duty."[43] Below are stanzas from *Babad Diponegoro* from which the scenes are portrayed.

Returning home to Tegalreja after visiting his brother, Diponegoro was greeted by his wife (Sang Retna) on the verandah.

Sinom
99. He embraced her, who resembled Supraba,
and brought her into the sleeping apartment.
The Prince then fell asleep,
and slept through the hours of prayer and of food,
all day into the night.
Sang Retna did not dare to wake him,
but simply kept watch.
Then, in the middle of the night
a sign of the wrath of God descended.

100. Mount Merapi burst into flames
which seemed to reach to heaven itself.
Jogjakarta seemed full of it;
the sky turned into fire;
the noise was frightful,
thundering and roaring.
The fire danced,
and everyone was filled with fear,
and earnestly looked for a place of shelter.[44]

Dhandhanggula
1. They fled seeking shelter scarcely knowing what they did:
the sky was now completely dark.
Now we tell that it happened
that the Prince did not wake,
but slept sweetly.
Sang Retna did not know what she should do:
she feared to leave him, in case he should be killed
and yet she hardly dared to wake her husband.
So she just kept watch over him.

2. Sang Kusuma [Retna] determined
to watch over her husband,
in case he should be killed.
Her only thought was to share his fate:
in truth, she did not intend to be left behind.
We say no more of this.
Sang Retna
had a servant who was very light-headed, and knew no proper respect.
Her name was Bok Buwang.

3. Looking at the sky, she became very afraid,
and when she heard the noise she lost control of herself
and simply screamed.
The other servants all joined in,
while their master and mistress
still remained inside the sleeping apartment.
Now we tell
that when the Prince heard the noise of all the servants screaming,
he woke with a start.

4. When he saw his wife
sitting at his feet, the Prince asked:
"What is happening, little one?"
She said gently:
"I don't really know.
I have not been outside."

Then the Prince
went out, hand in hand
with Sang Retna.
When they came out into the square in front of the house
they looked at the sky

5. and the burning mountain,
and the shifting earth.
The Prince smiled,
and spoke
to all the servants,
[saying] various things [to calm them].
Afterwards
the Prince took Sang Retna
and brought her back to the sleeping apartment,
where he had his wish (*dumugekaken kang karsa*)].[45]

In the play, after the eruption, Diponegoro woke up, singing a couple of macapat verses describing the explosion, from stanza Sinom 100. At the end of his singing, the music of an archaic ensemble called kodhok ngorèk, whose primary function is to accompany the first official meeting of a bride and groom in a wedding ceremony, was played in a slow tempo, the second level *irama*, featuring *gendèr*. Then Diponegoro carried his wife to a sleeping chamber where they made love.

There is no question that the eruption of a volcano is a terrible event. However, it can also be a sign of fertility, as after the explosion the land will become fertile ground for agriculture. This symbolic meaning explains why, witnessing the burning of the mountain and the shifting of the earth, Diponegoro responds to it first with rage, then a calm disposition.

Another symbolic meaning is contained in the last three lines of the final verse. After the eruption, Diponegoro took his wife back to the sleeping chamber, "where he had his wish." Kumar does not explain what wishes Diponegoro had, but Sardono interprets this sentence as a meaning "wishing to fulfill his sexual desire"; hence the love scene. In any event, two symbols of fertility are combined: the eruption of Mount Merapi and the act of procreation.

In the play, the love scene began with Diponegoro literally carrying his wife and placing her, lying down, on the stage. Accompanied by the melody of kodhok ngorèk, Diponegoro then took off his turban as his wife uncoiled her hair. The scene proceeded to a series of highly stylized lovemaking movements; while presented without nudity, by the standards of traditional Javanese theatre this lovemaking scene is indeed very graphic. It is, for lack of a better term, a "modern" portrayal of lovemaking on stage. This love scene is one of the many examples of the hybrid nature of this play: traditional theatrical idioms infused with references to contemporary performance practices.

It is worth reiterating Sardono's background as a Javanese dancer and his deep knowledge of and familiarity with traditional Javanese theatre. As stated in the Program Notes, Sardono acknowledges that much of the idiom for the Opera was drawn from wayang and kethoprak. The scene of Diponegoro in meditation is suggestive of a wayang scene in the story of Arjuna Wiwaha (The celebration of Arjuna), where Arjuna, the middle brother of the Pandhawas, seeks to acquire a power from the gods in order to eliminate the giant king Niwatakawaca, a symbol of evil. To do so, Arjuna must meditate in a cave, during which he is tempted by various spiritual beings: the gods also send nine celestial nymphs for this purpose. After he has resisted all temptation, the gods bestow on Arjuna a powerful, self-propelled arrow called *pasopati*—the sole weapon powerful enough to kill Niwatakawaca, it can be dispatched only by the mind of its owner.

The following passages from *Babad Diponegoro* provide further scenes of Diponegoro asceticism that make reference to wayang stories.

Sinom
17. On the next morning he set out
up the steep mountain,
intending to go to a cave called Langsé,
heedless of difficulties before him.
He traveled until he reached
the cave called Langsé,
and there Sheik Ngabdulrahkim [Diponegoro]
stayed to perform asceticism.
He was in the cave for about half a month,

18. seeking after enlightenment.
The visible world vanished from his sight:
Sheik Ngabdulrahkim
only took care for the Life [within him],
and the Life took care of Him.
He had returned to the Life
which is such
that it cannot be described.
Let us tell of her whose palace was beneath the sea:

19. Ratu Kidul appeared
before Sheik Ngabdulrahkim.
All was light and clear in the cave,
but Ratu Kidul knew
that Sheik Ngabdulrahkim
was as one dead to the world,
and could not be tempted.
So she spoke to give a promise
that she would return in the future when the time came.

21. He was sunk in meditation on the South coast, leaning against a stone,
half dozing, when he heard
a voice which spoke thus:
"O Sheik Ngabdulrahkim,
change your name.
You are now Ngabdulkamit.
Further, I say,
in three years will come a time
of great disturbances in Jogyakarta

22. It is the will of God
that the beginning of the disturbances in the land of Java
will be in three years.
And it is determined that you
will play the chief part.
I give this sign
to you, Ngabdulrahkim,
it is the arrow Sarotama.
Wear it.

The voice continues, explaining Diponegoro's fate in the disturbances, and instructing him to return home. Then:

25. Ngabdulkamit woke with a start. He looked around but all was clear,
there was no one speaking to him.
Then, high up in the clouds,
something flashed like lightning,
and fell in front of him.
It was Ki Sarotama.
When it had found its mark in the stone,
he took it at once.
Day broke, and Sheik Ngabdulkamit set out.[46]

We learn that Diponegoro practices asceticism in various caves, as does Arjuna. While in meditation, Diponegoro is met by Ratu Kidul, and soon after receives a powerful arrow called Sarotama, one of Arjuna's arrows. Through meditation, Diponegoro recognizes that his human character was an impediment to reaching union with god, as women often tempted him, just as the celestial nymphs tempted Arjuna.

It is worth comparing Diponegoro's meditation scene in the play, his *babad* about it, and the scene of Arjuna's penance in the *Arjuna Wiwaha* wayang. In the wayang performance, Arjuna is first tempted by different kinds of frightening spiritual beings, then by nine celestial nymphs. In *Opera Diponegoro*, Diponegoro was first disturbed by two contrasting manifestations of Ratu Kidul, the fierce and the gentle; where Arjuna was tempted by nine celestial nymphs dancing sensuously and gracefully, in the *Opera Diponegoro* was tempted by a female dancing in a fast and sensual manner, reminiscent of Middle Eastern belly dancing. The accompaniment for this scene is the *terbangan* ensemble (a music associated with Islam), along with rowdy Javanese singing. This once again demonstrates the hybrid nature of the play: a scene inspired by a wayang story is juxtaposed with a Middle Eastern dancing style and accompanied by Javanized Islamic terbangan music in the dangdut popular music style.[47]

Confrontation

The second part of the play began with a confrontation between farmers in Tegalreja and the Dutch. The scene was presented in a humorous manner, following the style of a traditional kethoprak drama. Speaking in Indonesian, the farmers spoke with each other about high taxes and the construction of a road through Tegalreja which had caused many of them to lose their land. When one of the farmers referred to the new road as a "jalan tol" (toll road), the audience immediately laughed. Sardono was alluding to the widely alleged corruption and cronyism on the part of President Suharto and his family surrounding highway construction in Java. This kind of anachronistic effect—the juxtaposition of two historically unrelated elements—is a common theatrical practice in wayang and kethoprak.

The confrontation continued with a feud between the farmers and a figure named Surabraja, a leader who was torn between siding with the Dutch and with Diponegoro. The second part of the confrontation began with the sound of a trumpet fanfare signaling the appearance of a group of Dutch soldiers. Riding on plaited-bamboo hobbyhorses, they appeared on the stage to the accompaniment of a melody by the archaic *monggang* ensemble, but with animated *ciblon* drumming. One of the Dutch soldiers then sang in the style of a Javanese langendriyan operatic play. After throwing his lot in with Diponegoro, Surabraja became the first casualty of the battle, killed by shots from the Dutch soldiers.

The audience members were presented with a mixture of various theatrical idioms. The plaited-bamboo hobby-horses immediately remind us of réyog, which involves various spectacles, including a dancer riding on a bamboo hobbyhorse in a state of trance, eating rice chaff or sometimes broken glass. Do European soldiers mounted on hobbyhorses connote the emasculation of the Dutch colonial power? One must also consider the musical accompaniment: monggang is considered to be one of the most sacred types of gamelan, played to mark the most important court events, including the death of a member of the royal family. We quickly realize, however, that the sacred ensemble is not using its traditional, simple patterns, but rather the animated, rowdy ciblon drumming used to accompany the réyog folk dance.

The performance was held in Jakarta, attended by an audience from varying regional and cultural backgrounds. I would suggest that the ability of a member of the audience to give meaning to the performance's conflicting elements would depend on their level of knowledge. The audience is probably on about the same level of familiarity concerning the historic figure Diponegoro, but not all of the attendees will share the same knowledge of traditional Javanese music, theater, and dance. Following Schechner, we could categorize the audience into two groups: accidental and integral.[48] The former consists of those audience members who attend a performance with little or no background knowledge of what they will be seeing. The latter are those "in the know" about the performance they will watch.

Islamic Elements

Scene: a song is sung, accompanied by the kodhok ngorèk gamelan in *pélog barang*, featuring gendèr and suling. The song is about Surabraja's bravery, as he prepares for battle. As he confronts his enemy, moving around in a defensive position, a shot suddenly pierces his body. He collapses. More shots strike him. A group of Dutch officers on horseback trample him. Surabraja lies on the floor, dying, while Javanese soldiers drag away the dead bodies of their friends. Surabraja dies. Diponegoro takes up the fight, a whip in each hand, cracking them repeatedly as he moves around. Dutch soldiers encircle him, but he escapes. Silence. Surabraja recites *takbir(an)*, calling the name of God—*Allahu Akbar*, God is Great—several times, as his spirit ascends. Diponegoro stops, standing up in the posture of an Islamic prayer.

Throughout the play, Islamic elements are visible: the long white robes and turbans worn by Diponegoro, his entourage, and the wali are all icons of Islamic culture. A terbangan ensemble, music commonly associated with Islam, accompanied some scenes of the play. The recitation of takbir(an) adds to the prominence of Islam.

Other moments where the presence of Islam was conspicuous include the scenes before and after the capture of Diponegoro, which takes place during the celebration of the end of Ramadan (the Islamic month of fasting). The scene begins with takbiran sung in a steady tempo to the accompaniment of a terbangan ensemble, evoking the jolly atmosphere of the feast as people are seen exchanging warm handshakes with one another. Still in a celebratory mood, Diponegoro attends a meeting with the Dutch officials, where he is seized—the Dutch authorities had tricked him into attending by pretending to call for a truce.

In the concluding scene, Diponegoro, his family, and his entourage are sent into exile. The group walks in a stylized, slow movement, accompanied by an Islamic-influenced flute interpretation of Sumatran music (*saluang*, the music of a bamboo flute from Minangkabau, West Sumatra) and a simple rhythmic configuration of *terbang* (frame drums). Approaching the end of the play, the narrator (Sardono) reads a report from the Dutch authorities about the death of Diponegoro in Menado from old age. In the final act, Diponegoro and his entourage return to their positions from the opening of the play, mirroring Sardono's adaptation of Raden Saleh's painting.

Given that each of the idioms employed in the play has certain regionally constructed meanings, the question is: in what ways does the audience locate and reconstruct them, or create new meaning? For instance, to the Javanese audience, classical central Javanese dance is to be appreciated as highly stylized and rich in symbolism, while kethoprak folk drama is seen as a proletarian social drama with a more direct correlation with daily life. The Javanized Islamic terbangan ensemble has certain social and religious meanings for the Islamic community in Java.

What effect does it have when these idioms are juxtaposed as in *Opera Diponegoro*? Perhaps understanding contemporary Indonesian theatrical arts in terms of an "aesthetic drama," in contrast to a "ritual process," will help us answer the question. Victor Turner proposes two abstract categories of cultural performances: (1) those of "tribal" societies, linked to recurrent calendrical events; and (2) those of industrial societies, as leisure activities.[49] The former evokes "liminality," the state of ambiguity, of being "out of time" or in "social limbo," that both performers and audience (in the general sense of the words) experience during a ritual process. The latter creates a "leisure" event, a "play," that "provides the opportunity for a multiplicity of optional, liminoid genres of literature, drama, and sport, which . . . are to be seen as Sutton-Smith envisages 'play,' as 'experimentation with variable repertoires,' consistent with the manifold variation made possible by developed technology."[50] Turner maintains that in aesthetic drama the liminoid is removed from ritual process and also "individualized." He goes on to say that "the solitary artist *creates* the liminoid phenomenon, the collectivity experiences collective liminal symbols. This does not mean that the maker of liminoid symbols, ideas, images, etc., does so *ex nihilo*; it only means that he is privileged to make free with his social heritage in a way impossible to members of cultures in which the liminal is to a large extent the sacrosanct."[51] Sardono's *Opera Diponegoro* is liminoid without disregarding liminality. The play can be characterized as a collection of juxtapositions: the synchronic-diachronic, on the one hand, and a presentation of the intersections between regional, national, and international perspectives on the other. The former consists of the collage-like presentation of past and present issues and perspective; the latter, the incorporation of diverse idioms from regional and foreign genres.

Part Two

Gamelan as Intercultural Object

Chapter Four

Deterritorializing and Appropriating Gamelan

Sir Thomas Stamford Raffles, British colonial governor of Java from 1813 to 1816, published *The History of Java* in 1817.[1] This two-volume work contains a rich discourse on many aspects of Javanese life, complete with many lavish illustrations. The book celebrates Java for its pomp and glory, incorporating descriptions of court life, the royal family, performing arts, weaponry, architecture, antiquities, the life of the commoners, the animal kingdom, and more.

It is commonly held that Raffles's book is inextricably linked to his political goals. As James Boon suggests, the book "is designed to convey in print and illustration a concrete model of his policies' ideals, a portrait of the wonder that Java promised, had his administration endured."[2] Anthony Forge confirms this line of thought in his study of the book's illustrations. Analyzing the color plates, he asserts that six of them "are in twisted perspective, the heads being shown in profile, the bodies more or less full on and the legs and feet again in side view, moving to the left or right. At first sight this suggests Javanese work, as these conventions are characteristic of *wayang kulit* yet to me these drawings do not feel Javanese at all."[3] After examining several other drawings, Forge concludes: "Raffles used his illustrations to reduce facile exoticism and present the Javanese as 'civilized' in a European sense."[4] He goes on to argue that "Raffles's visual material can be said to have minimized, almost domesticated, the genuine 'exoticness' of Java. Partly in order to justify himself and his policies, he presented the Javanese as having the same sort of bodies, albeit with different clothing, as the English."[5]

This reminds us of Edward Said's *Orientalism*, wherein he argues that discourse on non-Western culture by Western scholars tends to result in a kind of essentializing project and the domestication of the exotic. Said identifies ways in which Western formulations of non-Western culture "were integral to Western ideological, political, and colonial domination, and this observation has provoked a tremor of critical self-reflection through the entire 'Asian studies' profession."[6] In 1994, a conference proceeding entitled *Recovering the Orient* was published, countering Said. In the preface, the editors write that

"Said's *Orientalism* has encouraged a sense of embarrassment among those scholars concerned with the investigation of culture. In drawing attention to the essentializing tendencies of some writing about Asia and to its potential political consequences, he made us wary of delineating cultural differences. This wariness is not merely moral in origin: indeed Said's stress on the constructed character of the Oriental 'other' brings into question the theoretical basis of all cultural analyses."[7] Following James Clifford, the editors assert that Said's *Orientalism* "communicates an homogenizing view of humanity."[8]

Do the images used by Raffles fit Said's line of thought? Probably, but instead of exoticizing the "other," Raffles made his illustrations to fit European perspectives; the images attract his European readers not because of their exotic otherness, but rather their familiarity.

I will now examine the response of Western audiences, artists, and scholars toward the presence of gamelan in their lands. In light of the above argument regarding Said, does gamelan represent "the strange Orient," "exotic Otherness," or an object made "strangely familiar"? The answer is all of the above. Heterogeneity, not homogeneity as suggested by Said's *Orientalism*, is the salient character of intercultural encounters.

The Earliest Interaction

Thomas Stamford Raffles was the first European to introduce gamelan to the West in a significant way. After completing his term as governor in 1816, he returned to England bringing tons of items, including two sets of gamelan. What motivated him to do that? What type of gamelan did he bring? How did Raffles represent gamelan to Europeans? To address these questions, I would like to begin with a brief historical background.

Javanese contact with European traders began in the Mataram period in the seventeenth century. From the mid-eighteenth century to the early nineteenth century, power conflicts within the royal family and the interference of Europeans (especially the Dutch, and only briefly the British) caused, in 1755, the permanent partition of Mataram into two major courts and two minor courts: the major courts were Kasunanan of Surakarta and Kasultanan of Yogyakarta, and the minor courts were Mangkunegaran of Surakarta and Paku Alam of Yogyakarta. From this point on the Javanese rulers were under the control of the Dutch, and full colonization eventually took place in the 1830s. Throughout this period, Java was the headquarters of the colonial government. It is no wonder, therefore, that European interest in Indonesian cultures was first focused on Java.

As a consequence of the Napoleonic wars, the Dutch relinquished Java to the British in 1811. This period marked the beginning of European scholarship on Indonesia, thanks to Raffles. Raffles includes in his *History* a rather lengthy description of Javanese music and theater, indicating his keen interest in the Javanese performing arts. It seems that Raffles's gamelan were mostly used for exhibition, not for playing: only once does he mention that the Javanese chief Raden Rana Dipura, who accompanied him to England, played "several of his national melodies before eminent European composers, all of which were found to bear a strong resemblance to the oldest music of Scotland."[9] Writing in 1828, Charles Wheatstone refers to a sketch of gendèr taken from Raffles' gamelan.[10] The instrument also became a subject of the study of musical scales by Alexander Ellis, who examined the gamelan while it was on a display at the Royal Albert Hall, and produced an article entitled "On the Musical Scales of Various Nations."[11] William Crotch also examined Raffles's gamelan while the set was at the Duke of Somerset's residence, and found that the gamelan scale can be "produced by the black keys of the piano-forte, the scale that can also be found in many of the Scots and Irish, all the Chinese, and some of the East Indian and North American airs."[12] Raffles's gamelan became objects to be studied and displayed.

There is not much known about the extent to which Raffles was interested in gamelan music. We do know that he commissioned a gentleman from Semarang to notate a couple of gamelan compositions.[13] His lavish illustrations of gamelan instruments and wayang puppets show that he thought of Javanese culture as highly civilized. His comparison between Javanese society and those of two other islands makes his point clear: "Of the three chief nations in these islands, occupying respectively Java, Sumatra, and Celebes, the first has, especially by its moral habits, by its superior civilization and improvements, obtained a broader and more marked characteristic than the others."[14]

One set of Raffles' gamelan is now in the British Museum; the other is at Claydon House in Buckinghamshire.[15] From today's perspective, the size of the instruments in the British Museum set is larger than usual, and each of the instruments features ornate carving and lavish gilding. The frames of many instruments are shaped and carved in exquisite zoomorphic designs, such as dragons and peacocks, a motif that is—and was—atypical. Raffles probably commissioned the gamelan: as Sam Quigley shows us, a list of instruments is attached to the 1861 document of sale and transmittal of the gamelan.[16] The list includes a brief note: "Javanese Band of Musical Instruments made to the order of Sir T. Stamford Raffles and brought by him from Java 1816." That Raffles commissioned these instruments helps explain many questions: why were they so exquisitely made? Why is the decoration so appealing to Western eyes? Why are they in such an extraordinary condition? Why is the instrumentation not complete?[17] And why is the gamelan tuned to a diatonic scale? Quigley's answers deserve to be presented fully here:

> Owing to his political position, his military supremacy and his comparative wealth, Raffles would have been viewed by the Javanese as the most powerful

lord of the land. He was known to speak and read Malay and Javanese and, for a Westerner, to have an unprecedented interest in Malay traditional culture. Thus, when he ordered a gamelan, we can assume that the finest artisans were approached to carry out the work and that, as if for a royal patron, the set would be lavish and impressive. Further, as is the custom, he would have been expected to specify elements of the carved decoration, the paint colors, and the character of the tuning, the latter being not as standardized in Java as it is in the West.

Raffles seems not to have left much to chance. This inveterate collector traveled widely within Java and, as a keen observer, might well have assembled a portfolio of decorative schema which could be referenced when commissioning a gamelan. It is quite possible that he specified indigenous decorative vocabulary, which appealed to his European taste; he may even have suggested some Westernizing alterations and then left it up to the artisans to incorporate his ideas. Among the traditional motifs he could have easily stipulated are: the intersecting flower-petal grillwork (common to many batik designs) and the upholstery-like decorative beading on all the instruments, the undulating *C* scrolls, and spiral-fluted precious treatment of the finial at the end of both the gong stand and the gendèr key holders. The care with which the decoration was planned as an integral part of each case piece and the quality of its execution are stunning. The carved decoration is restrained but opulent; its gilding has great depth and complements the deep ochre-painted ground. The heavily patinated bronze keys silently convey the great age of the set, while the superb condition of the teakwood (*Tectonis grandis*) cases leads one to wonder how much, if ever, the gamelan had been used before it was brought to the more temperate climate of Great Britain.[18]

Raffles's gamelan, with its ornate decoration that seems to be designed according to his European tastes, the highly zoomorphic design of the frames, and the lavish illustrations of the gamelan in his book, all confirm an essentializing tendency when presenting Java and Java's compatibility with civilized Europe.[19]

Raffles also presents us with a counterpoint to Java's glory. His description of *gambang* (wooden xylophone) is a case in point. As mentioned earlier, after a demonstration of Rana Dipura's gambang playing, the eminent composers in attendance commented on a strong resemblance between gamelan music and the "oldest music" of Scotland. Raffles elaborates by saying that both gamelan and Scottish music, and also Indian music, are similar to their "being determined by the want of the fourth and seventh of the key and of all the semitones."[20] He continues, about the gambang playing: "By reiteration several of the sounds are artfully prolonged much beyond their noted length, which produces an irregularity of measure that might both *perplex and offend the educated ear of an accompanying timeist. The rhythm of the sections (from extension and contraction) appears very imperfect.*"[21] His comment may have been based only on Rana Dipura's playing, but the digression shows that he could also see flaws in Javanese arts.

The initial encounter of Europeans with Javanese music took place more than two centuries before Raffles became governor of Java. The arrival of British explorer Francis Drake in Cilacap (a port on the south coast of Java) in 1580 is considered the earliest encounter between Javanese and Europeans and their respective music. Although the authenticity of Drake's report is somewhat sketchy,[22] it seems clear that there was an exchange of musical presentations between locals and Drake's musicians. Ian Woodfield summarizes this encounter as follows:

> Drake's final port-of-call in the Far East was the island of Java, where he stayed for two weeks in March 1580. His musicians were in greater demand than ever before. After an initial meeting on shore during which Drake presented his "musicke," the *Golden Hind* received frequent visits from Javanese, anxious to view the curiosities on board the English ship: "Few were the dayes that one or more of these kings did misse to visit us." Drake showed the commodities on board and demonstrated the weaponry, "his musicke also, and all things else whereby he might do them pleasure, wherein they tooke exceedingly great delight with admiration." On 21 March one of the local chiefs came aboard and "in requitall of our musick which was made to him, presented our Generall with his country musick, which though it were of a very strange kind, yet the sound was pleasant and delightfull."[23]

There is no record of whether the music played for Drake and his group was gamelan, and indeed there is not much evidence of gamelan ensembles at all in this period. Evidence of an ensemble consisting of gongs and metallophone instruments was reported by a Dutch expedition to Banten in 1595–97. The report includes a drawing of an ensemble consisting of both horizontal and hanging gongs and a metallophone-type instrument (gendèr type) accompanying female dancers. Two other accounts from the same period corroborate the existence of this type of gong ensemble: Edmund Scott, the first Englishman to oversee a factory in Banten, describes local music as follows: "Their musique, which was ten or twelve pannes of Tombaga [Tembaga, brass?], carried upon coulstaffe between two; these were tuneable, and every one a note above another, and always two went by them which were skillful in their Country musique, and played on them having things in their hands of purpose to strike them."[24] This evidence suggests a processional gong ensemble, but it is possible that the ensemble performed in a stationary position, as shown in a contemporary drawing of a similar ensemble in Tuban, accompanying a horse tournament. Contemporary evidence of this type of gamelan—*cara balèn* ensembles in the courts of Surakarta and Yogyakarta—also shows that these were performed in either stationary or processional settings.

It is not my intention to proceed further with the history of the ensembles drawn and described by European visitors to Java: what is relevant to the present study is the presentation of cultural differences. As mentioned earlier, Drake seemed delighted to hear Javanese music, but he also perceived the music as "strange." A number of reports from the sixteenth through eighteenth centuries show more intolerant responses to Javanese performing arts.[25] The report from Banten mentioned above also describes the daughters of high nobility dancing in a "disgusting" manner, "pulling their arms and legs about, and twisting their whole bodies, like dogs when they creep out of their nest." Valentijn, author of the encyclopedia of the Dutch East Indies, describes Javanese music as a "horrible rumbling of gong and drums." He also says that "all of their music as merely consisted in bawling out the tones *re mi re* . . . and in cadences in fourths, thirds and fifth, in a most disagreeable manner, and with a drawl that irritated me beyond words."[26]

However, not all reports show an unreceptive response. I have previously described Rijcklof van Goens's rather lengthy description of dances and a number of ensembles during his residency in the Mataram court in the eighteenth century.[27] Jaap Kunst describes him as "the keenest observer of, and most receptive to, Javanese music."[28] From these earliest responses to this cultural difference, we find heterogeneous views of Javanese music.

Gamelan in the Early World's Fairs

World's Fairs were an early arena for introducing gamelan to the West. Historians, musicologists, ethnomusicologists, anthropologists, and other scholars have examined these events, especially as postcolonial studies have grown in popularity.[29] As a new mode of communication in the nineteenth century, the fairs "aroused high expectations, in much the same way as the arrival of the internet at the end of the twentieth century."[30] World's Fairs had the same role and significance as today's Olympic Games and World Cup tournaments: they were concerned with nationalism, rivalry, ethnographic display, and commerce on a global scale. Studies such as Marieke Bloembergen's "Colonial Spectacle," Corbey's "Ethnographic Showcase 1870–1930," and Burris's "Exhibiting Religion: Colonialism and Spectacle at International Expositions," to mention just a few, discuss the importance of World's Fairs as ethnographic and anthropological displays of civilization and representations of cultural difference.

Corbey concludes his essay, in part, by saying that the context of World's Fairs involves "complex interdependencies between the colonialist, scientists, and visual appropriation of cultural others" in which "Person[s] from tribal cultures, on show in the West, were commodified, labeled . . . , scripted, objectified, essentialized, decontextualized, aesthetisized, and fetishized. They were cast in the role of backward, allochronic contemporary ancestors, receivers of true civilization and true religion in the stories told by museums, world fairs, and imperialist ideologies, thus becoming narrative characters in the citizen's articulation of identity—of Self and Others."[31] An elaborated form of Corbey's last point can be found in Breckenridge's essay, in which she sees nineteenth-century World's Fairs as

> part of a unitary, though not uniform, landscape of discourse and practice, that situated metropole and colony within a single analytic field, through precisely such cultural technologies as the inter-national exhibition. Such technologies created an *imagined ecumene* (in much the same way that Benedict Anderson [1983] talks about print media creating imagined communities underlying the nation-state). I will call this the *Victorian ecumene*. This Victorian ecumene encompassed Great Britain, the United States, and India (along with other places) in a discursive space that was global, while nurturing nation-states that were culturally highly specific. One condition for the construction of cultural specificity, particularly in relation to the development of the nation-state, was a concept of the cultural other, for these new technologies, routines and rituals of rule were frequently developed in relation to this imperialized or imperializing other.[32]

International expositions were thus about more than the display of colonized peoples and cultures; they also tell us how images of indigenous culture were related to the host's self-image, the development of its nation-state, and economic development. In the mid-nineteenth century Europe had moved toward the development of capitalist societies in urban complexes, accompanied by the appearance of the modern entertainment industry. Breckenridge continues: "Trains, the latest in transport inventions, facilitated the temporary movement of people for leisure, and advanced the idea of the excursion as a sign of an accomplished middle-class person. . . . Advertising, a term coined in this period, enlarged and recontextualized the world of the object, and patronage relations became entangled with transnational practices in which the accumulation, display, and admiration of objects from near and far came to be highly valued."[33]

One of the points of the studies is that World's Fairs were designed to show the evolution of humankind from a so-called primitive stage to the modern world. There are exceptions, though, and a gradual shift of emphasis in representing indigenous cultures at these exhibitions, from "a single all-embracing, 'primitive' and exotic entity, as presented under the collective label of 'ethnography' in the 1880s," to "a range of more complex artistic products on the Hindu-Javanese 'civilization,'" in the 1890s fairs.[34] In fact, the display of Indian cultural objects in the first World's Fair, the 1851 Great Exhibition at London's Crystal Palace, featured not primitive India, but rather a modern court of India and its glory. "India was characteristically represented by regalia including such transport and enthronement paraphernalia as palanquins, elephant trappings, thrones, crowns, scepters and vestments.... The elaborately carved throne was upholstered in green velvet and embroidered with gold.... The throne was accompanied by fine carpets, shawls, saddles, and parasols."[35] The presence of court gamelan and dances in the 1879 National and Colonial Industrial Exhibition at Arnhem is another case in point: the music and dance represented not primitivism, but a contemporary "high culture" of Java. For another example, in 1882 Javanese gamelan from the court city of Yogyakarta was performed daily in the Royal Aquarium in Westminster, England.

Before a detailed examination of gamelan in the early exhibitions, it is worth mentioning the degree to which the European public understood gamelan prior to first hearing it at the 1879 Arnhem exhibition. The mid-nineteenth century witnessed the development of a liberal policy by the Dutch colonial government, which considered local rulers to be close allies rather than enemies: it was therefore necessary to seek a better understanding of their customs and traditions. Before taking up their postings, Dutch officials were required to learn the local culture and language, a learning experience which led to the emergence of a number of prominent scholars of Javanese art and literature. It was from them that knowledge about the gamelan circulated in the Netherlands. Jan Willem Terwen has written about these scholars, and the following discussion is drawn largely from his *Gamelan in the 19th-Century Netherlands.*

Cornets de Groot, the Dutch Resident (governor) of Gresik (in East Java) in 1825, was the first scholar-official to write a rather extensive report on gamelan in its cultural context.[36] He describes different gamelan ensembles and a list of the pieces they performed, with a description of the individual instruments and their playing techniques. In addition, he provides drawings of the instruments in six different types of gamelan, and a chart showing nine ensembles with a list of pieces and their usage in performance. For example, thirty-three gendhing are listed in the *Salendro* gamelan used for accompanying wayang. The nine ensembles in the list are gamelan *Senen, Kodok Ngorek, Tjara Bali, Bonang Renteng, Salendro, Mentaraman, Pelog, Soerabayan,* and *Salompret.* Elsewhere in his report he mentions *gamelan sekaten,* a large and loud gamelan tuned in *pelog* and used for the Islamic festival commemorating the life of the Prophet Muhammad. His work became a reference for later authors.

J. A. Wilkens was another Dutch scholar-official to write on gamelan, producing an essay entitled "Sewaka" which appeared in the Dutch journal *Tijdschrift voor Nederlandsch-Indie* and provided elementary but rather insightful information about the sléndro and pélog tuning systems, *pathet* (the modal system), and Javanese poems.[37] Wilkens's information came partly from Prince Pangeran Harya Kusumadilaga, who had unsurpassed knowledge of gamelan and wayang and was the author of a manuscript on the subject entitled *Serat Sastramiruda.*[38]

In addition to these scholar-officials, two Dutch missionaries, H. Smeding and C. Poensen, also contributed to the knowledge of gamelan in the

Netherlands in the early 1860s. Having encountered gamelan in the village of "Kepanjen" (Kediri?), East Java, Smeding observed the importance of singing in the ensemble, and also mentioned bonang and gambang. He noticed that the *rebab* is the leader of the ensemble, playing the same melody as the singer and followed by the rest of the group; this is interesting since in today's practice, rebab is rarely used in East Javanese gamelan. Poensen provided a lengthier account. He lived in Kediri for 27 years as a minister, schoolteacher, and community worker, and authored a number of articles, including a forty-page essay on wayang which describes different kinds of ensembles and the tuning system of the gamelan.

In the Netherlands, the Koninklijk Nederlands Aardrijkskundig Genootschap (Royal Dutch Geographical Society) committed in the 1870s to researching and disseminating knowledge about the Dutch East Indies. One of the society's projects was to send three of its members on an expedition to Sumatra, where they collected and studied musical instruments, among other ethnographical objects. One of them was C. D. Veth; the experience prepared him to later plan and mount the display of cultural objects at the 1883 International Colonial and Export Trade Exhibition in Amsterdam. His father, Professor P. J. Veth, was known for his intensive studies of the Dutch East Indies; he wrote an essay on gamelan, attempting to compare it with European music and bemoaning the poor reception that gamelan generally met with from Europeans.

On two occasions in 1857 students of the Dutch Royal Academy of Engineers and Civil Servants of the Indies reconstructed a processional gamelan—with the resources at their disposal and a certain amount of imagination—to simulate a religious procession of the Yogyakarta court, the *garebeg*. It happened that the Royal Academy owned a gamelan set, and they performed along the streets of Delft, with two dancers (a female and a masked male) preceding the ensemble. The two engravings depicting this procession suggest that the ensemble was a simulation of a special processional gamelan, perhaps cara balèn and kodhok ngorèk.

Gamelan and other ethnographic objects were collected at the Rijks Ethnographisch Museum (built in 1837; now the Museum Vokenkunde) in Leiden. It was from this museum that a gamelan was sent to the 1878 Exposition Universelle in Paris and to the 1880 exhibition in Berlin.

Gamelan in the 1879 Arnhem Exhibition

Intellectual circles in the Netherlands thus must have had some knowledge about gamelan. The imagined sound of gamelan became a reality when it was heard for the first time at the 1879 Nationale tentoonstelling van Nederlandsche en koloniale nijverheid (National Exhibition of Dutch and

Colonial Industry) in Arnhem. Discussions with the Dutch Resident in Surakarta, central Java, led the committee to invite a group of musicians, singers, and dancers from the minor court of Mangkunegaran to the exhibition. Prince Pangeran Hario Gondo Siwojo and his son escorted the troupe. They were well received by the members of the fair's board, and met the king and queen before their journey continued to Paris and England.

From July to October the fifteen musicians and singers and two dancers remained in residence in Arnhem, performing almost daily in an outdoor bandstand specially designed for gamelan performance. The musicians wore attire not commonly wore by today's musicians in Surakarta: European-style jackets, with openings in the front so that their white shirts were exposed. A few musicians wore traditional *sampir* (a scarf-like cloth worn around the neck) with a European vest; one musician wore a necktie. The European-style jackets made one reporter speculate whether this un-Javanese garment was meant to protect the musicians from cold weather, but in fact Javanese courts had adopted European attire by the second half of the eighteenth century, wearing them for formal occasions "to share in the strange power that the persistent presence of the Dutch must have represented to Javanese rulers by the late eighteenth century."[39] Even in Java the Javanese found themselves between two worlds.

It is possible that the gamelan dispatched to the exhibition was chosen for its portability: it was a sléndro-pélog set, which in contemporary gamelan practice is called *gamelan klenèngan*. The absence of the main loud instruments (bonang and demung) typifies this set, allowing the musicians to focus on softer pieces featuring elaborate melodies. The sléndro-pélog set consisted of: three kendhang, one rebab, *gendèr barung*, *gendèr panerus*, gambang, celempung, suling, slenthem, two saron barung, peking, *kethuk-kempyang*, kenong, a set of kempul, and *gong kemodhong*.[40] The two programs reprinted in Terwen's book mostly show pieces in the *ketawang* and ladrang forms (16 and 32 pulses per gong cycle), except *gendhing Lobong* (64 pulses per gong cycle). But the program also mentions loud pieces suitable for accompanying dance or dance drama: pieces in the gong structure of *srebegan* (srepegan), *sampak*, and *lancaran*.

Questions were raised about a dancer wearing a costume with exposed shoulders. The dancer in question was a ronggèng,[41] a dancing-girl in tayuban (a dance party at which the males in attendance take turns dancing with professional ronggèng dancers, who are also known to be prostitutes).

Only two Javanese dancers were present at the exhibition: eighteen-year-old Warsi and fifteen-year-old Reki, and the dances they were to perform were bedhaya or serimpi. It is possible that the dancers performed a fragment of serimpi, although usually this dance is performed by four dancers. The two photos available to us indicate that the dancers wore serimpi dance costumes.[42] Another newspaper mentions that the dancers sang, although "their songs might not be that fitting to us Europeans, who furthermore do not understand a word of them."[43] This mention suggests that the dancers were dancing as well as singing.

The reporter from *Algemen Handelsblad* condescendingly wrote: "They played a battle song: *Srebegan*. If our shooting clubs ever need a war song, then this calm, monotonous, frequently repeated melody (if there were such one), repeated ad nauseam would be highly recommended."[44] About the dance, he says: "They call the *ronggengs* dancing-girls. I would like to refer to them as walking-girls. Their distorted way of moving is not dancing. They walk while they are bending in all kinds of snake-like curves, making sounds in the process that seem to pass for singing, constantly repeating the same tune."[45] Rejecting this, an old Dutch colonist named Kehrer pointed to the fact, as he understood it, that *tandak* dancing is "a preeminently important issue to the Javanese people." It seems that Kehrer knew the importance of tayuban in both village and court tradition at this time. He was happy when a native ruler offered him the opportunity to enjoy some good tandhak dancing and to hear a good gamelan: "often I have picked up the offered *slendang* and participated myself."[46] Kehrer goes on to explain that the word "squatted" is an inappropriate translation of the term "sila," describing the cross-legged sitting position of the musicians. His explanation of sléndro and pélog tuning—not *slindo* as meaning a double orchestra differing from a *pilok* gamelan, as stated by one reporter[47]—demonstrates his intimate knowledge of this music.

Upon hearing gamelan for the first time, Daniel de Lange, of the *Nieuws van de Dag*, declared: "What I did suffer at that occasion is difficult to describe. I think I can give the best description by saying that the Cacophony brought about by the simultaneous performance of two different pieces on two Pianos that are not wholly in tune with each other, which I witnessed when I walked through the main building of the Exhibition, seemed to be even more bearable than the miserable 'tick-tock' mixed with heavy beating of kettles of the music played by my Javanese fellow artists."[48] De Lange's comment is sarcastic and condescending indeed, but there was something in the music that led him to desire to know more about gamelan. Upon a second listening, the pieces with singing were still "awkward" to his ears, and the nasal singing was unbearable, "And yet I cannot say that this music is without meaning," he says. Repeated listening led to the progression of his understanding of gamelan, to the extent that he describes the music using as a metaphor the abstract patterns of cashmere scarves, in which "great order" and "method" are undeniably present.[49] His questions about gamelan deserve full mention:

> I do feel I need to ask a few questions. The *rebab* (. . .) plays the motifs, like a leader, the other instruments, such as the *suling* (. . .) and the *gambangs* (harmonica with wooden metal sticks) play the same motifs, but in a figured way, each on their own in a different manner; the *saron* provides a summary of the motif. Add the idea of a kind of 'basso ostinato' (ground bass) and a

rhythmic movement of the drum, everything divided in regular sections and sub-sections by the periodical beats of the *gongs* and the *kenong*; and now I wonder: does this music need to be considered as melodic music exclusively? It is true that all these instruments only play the same motifs in a varied way, and that these variations sometimes result in often barbaric discords, but this does not alter the fact that a kind of simultaneous sounding exists which, however hard on the ear, may be considered a harmony. The second question is: should I not presume that the harmony created by the variations of the motif is bound by certain rules? To prevent a misunderstanding, I add that I do not refer to an arrangement of the tones sounding together, but an arrangement of the variations played by each instrument in the various pieces, of which a harmonic (read 'often in harmonious') arrangement is the natural result.[50]

At last De Lange understood how gamelan music works organizationally, but his European musicality bound him to listen to gamelan in its vertical relationship. It seemed that he was able to grasp the concept of motifs or melodic patterns in gamelan, was amazed that musicians did not use notation, and admired the melodious sound of the gongs. Gamelan had a definite impact on Lange's musical life, spurring him to theorize and lecture about the gamelan tuning system, and to compose a cantata which was somewhat influenced by his gamelan experience.[51]

From Court to *Kampong* Culture

The evidence shows that in the earlier fairs, the Royal Aquarium in 1882 and the 1879 Arnhem exhibition, Javanese dances and gamelan represented not primitive art, but contemporary cultural performances of the high art of Javanese court culture. Then there was a shift in focus in the representation of culture from court to village, from high art to folk art. Below I will discuss three of these later fairs: the 1883 International Colonial and Export Trade Exhibition in Amsterdam, the 1889 Exposition Universelle in Paris, and the 1893 World's Columbian Exposition in Chicago.

Enhancing industry and trade was one of the main objectives of all World's Fairs. This is why life in villages (the producers of goods) became a spectacle of the fairs. Another main objective of the fairs was to introduce the colonies and its people to Europeans. Combining these two objectives, especially beginning with the 1883 Amsterdam exhibition, the fairs displayed the colonies as ethnographical and anthropological objects in which the village represented a primitive life style, that of the lower strata of society.

The village spectacles also related to colonial policy in the Dutch East Indies. In 1830 the Dutch government stepped up its exploitation of the natives and their resources, and a policy called *cultuurstelsel* (cultivation system) was launched by the colonial government. Basically, this system forced the villagers to use their lands to grow crops for the benefit of the colonial government. In 1870, as Dutch liberal policy gained momentum, the Cultivation System was abolished, but the village nevertheless remained important as a producer of crops and export goods such as tea, coffee, and spices. In this regard Bloembergen asks the following question: "Was the spectacle of the Javanese village designed to lay bare the splendid origins of the Cultivation System, or did this informative display reflect changing attitudes to the culture and social institutions of the colony's local population?"[52] In either case, the importance of the village as the producer of economic goods remained. The question, then, was: what kind of music and dance should be presented in this village spectacle? We should begin by examining performing arts at the 1883 Amsterdam exhibition.

The exhibition took place on the grounds behind the Rijksmuseum, and twenty countries were represented. In the Eastern part was the colonial palace, displaying colonial products. Then there was a complex of houses from the Dutch East Indies in a section known as a *kampong* (village), and a hall (*pendopo*) where gamelan performances were held.[53] Next to the hall was a replica of a European residence in a mixed Padang-European style, and a replica of a Tegal restaurant from where exhibition spectators could enjoy listening to gamelan.[54]

Bloembergen provides a nuanced interpretation of the kampong: "A diminutive apparition beside the Aceh monument, a rather awkward-looking arrangement of small bamboo and wooden houses from different parts of the Dutch East Indies constitutes the 'East Indies village,' complete with inhabitants who lived, we may assume, correspondingly awkward lives."[55] With regard to the hall for gamelan and dance performance, Bloembergen describes it as "a baroque summerhouse on the side of the exhibition grounds nearest Ruysdaelkade canal, [where] the musicians among the imported Javanese played gamelan between midday and 6 p.m. every day."[56]

This gamelan hall was actually an intriguing architectural hybrid of "eclectic curiosity, a mishmash of European and Arabic styles, and as such was a fitting byproduct of the main colonial palace, a grandiose edifice in Islamic style by the architect A. W. Storebeker."[57] The presence of the statues of Euterpe, Melpomene, and Queen Semiramis in the corners of the pendopo, standing in niches crowned with small Hindu domes, made this hall even stranger.[58] According to Terwen, this pendopo, so uncharacteristic of the East Indies, was built because the organizer thought that the native architecture was not "a fashionable exhibition hall: indigenous construction was too inferior and the compact forms of ancient Hindu temples made them unsuitable for use as exposition space. Islamic architectural forms were the next best thing, all the more so because one could point to the impressive secular structural design in the Islamic world."[59]

A kampong was chosen as the main ethnographic display to represent the early development of human life and dwellings. What performing art should accompany this idea? Evidence shows an interesting dimension of the kind of gamelan and its repertoire presented in the exhibition.

Some of the gamelan instruments used for the village gamelan performances (still in Leiden) exhibit unusual designs or size.[60] A few instruments resemble Raffles's gamelan: the stand for the rebab has a unique design, depicting two roosters standing back-to-back. The bonang is remarkably large, so much so that the musician cannot reach the farthest pots from his position. The kendhang is also extremely large. The kempul stand is also uncommon, in that it has two horizontal poles to which five kempul are hung, with the knobs facing the player. A set of five European bells hung on a stand similar to the kempul's was also found in the collection.

Unfortunately, no documentation can be found regarding the origin of the gamelan. It is likely that C. D. Veth, who was sent to the East Indies to select ethnographic objects to be displayed in the exhibition, ordered the gamelan to his own specification. That some of the instruments were modeled after Raffles's gamelan is a possibility, since Raffles's book on the history of Java was well-circulated and quoted in nineteenth-century gamelan literature. De Vale, who compared this 1883 gamelan with the gamelan displayed at the 1893 Chicago exhibition (the subject of her research), concluded that the colors of the stands and resonators of the 1883 gamelan—bright blue and gold accented in red—"appear to be modeled after European furniture designed with their legs turned in spirals, and the stands carved with ordinary serpents."[61] De Vale also suggests a Chinese influence on the decoration.

This jumble of decorations on the instruments, the large size of the bonang and kendhang for the sake of a visual impression, and the inclusion of bells (traditionally not part of a gamelan ensemble) are all in line with Veth's intent to display objects that would catch the eyes of European spectators. Like the mishmash of the pendopo, a combination of perspectives Eastern and European, ancient and modern, it was meant to make "exotic otherness" become "familiar strangeness"—similar to the drawings that appear in Raffles's book, discussed in the opening of this chapter.

The performance of "Wien Neêrlands Bloed" (the Dutch National anthem at that time) on the gamelan to herald the arrival of King Willem III was another realization of this hybrid perspective; the gamelan was reportedly tuned to a Western diatonic scale.[62]

Whereas the musicians were most likely also regular workers in the plantations, playing "Wien Neêrlands Bloed" on the gamelan must have been a challenge for them. But based on the repertoire presented by the group, they were very flexible in what they could play. Clearly, the musicians and dancers of west Java would have been most familiar with Sundanese music and dance, but the repertoire they performed included a Javanese wayang purwa shadow

Figure 4.1. Gamelan and musicians at the 1883 Amsterdam Exhibition. Reproduced with permission from Museum Volkenkunde, Leiden (RMV A-52-1-56).

puppet performance, *wayang krucil*, and a mask dance telling the story of Negri Blambangan. It is also said that the dancers Amsa and Eno performed serimpi instead of West Javanese dance.

The group's performances at the 1883 Amsterdam exhibition received much criticism from people who had heard gamelan from the court of Mangkunegaran at the 1879 Arnhem exhibition. De Lange, mentioned earlier, had nothing positive to say about the performance at the Amsterdam exhibition:

> I encountered only confusion and even note relationships that were completely out of tune. I waited eagerly for the beautiful rhythmic alterations, of which I remember more than one. In vain: I indeed heard many tempo changes, but coarsely and sloppily executed; here and there a kind of conductor even had to give signals. I anticipated the various sound effects, those representing joy or sadness, passion or intimacy. In vain: I heard them not. After hearing the gamelan a number of times here, I could not bring myself to return, as I was utterly disappointed.[63]

Even more frustrating to de Lange was the playing of the national anthem on gamelan. "I do not doubt that some listeners found it pleasurable, but hope I will be permitted to express my unmitigated horror. What kind of satisfaction indeed can a music-lover possibly experience from hearing 'Wien Neêrland's

Bloed' or the 'Wilhelmus' performed on this type of instrument, while any boy singing these songs will elicit more enjoyment than these players?"[64]

Paris Exposition: Rethinking Gamelan and Debussy

The 1889 Paris exposition and the 1893 Chicago exposition both had as their theme human evolution and social progress. Regarding cultural performances from the Dutch East Indies, the two exhibitions shared the same configuration: a gamelan and a dance troupe from the same plantation in western Java, with the addition of a few dancers from the court of Surakarta. Here I will focus on the 1889 Paris exposition, mentioning the 1893 Chicago exposition whenever comparison is necessary.

Taking place in the center of the city on the banks of the Seine, the Paris Exposition Universelle was an event held to coincide with the centennial of the French Revolution, a fact which made the Dutch government and other European nations (those that were controlled by the French as a result of the French Revolution) reluctant to participate. The eventual Dutch participation was largely backed by private institutions. At any rate, the ethnographic display of the Dutch East Indies was a success. The Dutch organizers built a pavilion and a kampong (East Indies village), which proved to be a tremendous attraction. The admission, five times more costly than the nearby Annamitic (Vietnamese) theatre, did not prevent 875,000 visitors entering the kampong over the six-month duration of the fair.[65] An average of four to five thousand visitors attended daily, closer to ten thousand on Sundays.[66]

Not unlike the 1883 Amsterdam exhibition, the theme of human evolution was part of the planning of the exposition. This was the era when the evolutionary theory proposed by Darwin was debated not only for its explanation of the natural world but also the human one, especially as regards religion and other aspects of culture.[67] There is no question that racism was the norm in the nineteenth-century European worldview, and music served to illustrate this. The exclamation of the journalist for *La Vie parisienne* about Arabic music accompanying the Egypt belly dancers that he saw at the Paris Exposition is one of the best examples of this perspective:

> Hey! Is this the dance of the Egyptian? Could it be such rude spectacles that the potentates of the crescent-moon relish in the secrecy of their harem? . . . How far from the smallest oriental ballet in the Opera, how vulgar, how unlike the descriptions of writers or the striking images of the painters are these obscene calls of girls moving rhythmically to a barbaric motive, the precise opposite of those accents that our Western musical language applies to express the infinite voluptuousness of the flesh.[68]

The notion of the evolutionary process had influenced the planning of the 1878 Paris exposition and was fully realized at the 1889 event,[69] with the 1883 Amsterdam exhibition as an intermediate step. In the case of the 1889 Exposition Universelle, organizers gathered anthropologists, ethnographers, archeologists, and scholars in the field of prehistory to assist in the planning.[70] "They helped, in special thematic and retrospective expositions, to chart existing knowledge regarding human nature and the age of humanity, and regarding humanity's physical features and states of civilization, as these had developed over time in a variety of circumstances, according to prevailing ideas, and as allegedly still visible among the earth's diverse ethnic groups."[71] But in what way did this conception influence the choice of performing arts to be presented?

I should remind the readers that economic interests remained an important aim of World's Fairs. This was especially true with respect to the participation of the Dutch, since private interests largely financed the Dutch pavilion and kampong. Another important aim of the exhibition was showing the culture and civilization of the colony. Taking the two themes into consideration, it must have been a challenge for the organizers to find the most appropriate performing arts to be presented at the exhibition. As a way to display economic interest, they decisively chose performing arts from areas where trading interests were located, namely the village plantation. However, knowing that their colony also produced well known performing arts created by the "high culture" of Javanese courts, they felt compelled to add the attraction with Javanese court dances. The Paris exposition followed this format—the format that was also carried out at the Amsterdam exhibition, as I discussed earlier. The kampong at the Paris exposition thus featured village life and the performing ensemble of the Parakan Salak plantation, but four dancers from the court of Mangkunegaran in Surakarta also joined the performing group.

It is safe to say that the contemporary European public did not fully realize that there are two distinct forms of gamelan music in Java: (1) Javanese gamelan, from the court cities of central Java and their vicinities, and (2) Sundanese gamelan, from west Java.[72] Both Javanese and Sundanese music (also Balinese, for that matter) are governed by four functional layers: (1) colotomic foundation in which the stroke of different gongs define cyclical structure of the music; (2) abstracted melody or melodic skeleton played by a group of instruments; (3) elaborate melodic form, and (4) drum patterns that reinforce the cyclical structure, regulate temporal flow, and synchronize its patterns with dance movements.

The most noticeable difference between Javanese and Sundanese gamelan is the drumming. Using three drums (a large drum and two small drums), with the manipulation of the sound of the large head of the large drum (by pressing it with the drummer's heel), the Sundanese drummer produces dynamic and lively drum patterns, more lively than the Javanese drummer.

In Javanese gamelan, the music is rather clearly defined: one group of instruments plays the melodic skeleton of the piece, while the other instruments elaborate or make reference to that skeleton to express their melodies. In Sundanese music, the boundary between melodic skeleton and melodic elaboration is not as clear as in Javanese gamelan. In fact, in Sundanese music "all melodic instruments (except kenong) involve some kind of elaboration upon the piece's core melody. Core melody is an especially abstract concept in Sundanese music,"[73] more abstract than the core melody in Javanese music.

Gendèr, one of the leading instruments in Javanese gamelan, is absent from Sundanese gamelan. Singing and rebab stand out musically and texturally in Sundanese gamelan, more so than in Javanese gamelan. Larger than the Javanese rebab, the Sundanese rebab produces a louder sound. It plays in a freer rhythm than the Javanese rebab does. The practice of the rebab and singer to superimpose an alternative, pélog-like tuning system to the sléndro gamelan tuning is another distinctive feature of Sundanese music; this practice also occurs in Javanese gamelan, but only incidentally. All in all, when Javanese musicians are asked to play Sundanese gamelan, or vice versa, they have to learn a new concept of the melodic structure and new playing techniques for many of the instruments.

Which gamelan and what type of gamelan and dance repertoire were presented in the kampong? Obviously, Sundanese music, dance, and *wayang golèk* would be the main repertoire, since the musicians and dancers were Sundanese from the Parakan Salak plantation. In addition, a Sundanese processional *angklung*, an ensemble of instruments made of bamboo, took part in the exhibition: its function was to call visitors' attention to the performance, accompanying them while entering and exiting the performance space. But the presence of four court dancers from Java, named Wakiem, Seriem, Taminah, and Soekia, raises a series of questions: how could Sundanese musicians accompany Javanese dances? What dances did the four court dancers perform? Did the gamelan group also perform Javanese gamelan repertoire? In other words, what did the visitors to the exposition actually hear and see in the kampong? These are questions that many music scholars have tried to answer, due to the prevailing opinion that gamelan at the exposition influenced the work of Claude Debussy.

Establishing which gamelan was used in the exposition has been one of the challenges for scholars. No photographs of the gamelan can be found, and there are only a few drawings showing some of the instruments on stage. Drawings of bonang, gongs and their stand, rebab, and kendhang were posted in the Dutch pavilion (not the kampong where the gamelan performance was held), juxtaposing them with other objects. In this drawing, the gongs and their stand and the bonang were clearly modeled after the gamelan in the possession of the Paris Conservatoire, a gamelan set from Cirebon donated by East

Indies Minister of the Interior J. M. van Vleuten in 1887. Given the evidence she was able to gather, Rachel Thompson concludes that the Conservatoire gamelan must have been the one used at the exposition.[74] However, based on various evidence, including drawings of the instruments, an archival document from the Mangkunegaran, and photographs of the dancers, Jean-Pierre Chazal concludes that in fact a Sundanese sléndro gamelan from Bandung was used at the exposition.[75] According to a document from the Mangkunegaran archive, the gamelan was provided by a certain M. Bernard of Bandung.[76] Apparently Bernard had lived in Java for seventeen years, and was the manager of the kampong at the exposition.[77]

Chazal provides the following list of instruments: bonang (probably two), gambang, gendèr, gong, kempul, *jengglong*, kendhang, rebab, saron, and *tarumpet*. The listed instruments, sometimes with a specific description indicating their Sundanese type, conform to a typical Sundanese gamelan set, except the gendèr. Chazal acknowledges that evidence for the presence of gendèr is very weak. In a message to me, Chazal mention that "gender" is mentioned in three texts, but (respectively) in a confusing context, a fanciful story, and in the context of a general description of Javanese music.[78] He is convinced that gendèr was not part of this Sundanese gamelan at the exposition.

Contemporaneous accounts inform us that the dance performances were famous, but there is no solid evidence indicating what repertoire was actually performed. These accounts also offer a tantalizing, but often confusing, glimpse of dance performances. For example, bedhaya, serimpi, and tandhak are terms used interchangeably to describe dance performances in the kampong. Bedhaya refers to a genre of female ceremonial dances in the courts of central Java: considered to be the most exalted (even sacred) dance, it is performed by seven or nine dancers. Performed by four dancers, serimpi is a less exalted female court dance, but its status is close to that of bedhaya. As mentioned above, tandhak or ronggèng refers to female dancers hired for male dance parties in which the men present take turns dancing with them; often the dancers are also prostitutes. These distinctions were not reflected in documents about the dances at the exposition: for example, some documents indicate that both bedhaya and tandhak were court dancers or dances. Even if these two dancers were under the care of the court, bedhaya had a higher status than tandhak.[79] There must have been much miscommunication between the authors and their Javanese informants, given that three languages were used: Malay, Dutch, and French.

From examining the costumes and postures of the dancers from engravings, I notice that a preference was given to dances other than bedhaya and serimpi. This is strengthened by the fact that, as Chazal shows us, the costumes for bedhaya or serimpi dancers were not listed in the archival document from the Mangkunegaran. The Mangkunegaran document lists mostly dance costumes for the characters of three different wayang dance dramas. The list mentions five costumes for dancers of wayang wong, with a specific mention of costumes for Baladéwa and Karna (characters from the Mahabharata story); two costumes for a *ksatriya* or knight dancer; one costume for a female dancer; three costumes for the dancers of *wayang gedhog*, with two specific mentions of costumes for the Panji and Bugis dancers; two costumes for Ménakjingga and Damarwulan (the main characters of Damarwulan story); and one costume for Bondabaya, a dance portraying a military drill. Ten masks and forty-seven wayang puppets were also on the list. Given that ten masks were listed, it is possible that mask dances were performed in the kampong; similarly, wayang kulit performances might also have been staged.

After matching the dance costumes listed above with the costumes in the engravings, I learned that many of the dancers represented characters from the story of Panji and Damarwulan. However, the headdresses of Damarwulan and Menakjingga in the 1889 performance are different than in today's representations of these characters. Both dancers wore *tekes*, a large headdress in a semicircular shape, topped with black fur (see fig. 4.2). I have consulted a Mangkunegaran dancer, Bambang Suryono, who after checking archival documents at the Mangkunegaran court, confirmed that the engraving represents (see fig. 4.2, from left to right): Ménakjingga, Princess Wahita, Princess Puyengan (the two captive princesses), and Damarwulan.[80]

From contemporary dance practice we know that these headdresses in a semicircular (from left to right) are worn only by characters from the Panji story: nowadays Damarwulan wears a similar headdress, but the circular shape is from front to back. Ménakjingga wears a headdress of a different shape, called *pogogan*. I suggest that there has been a change of headdress design from one era to another. Researching Javanese performing arts in the 1950s, Claire Holt includes a photograph of these two characters in her book; they wore headdresses that differ from both today's and nineteenth-century costumes.[81] Pigeaud reports that, inspired by Bima figures drawn on the wall of the Candhi Sukuh temple, Mangkunegara V, monarch during the 1889 Paris exposition, ordered artists to design new headdresses for wayang wong dancers: the Bima figures wear a circular hairstyle, which presumably inspired the tekes headdress.[82]

If the Damarwulan story was staged at the Paris exposition, it might well have been in langendriyan style. If they indeed performed langendriyan, how were the Sundanese musicians able to accompany this Javanese dance opera? Unfortunately, no firm answer can be found. As I mentioned earlier, there are significant differences between Javanese and Sundanese gamelan; and langendriyan requires a rather elaborate musical accompaniment, which I explain below. Annegret Fauser suggests that there had been a cultural (and musical) exchange through marriages and trade between central Javanese and Sundanese, making it likely that the Sundanese musicians could play Javanese

DETERRITORIALIZING AND APPROPRIATING GAMELAN 97

Figure 4.2. The four Mangkunegaran dancers at the 1889 Paris Exposition, representing the characters of (*from left to right*) Damarwulan, Waita, Menakjingga, and Puyengan. B.H.V.P., Dossier photographique *Divers XXI*, 364.

music with some modifications. However, Fauser does not provide us with any examples of such marriage or trade diplomacy. The only evidence she offers us is Ernst Heins's speculation: "In those days Sundanese gamelan players could, with some modifications, meaningfully perform Javanese music (and sing Javanese *tembang macapat*)."[83] But Heins doesn't provide any evidence either.[84] Following Chazal's assertion, Fauser maintains, however, that music for langendriyan must have been performed in the kampong.[85] Based on contemporaneous written accounts, she presents evidence of the staging of the story of Damarwulan by four dancers, summarizing the accounts as follows:

> On the small stage, Wakiem, Seriem, Taminah, and Soekia were already seated in front of a row of marionettes (used in separate performances of Sundanese marionette theater). The four dancers, aged between thirteen and seventeen, ignited the fantasies of the Parisian audiences: they were perceived as nubile courtesans from the "harem of a sultan," the Solonese prince Mangkunegara VII [V].[86] As the gamelan began the first piece, the four *tandak* [dancers] rose slowly and began the courtly dance. Their dance

represented an episode of the Javanese epic *Damarwulan*, in which the hero tries to rescue two captive princesses from his enemy, Menakjingga. The dance from the princely court of Surakarta was performed in the characteristic formation of four *tandak* to the accompaniment of the Sundanese gamelan, including a singer.[87]

In what way the four dancers reenacted the story of Damarwulan is not known, and the accounts do not mention whether the dancers were singing while dancing, as in langendriyan, but the evidence points to the probable presentation of the genre.

As mentioned in chapter 3, langendriyan songs are sung interactively by two or more dancers, representing a dialogue. Langendriyan dancers must thus be able to simultaneously dance well and sing from memory. In addition, dancers portraying primary characters must perform the character's special introductory dance, and the performers also have to dance in a battle scene. Because of the challenging task of combining singing, dancing, and choreography, a langendriyan dancer is greatly admired for her artistic accomplishment. Because of its appeal, the operatic langendriyan singing style is often incorporated into some scenes of wayang wong panggung and kethoprak.

The search for aspects of gamelan that supposedly inspired French composers has been an important subject in musicology. Fauser has investigated the gamelan sources for Benedictus's transcription for piano entitled *Danse javanaise*. Predating and prompting Fauser's treatment is Mueller's essay, in which he links a gamelan piece called Vani-Vani (Javanese, Wani-Wani) with Debussy's *Fantaisie* for piano and Benedictus's *Danse javanaise*.[88]

One of the pivotal points of Mueller's argument is that the ostinato theme of the final movement in the *Fantaisie* is a realization of Debussy's remembrance of a repeated section of melodic skeleton (balungan) of Wani-Wani.[89] The clue that has led to his proposition lies in passages written by an author and friend of Debussy, Julien Tiersot: "There is one dance, however, that, from the point of view of music as much as of choreography, seems to enjoy the special favor of the Javanese, for it is the one they mention more often and play more willingly as a typical example of their music. It has the name *vani-vani*. . . . Its principal theme . . . represents one of the more characteristic forms of the music proper to the gamelan."[90] After establishing that, though written in 1889–90, the "Fantaisie" was performed in public for the first time only in 1919, and was published by Fromont in 1920, Mueller explains that "the peculiar fate of the *Fantaisie* has previously been believed to be the result of Debussy's dissatisfaction with its orchestration and its conventional form."[91] However, his article argues that "the cyclic theme of the *Fantaisie* is based on a Javanese melody and that Debussy withdrew the work more because he was not content with its assimilation of Javanese influences."[92]

But which Wani-Wani did Tiersot transcribe and Debussy hear? Beside Tiersot's transcription of an excerpt of Vani-Vani, Mueller uses the transcription of the melodic skeleton of Wani-Wani from the court of Yogyakarta, quoted from the work of Groneman and Hood.[93] Citing Edward Lockspeiser's *Debussy: His Life and Mind*,[94] Mueller is wrongly convinced that the music played at the Exposition Universelle came from the court of Yogyakarta. As I have discussed earlier, the gamelan and Sundanese musicians and dancers at the Paris Exposition, in fact, came from west Java, with four additional dancers from the minor court of Mangkunegaran joining the group. But there is no evidence to show that the Sundanese musicians performed Vani-Vani to accompany Javanese dance. The only evidence at hand is Jean Kernoa's and Julien Tiersot's transcription (the later is only an excerpt of the piece). Closer examination reveals that Tiersot's transcriptions represent Sundanese, rather than Javanese, music. The melodic identity of Jean Kernoa's transcription is very hard to decipher, however.

Henry Spiller (whose study focuses on Sundanese music and dance) says that Sundanese musicians consider Wani-Wani as one of the archaic or "large songs" (*lagu gede*), which is rarely, if ever, performed nowadays.[95] Spiller mentions that he found only one teacher, Otong Rasta, who took pride in preserving these older songs and includes them in his gamelan teaching. This makes it difficult to find information about lagu gede. The only notation of lagu gede pieces available to me is in a booklet written by Sundanese gamelan scholar Koesoemadinata entitle *Lagu-Lagu Gede Sunda*, containing 33 songs.[96] As can be seen in example 4.1 below, Tiersot's transcription of Vani-Vani resembles Koesoemadinata's Wani-Wani. It is most likely, therefore, that Wani-Wani performed at the Paris Exposition was a Sundanese, not a Yogyakarta piece. This finding does not necessarily negate Mueller's proposition, however, since his main argument is to prove that certain characteristics of Debussy's *Fantaisie* were inspired by the cyclic theme and pitch structure of gamelan composition. But he arrives at a conclusion by using certain pitch structures of Yogyakarta Wani-Wani (which Debussy never heard), although he also makes brief reference to Tiersot's Vani-Vani.[97]

Fauser criticizes Mueller for neglecting to mention a version of Vani-Vani from the program of the performance.[98] Fauser also suggests that there is no basis for Mueller to assert that the Benedictus piece is a version of Vani-Vani. In contrast, she argues: "Benedictus is offering a version of the first dance from the langendriyan."[99] She cites Jurgen Arndt's *Der Einfluß der javanischen Gamelan-Musik auf Kompositionen von Claude Debussy*, which "to a certain extent," supports her proposition.

Fauser speculates that one of Tiersot's untitled transcriptions is music for this Javanese dance opera. However, a thorough examination of the transcriptions reveals Sundanese music: the transcription that Fauser identifies as "Beginning of the piece, melody played by rebab" is typical of the introductory melody of a Sundanese piece. The second example, which she identifies as "Beginning of melody line (sung?), starting slowly," is actually a saron part for

Example 4.1. Comparison of Julien Tiersot's transcription of Vani-Vani and Koesoemadinata's Wani-Wani. Reproduced from Julien Tiersot, *Musiques pittoresques: promenades musicales à l'Exposition de 1889*; and R. M. A Koesoemadinata, *Lagu-Lagu Gede Sunda.*

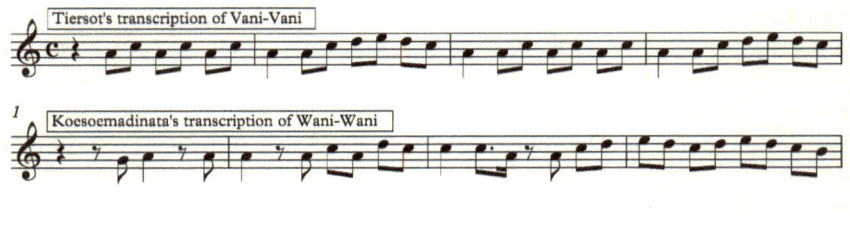

a Sundanese piece called *Bendrong.*[100] The identity of the music she represents as "Melodic fragment played by rebab, and bonang-ageng, with saron-barong, low bonang and gongs" is not as clear, but not in the style of Javanese music.[101]

Regarding Benedictus's transcription, the whole piece is a repeated variation of a melodic passage that consists of D, E, F#, A, B in upper octaves (right hand) and lower octave (left hand), with occasional temporal and textural changes and special endings.[102] As has been noted earlier, the main presentation of music for langendriyan is the singing of the dancer and highly interactive activities of the dancers and the musicians. In what way does this music reflect music of the langendriyan? Obviously, it is not a reflection of the music for langendriyan which I have described above and in chapter 3; if anything, it might be a reflection of a particular gamelan piece composed in a compact structure. The difficulty of finding the answer is compounded by the fact that we do not know what kind of langendriyan was performed in the exposition; this is a topic I will return to later.

In spite of this issue, Fauser's study succinctly synthesizes thirty years of discourse on the topic of gamelan and its influence on Debussy. Fauser notes that scholars have focused on Debussy's works for piano and orchestra that have commonly been labeled as being influenced by gamelan: *Pagodes* (from *Estampes*), the prime instance of such work; the *Nocturnes* and *La Mer*, which have been described as a "stylized gamelan,"[103] and others. She expands the discussion of Debussy beyond the influence of gamelan, asserting that other non-Western music had an impact on his work. In particular, she calls attention to the impact of the music of the *Theatre Annamite* from French Indochina (now Vietnam) on some of Debussy's works. Her point is that "Debussy did not transcribe the music he heard at the Exposition Coloniale into an immediate referential piece—not even in the case of the 1890 *Fantaisie*. Rather, he appropriated structural concepts and compositional procedures from his exposure to the gamelan that became amalgamated with other influences in the 1880s, such as the music of Mussorgsky and Wagner, both of which he also heard in 1889."[104]

It goes without saying that Debussy's musical background prior to hearing gamelan and other music at the 1889 Paris Exposition was essential to his works. In her reexamination of the relationship between gamelan and Debussy, Thompson points to the importance of the collection of memories as a source of his artistic expression.[105] "In any of Debussy's supposedly 'Javanese' influenced works, it seems that the composer was not seeking to faithfully incorporate what he heard in the *kampong* at the 1889 *Exposition Universelle*; rather, such compositions could be viewed as exhibiting Debussy's indulgence in his own aesthetic fantasies which involve a filtering and creative assemblage of various memories and dreams."[106]

But Thompson approaches the subject differently from most of the previous studies. She moves away from the theory of "exotic" influence on Debussy, and instead addresses "the idea of a shared aesthetic purpose between Debussy and the music of the 'Javanese' gamelan."[107] She proposes that Debussy's perception of Javanese music is in parallel with his conception of "arabesque" melody, a conception that coincided with certain themes in Debussy's overall aesthetic outlook, especially its link to the Art Nouveau movement, "whose proponents based their conception of the ornamental on the organic curvature of floral lines found in nature."[108]

Thompson begins her discussion by laying out chronologically the positions scholars have taken on gamelan. In the beginning, the balungan or melodic skeleton was considered the overarching determinant of melody for the whole ensemble. Later studies recognized the importance of *gatra*, the constituent four-note units of balungan, as a formulaic ingredient from which a gendhing is composed. Subsequent studies have advanced the notion that there is a melody in the minds of the musicians, called inner or implicit melody, from which other instruments are inspired in expressing their melodies.[109] Thompson is correct in stating that Western studies have situated elaboration or embellishment as a fundamental concept in understanding gamelan; it is the very life and substance of Javanese music.

Thompson conveys Debussy's thoughts on music by quoting the composer's own words, written twenty-four years after hearing gamelan at the Paris exposition.

> And if we look at the works of J. S. Bach . . . on each new page of his innumerable works we discover things we thought were born only yesterday—from

delightful arabesque to an overflowing of religious feeling greater than anything we have since discovered. And in his works we will search in vain for anything the least lacking in "good taste."

Portia[110] in *The Merchant of Venice* speaks of a music that everyone has within them: "The man that hath no music in himself... let no such man be trusted." Those people who are only preoccupied with the formula that will yield them the best results, without ever having listened to the still small voice of music within themselves, would do well to think on these words. And so would those who most ingeniously juggle around with bars, as if they were no more than pathetic little squares of paper.... We should distrust the writing of music: it is as an occupation for moles, and it ends up by reducing the vibrant beauty of sound itself to a dreadful system where two and two make four.[111]

As Thompson observes, Debussy's discussion of "a music that everyone has within them" can be seen as an allegory for the development of theories of gamelan. The notion of one's preoccupation with the formula and juggling around with bars could refer to the idea of the creation of gendhing as a process of rearranging gatra; the "small voice" of music within ourselves is the inner melody in the mind of the musicians; and the reduction of "vibrant beauty" of musical sound can be seen as the misinterpretation of balungan as the "core melody," from which other parts are derived, an idea that appeared partly as a result of the introduction of notation for gamelan.

It seems apparent that Debussy's criticism of certain European composers came about as a consequence of his listening to gamelan. Debussy expresses his admiration of Javanese music, mockingly comparing it to European music.

There used to be—indeed, despite the troubles that civilization has brought, there still are—some wonderful peoples who learn music as easily as one learns to breathe. Their school consists of the eternal rhythm of the sea, the wind in the leaves, and a thousand other tiny noises, which they listen to with great care, without ever having consulted any of those dubious treatises. Their traditions are preserved only in ancient songs, sometimes involving dance, to which each individual adds his own contribution century by century. Thus Javanese music obeys laws of counterpoint which make Palestrina seem like child's play. And if one listens to it without being prejudiced by one's European ears, one will find a percussive charm that forces one to admit that our own music is not much more than a barbarous kind of noise more fit for a traveling circus.[112]

Javanese music was only one part of the gamelan repertoire at the Paris exposition. The other part, perhaps even the majority, was Sundanese. This does not negate Thompson's argument, however, since Sundanese music embodies a concept closely related to central Javanese gamelan. Even if Sundanese music gives more weight to "essential pillar pitches,"[113] elaboration or embellishment is also a key concept in the music. In fact, almost all instrument types in Sundanese gamelan (more so than in central Javanese gamelan) involve some kind of elaboration of the core of the melody.[114] Moreover, the Sundanese repertoire is not limited to music solely defined by essential pillar pitches. There is a genre of longer pieces called *lagu gede* (large tune) or *sekar ageng* (large song) that use set melodies as a basis from which all the musicians play simultaneous variations.[115] As I mentioned earlier, Vani-Vani falls into this category.

In both Javanese and Sundanese gamelan, rebab plays a leading role. Iconographic evidence of the rebab in the Paris exposition ensemble shows that it is Sundanese. Did the Sundanese musicians play rebab in the style of Javanese music? There is no answer. However, in the case of the gamelan performance at the 1893 Columbian exhibition, we know from Gilman's wax-cylinder recording that rebab was played in a Javanese lancaran piece, although in Javanese gamelan practice rebab is not played in a lancaran piece performed in the first level of irama.[116]

Sundanese rebab plays a more important role than Javanese rebab. As I mentioned earlier, one of the features of Sundanese rebab is the player's ability, when playing a sléndro piece, to perform with ease a scale that deviates from the sléndro. This brings about musical passages juxtaposing a pélog-like tuning of the rebab melody with the sléndro tuning of the gamelan. This practice is also common in Javanese gamelan, but the extent to which it occurs is far more prevalent in Sundanese music. In fact, a Sundanese rebab player might play the entire sléndro piece with this altered tuning.

At the Exposition Universelle, there was deep admiration of the dancers. As reported by Fauser, some eleven years later Judith Gautier recalled that the dancers danced with their "splendid costumes and jewels, the careful makeup, the controlled poses both before and during the dances, together with the young age and exotic beauty of the dancers, created a spectacle which kept the audience spellbound, while 'the foam of the beer withered and the sorbet melted under distracted spoons.'"[117] Judith Gautier's estranged husband was inspired to capture the dancing "in a *rondel* that used most of the images derived from nature and mythology that were associated with the *tandak* [dancers]"; painters used the dancers as models for their works, while musicians were fascinated by the unfamiliar sound of the gamelan.[118] These exotic people provided the audience with an experience of the imagined timelessness of the Far East,[119] and its "penetrating and unknown sensations," allowing them "to breathe a new air impregnated with exotic perfume."[120]

What was the music which Wakiem, Seriem, Taminah, and Soekia danced to? Did they dance langendriyan to music performed by Sundanese musicians? Although the accounts summarized by Fauser mention a reenactment of the story of Damarwulan, there are no accounts of the dancers singing while dancing—the defining feature of langendriyan.

Four years later, we find evidence that a fragment of langendriyan was possibly performed at the 1893 Chicago Columbian exhibition. Since the Columbian exhibition had the same concept as the Paris exposition and employed performers from the same plantation, this evidence deserves close inspection. We have access to a set of wax cylinder recordings of the gamelan from the exhibition, intriguing not only because of their content, but also for their implications concerning the issue of langendriyan that we have discussed so far.

The planning committee of the Chicago fair sent two prominent anthropologists to Paris in order to seek guidance.[121] Like the Paris exposition, the Columbian fair displayed a west Javanese kampong and its people, likely meant to represent a lower level in the hierarchy of human races and dwellings according to the social Darwinism of the period. As Robert Rydell writes, drawing on the writings of Edward McDowell in 1893, "Javanese men were described as industrious workers, the women as untiring in their domestic duties. Described as cute and frisky, mild and inoffensive, but childlike above all else, the Javanese seemingly could be accommodated in America's commercial empire as long as they remained in their evolutionary niche."[122]

The performances of gamelan, wayang, and dance were some of the most popular attractions in Chicago. Four dancers from the court city of Surakarta joined the performing group. Instead of creating a native environment, performances were held in a specially built European-style proscenium stage, with backdrop scenery of mountains and trees. At the rear of the stage, the gamelan instruments were placed on a raised platform in three graded levels, while the front of the stage was reserved for dance or wayang performance.

The first wax-cylinder recording devices came on the market at this time. Benjamin Gilman, sponsored by the Harvard Peabody museum, recorded musical performances at the exhibition. He made 101 cylinder wax recordings of the Samoan Exhibit, Java Village, and Kwakiutl or Vancouver Island Indians.[123] Forty-three of the recordings are from the "Java Village," and from them we learn much.

Among the ten different performances, cylinders 26–33 are titled by Gilman as a genre of "Javanese wayang," but he also refers to the dancers as "*serimpi*." Here are Gilman's notes of the order of the dance.[124]

#26. End of Soendanese Wayang
Beginning of Javanese wayang.
Entry of first Serimpi
#27. Posturing of first Serimpi
#28. This is the voice of the first dancer (if audible)
Entry of second Serimpi
#29. Dialogue between first and second dancers
Dispute between first and second dancers
#30. One dancer draws a dagger

#31. Fight: the two dancers arm themselves, one with a stick, the other with a sword; the one with sword is wounded.
#32. Third and second dancers (the wounded one) have a colloquy seated. They go out and reenter.
#33. The fourth dancer sings.
End of the native performance.
Now American airs.

It is most likely that Gilman used the term serimpi as a generic word for female dancers or dance, a very common use of the term outside of the court tradition. From a close listening of the recordings, I think that Gilman described a fragment of dance drama involving four dancers, consisting of singing or dialogue and a fight with weapons. Was this langendriyan? The order of the appearance of the dancers seems to follow a story line of a fragment of langendriyan. The first dancer entering the stage was the villain king Ménakjingga, and the second was the protagonist Damarwulan. They fought, Damarwulan arming himself with a stick (probably a club), Ménakjingga using a sword (the same weapon used by this character in contemporary langendriyan). The one with the sword, Ménakjingga, was wounded. The identity of the third and fourth dancers appearing in cylinders #32 and #33 is not clear to me, but knowing that the third dancer had a discussion with the wounded one (Ménakjingga), she might be one of Ménakjingga's captive princesses, Wahita. The fourth dancer could thus possibly have been his second captive princess, Puyengan.

This dance and its story remind us of Fauser's summary of the 1889 Paris exposition. The dance had the same storyline and the same number of dancers: Damarwulan, Ménakjingga, and two captive princesses (Wahita and Puyengan). However, in the description of the Paris performance there is no mention of speech or singing by the dancers. This could be a matter of carelessness on the part of the authors who wrote about performances at the Paris Exposition. The possibility of the performances at the Paris Exposition and the Chicago World's Fair being the same cannot be ruled out, since the musicians and dancers in both exhibitions came from the same places: the musicians from Parakan Salak plantation in west Java, joined by dancers from the court city of Surakarta.

As mentioned earlier, the music of langendriyan is quite elaborate, involving gamelan accompaniment to poetic dialogues sung by the dancers. The feature of musical accompaniments and the changing of the temporal and density flow (irama) of the music convey the dynamic of the dramatic action. However, in the piece performed at the Columbian exhibition, as Gilman's recordings show, the accompaniment consisted of only a single piece composed in a short gongan structure, *lancaran*. Consisting of five gongan cycles, the lancaran Kembang Jeruk in *pélog* is repeated many times. Occasionally, the irama of the piece changes momentarily to the second level of irama in *sirepan* or soft-playing style. At this point, the dancer sings a few phrases (sirepan followed by the poetic singing of the dancers is a feature of langendriyan). As far as what can be heard clearly in cylinder #32, the singing is in sléndro.[125] The two recordings do not contain more than a few phrases of singing, which ends abruptly due to the two-minute limit of the wax cylinders. I suggest that what we are hearing is a fragment of langendriyan with a simplified musical accompaniment—a single piece performed repeatedly. The piece was in pélog barang, but the singer sang in sléndro. The simplified langendriyan at the Chicago Columbian Exposition was mounted using whatever resources were available to the performing group.

Did Debussy and others hear the same simplified fragment of langendriyan in Paris? Given the many shared characteristics of the performances at these two exhibitions, the possibility cannot be ruled out. If this was the case, it is worth noting that this confusing musical mixture of heavily simplified dances of the langendriyan have had such a great impact on the works of Parisian writers, painters, and composers. The implication is that the gamelan presented at the World's Fairs reflected an intriguing mixture of various elements, reflecting the nature of the exhibitions themselves: a mixture of various interests—trade, national image, ethnographic show, colonialism, human evolution, and so forth. In other words, the music of langendriyan in the World's Fairs is an allegory of the fairs themselves.

Visitors to the exhibition did not necessarily see the performing arts as arising from the evolution of civilizations. But "a number of the kampong visitors, in spite of—or because of—their anthropological and racist prejudices, were impressed by the beauty and refinement of these [colonized] people, by the fact that they possessed nobility, by the products they made, and by their music and dancing."[126] Listening to and watching the exotic others, in whatever form, is not so much meant to imagine and construct Orientalism as it is "a way of escaping from the rigid conceptual frameworks of evolutionism and colonial domination."[127] In the next section, I will discuss a new context for gamelan that emerged in the mid-twentieth century: Western academia.

From Orientalism to Interculturalism: The 1931 Colonial Exposition, "White" Gamelan Clubs, and Gamelan Study in the United States

> The Exposition was extraordinary. People from the East were being introduced to the bourgeoisie of the Western world in order to disclose their civilization. But they were displayed in such a manner that in the eyes of Western people they nonetheless looked like savages without manners, except in one or two cases. The Indo-Chinese received a lot of attention because of their dancing and music, as did the musicians and . . . dancers from . . . Bali, from whose sounds Western musicians profited greatly.[128]

The quotation is from an Indonesian novel written by Matu Mona: a story about a leader of the Indonesian Communist Party, Tan Malaka, who is exiled for decades by the Dutch government. His comrade, searching for him, travels to Paris, where Malaka lives with a leader of the French Communist Party at the time of the 1931 International Colonial Exposition, held in the Bois de Vincennes.

In the eyes of this novelist, the exposition was no more than a form of colonial exploitation.[129] The exposition was indeed a celebration of colonial power, but the backdrop to the exhibition became more complicated than at previous fairs. In the first place, the exhibition coincided with the Indonesian national awakening, a movement backed by those Dutch who supported the Ethical Policy.[130] The Dutch colonial government also granted more voice and promised better education to the Indonesians, which brought about the founding of Indonesian nationalist organizations such as Budi Utomo and Sarekat Islam. More progressive, anticolonial organizations also appeared, including the Indonesian Communist Party (Partai Komunis Indonesia) and Indonesian Youth Organization (Pemuda Indonesia). In this context, it was necessary for Indonesian voices to be heard in the planning of the display at the exposition. Two Indonesians involved in the initial planning in 1927 were the regent of Serang, Djajadiningrat, and the son of the ruler of the Surakarta court, Hadiwidjojo. They wanted the Indonesian display to be the responsibility of Indonesians.[131] Their suggestion was ineffective, however.

After the exposition was postponed to 1931, in 1929, an Indonesian committee was reinstituted, working in collaboration with the Dutch committee in the Netherlands. In spite of this supposedly collaborative effort, however, Dutch consciousness dominated the conception of the exhibition, which sparked opposition from the Indonesian members of the committee. Prince Hadiwidjojo asked to be discharged from the committee, and the courts of Surakarta and Yogyakarta withdrew their pledge to dispatch their dancers and gamelan musicians to the Exposition.[132]

The idea of presenting court music and dance at the Exposition was also contested by members of the Dutch community. One wrote anonymously to the editor of the Javanese newspaper *Het Soerabajasch Handelsblad:* "Would such a finely tuned soul [referring to court dancers] feel merely embarrassed or truly humiliated [to dance] in front of an endless stream of 'tourists, who saunter from one spectacle to the next, alternating the sounds of African drums with the sights of voluptuous belly dancers and self-lacerating fakirs?'"[133] Another author, who had memories of colonized people being paraded in European cities, worried that Europeans would see them as animals in a zoo, and would consider the performance of court dancers and music to be a shameful sideshow.[134]

Amidst the controversy, the committee dispatched Balinese musicians and dancers to the exposition in the place of Javanese. It seems that the popular image of Bali in the West, and the robust development of Balinese arts in this period, made it the obvious choice: the Dutch government had popularized the island through the promotion of tourism.[135] Consequently, Balinese artists designed performances especially for tourists. An hour-and-a-half-long program consisting of an assortment of dances with musical interludes was a common program offered to Western tourists who stayed in the Bali Hotel in Denpasar. Picard says that the performance at the exposition was similar in design to the tourist shows in Bali hotels.[136] Aside from dances such as *kebiar, janger, legong*, and a shortened version of a dance drama telling the story of the wedding of Arjuna, the troupe also performed a condensed version of *Calonarang*.[137]

Balinese music and dance at the Exposition were received with amazement by the spectators. As Blombergen observes, this was the first Balinese performing group "to perform in Europe, and the huge audiences too were entirely new to them. Journalists and photographers jostled feverishly in their efforts to immortalize the gamelan orchestra . . . , which became renowned overnight . . . The house was sold out every evening, and the musicians and dancers were invariably regaled with the applause and cries of Bravo!"[138]

The well-known composer Olivier Messiaen was also fascinated by the Balinese music he heard at the exposition, so much so that he incorporated his recollection of it in sections of his *Turangalîla Symphony*.[139] Similarly, the dramatist Antonin Artaud's intuitive observation of Balinese dance and theater at the exposition led him to deeply appreciate it, calling it a form of "pure theater" that embodies a highly metaphysical dimension.[140]

In the mid-twentieth century the world of academia began to look at gamelan. One proponent of this study was Jaap Kunst, one of two Dutch scholar-officials whose interest in and study of Indonesian music had a significant impact on the development of the field of non-Western music studies as a whole.[141] Kunst arrived in Indonesia in 1919 as a violinist, playing light music throughout the archipelago with his trio.[142] When he arrived in Java, he was immediately fascinated by gamelan music: his pianist and singer returned to Holland, but Kunst stayed in Indonesia for fifteen years, studying music and working as an official of the Dutch colonial government. Although he wrote various essays and monographs on music from a number of other Indonesian islands, the focus of Kunst's work was on Java. His book *De Toonkunst van Java* (Music in Java), published soon after his return to the Netherlands, became a milestone in the study of Javanese music.

Kunst discussed music with learned Javanese elites and leading court artist-intellectuals, including Mangkunegara VII (r. 1916–44), the well-known Javanologist Purbacaraka and his brother Raden Kodrat, and Raden Mas Jayadipura. He consulted the works of Ki Hadjar Dewantara, Raden Bagoes Soelardi of Mangkunegaran, and an early Yogyakarta kraton gamelan manuscript, *Serat Pakem Wirama*. He also occasionally referred to the great nineteenth-century Javanese encyclopedic work, *Serat Centhini*.

The social structure of colonial Java made it easy for European men of Kunst's status to have a close relationship with Javanese aristocrats, but his relationship with musicians was less intimate. As one of his closest students, Ernst Heins, observes, "Jaap Kunst never touched [or played] a gamelan instrument except for measuring purposes. . . . Because of the colonial situation it was unthinkable for a European to play in a *gamelan* and thus become one of a group of Javanese musicians, or even to take private lessons with a tutor. The mutual social barrier . . . were insurmountable, no Dutchman or other foreigner would or could dream of entering the tightly-closed unit of a *gamelan*-group in those days."[143] Kunst's return to the Netherlands had an impact beyond gamelan scholarship. He is known as one of the founders of the academic discipline he named "ethnomusicology," replacing an existing subdiscipline of musicology called comparative musicology. He proposed that the study object of ethnomusicology "is the *traditional* music and musical instruments of all cultural strata of mankind, from the so-called primitive peoples to the civilized nations."[144]

Since the mid-nineteenth century a number of gamelan sets had been brought to Europe by the Dutch colonial government and by individuals. A number of gamelan enthusiasts in Europe formed groups to performd gamelan music, including accompanying dances or excerpts of wayang performance. As has been noted, in 1857 Delft Royal Academy students formed an ad hoc gamelan group to perform processional music. In the early twentieth century, other gamelan groups appeared whose players were either Javanese sailors or Javanese students studying in the Netherlands.[145] There was also the case of Jodjana, a Javanese student turned dancer, whose gamelan musicians consisted of his Indonesian and Dutch friends, his Dutch wife, and their children.[146]

However, the first "white" gamelan group was founded in 1946 by Bernard Ijzerdraat Jr., a war orphan whom Jaap Kunst cared for. He became fascinated with gamelan after listening to a performance at the Tropen Museum, a gamelan program that had been started by Kunst, and joined the group. Subsequently, he formed his own group, called "Babar Layar," whose members were Dutch teenagers.[147] The group performed regularly at the museum and toured throughout Europe until ceasing to exist in 1950. In 1954 Ijzerdraat left for Indonesia, where he was eventually naturalized as an Indonesian citizen, changing his name to Surya Brata: he became one of the most influential scholars in Indonesian music. In 1960s, gamelan activity in Holland resurfaced under the guidance of Ernst Heins, another student and assistant of Kunst.

Mantle Hood, who had moved from the United States in 1952 to Amsterdam to study with Kunst, joined the Babar Layar group, returning in 1954 to UCLA to teach ethnomusicology. In 1956 Hood went to Java for two years to conduct further research. He studied and learned to play gamelan with prominent musicians in Surakarta and Yogyakarta. Returning to UCLA in 1958, he brought with him a complete set of Javanese gamelan from Surakarta named

Kyai Mendhung (The venerable dark cloud).[148] As a founder of the Institute of Ethnomusicology at UCLA, he organized what were called "performance-study groups" of non-Western music ensembles. This experience led him to articulate an important concept in 1960 called "bi-musicality."[149] The concept is that Western students should acquire some practical experience of the music being studied. The participation of one or more native musicians or teachers was an important ingredient in the performance-study group. They served not only as a teacher or teaching assistant for the ensemble but also as a resource for research, and in return, they were given the opportunity to enroll as students. Hardjo Susilo is the earlist example of this endeavor, starting his career at UCLA in the late 1950s. The author of this book and a number of his Indonesian colleagues have had the same experience as Susilo, teaching and studying either in American or European universities.

Most of the graduates of the UCLA ethnomusicology program promoted the concept of bi-musicality, which was the root of gamelan activity in the United States. In fact, there is no gamelan group in the United States made up exclusively of Indonesians.[150]

Non-Western music performance is a relative newcomer to academia. Classical Western music composed between roughly 1720 and 1930 has long been the "central repertory" at American music schools and university music departments, but:

> Outside the central repertory, special designations are needed because there are courses on "jazz," "folk music," "popular music," and "ethnic music." The terms *early music* and *contemporary music* are used to separate the "normal" music from others in the art music sphere. It is implied that "normal music" (even in North America) means European music, whereas other kinds of music, both in the college and the library catalogs, are labeled by nation or area: "American music," "music—India," and "Indians of North America—music," for example. . . . The various musics that are not "central" have had to struggle over a period of decades for entry into the music school. They usually gained admission via the back door of musicology because faculty and administrators felt, on first application, that one should not teach them as fields of performance, but that it might be all right to teach "about" them because they could be helpful in fostering an understanding of the evolution of the central repertory or of the cultures of early, recent, contemporary, foreign, or rural peoples.[151]

In the 1960s, some universities began to recognize non-Western music performance as an academic pursuit. The introduction of ethnomusicology in universities in the same decade provided for a poly-musical experience. In the 1980s, this diversification of musical experience was considered part of the multicultural movement then in vogue. Originally, multiculturalism developed in response to the growing need to pay attention to minority groups and their cultures. The initial response to this development was specific programs, such as Afro-American Studies, Women's Studies, Asian-American Studies, and American Indian Studies. Thus, although gamelan programs seem to be a perfect fit with multiculturalism, it predates the multicultural movement of the 1980s and has a different aim: the study of music (especially non-Western music) in its cultural context, paying special attention to the notion of music as a communicative device.[152]

Despite this long history, questions about the appropriateness of performance as an academic course still linger. The recent book *Performing Ethnomusicology: Teaching and Representation in World Music Ensembles* provides an invaluable study of this topic.[153] Most authors are forthright in spelling out the dilemma that faces them as ethnomusicologists and instructors of a non-Western performing ensemble: "how do we represent the rich cultures we revere while we acknowledge and deal with the culture distance between us and our students, and between both of us and these cultures?"[154]

As public performance became routine, the boundary between "performance-study" group (Mantle Hood's original term) and performance group became blurred. But how is it possible, in just one semester, or one year, for a group to learn the music well enough for public performance? This practice would never happen with a symphony orchestra or jazz ensemble, for example.

Because of its conspicuous presence among academic non-Western music ensembles (not to mention its great appeal due to its size, appearance, and compelling sound), gamelan has become an icon of non-Western performing ensembles. Ricardo Trimillos lightheartedly says that "the acquisition of a gamelan as part of a 'proper' ethnomusicology program in the United States appears as iconic as the establishment of a national airline in a 'proper' nation!"[155] But gamelan performance on campus does not necessarily engender musical expectation on the same level as the university's orchestra, whose players have had many years of training before joining. As Keith Howard puts it:

> While our [non-Western] ensembles are typically classed as equivalents to orchestras and choirs, we readily accept students without audition, with no pre-requirements. While a violinist in a student orchestra will have taken lessons for many years, passing those indoctrinating and standardizing grade exams that Blacking famously critiqued, and probably competing for a place in the orchestra, the student in a world music ensemble is not expected to have any previous training. Yet, at the end of the semester or the end of the year, our ensemble are expected to perform in much the same way as every choir or orchestra performs. They give a performance before an audience. It is, then, not surprising that both ethnomusicologist and audience will engage in soul searching as they evaluate what has been achieved.[156]

The criticism does not take into account the different musical practices of gamelan and Western orchestras. While playing orchestral instruments requires a student to take lessons for many years, some gamelan instruments offer relative technical simplicity, allowing students who have never played any instrument at all to play quickly. The student might then go on to learn instruments which, like violin or piano, will take many years to master.

This does not mean that the problems of public performances by beginning gamelan groups go away. I would say that the original, less presentational model of performance-study groups is still valued. As an instructor of gamelan myself, I always mention this idea to my beginning students; in addition, I inform them that the gamelan class is not goal-oriented, but rather process-oriented learning. That is, the emphasis is on the experience in music-making during class, not the recital at the end of the semester. Solis's term "experience ensemble" describes this group well: the students "embrace a second (cultural) childhood, akin to the sort of entirely new musical experience most musicians underwent as children with their first piano lessons or sixth-grade band."[157] This differs from the "realization ensemble," or in Vetter's term "canonical ensemble," of Western orchestra, concert band, jazz band, and choral groups, whose student performers have already had years of experience in vocal production or instrumental technique, whose "rehearsal time is dedicated to musical matters; any cultural contextualization of the works is typically relegated to printed program notes. A high standard of musical presentation in public performance and the honing of the performers' technical skill and expressive potential are the primary goals of most canonical ensemble organizations in the academy."[158]

At any rate, a non-Western music ensemble, like any other ensemble on campus, is expected to perform publicly, a practice encouraged by the university's desire for good public relations. In the 1980s, incorporating non-Western music into the curriculum reflected universities' commitments to multicultural perspectives, and continued to apply when multicultural studies evolved into international or intercultural studies. Whether university administrations wholeheartedly support the presence of non-Western music on their campuses is a different story, however. Bruno Nettl observes that the administration "usually makes clear its allegiance to the central music. It is unusual, for example, for administrators to have musical roots that are not in the central music. Some do come from fields such as ethnomusicology or composition (viewed with some suspicion by performing faculty), but in each case, some kind of loyalty, in terms of early training or avocation, to the 'real' music is characteristic in the administrator."[159] Nettl goes on to say: "In choosing events to attend, deans or heads usually prefer central-repertory performances over performances of peripheral music or nonmusical events such as lecturers." There is no follow-up study to show if this perspective persists.

Against the marginal but important position held by their ensemble, ethnomusicologists and gamelan instructors search for ways that their ensembles can fit the academic program. For example, Gage Averill observes that "the current praxis of many world music ensembles is based on the aesthetic imitation (mimesis) or, in its most extreme form, musical transvestism."[160] He goes on to say that ethnomusicologists involved in non-Western ensembles "unwittingly indulge our student participants and our audience in a form of concert tourism ... without challenging preconceived notions of acknowledging the noisy clash of cultures, politics, and musics in contemporary world."[161] Averill is intensely critical of teaching and performing non-Western music, but he also offers a solution:

> To replace mimesis [the aesthetic of imitation] with a self-conscious distantiation; to involve student ensembles in the discourse about cultural representation; to use our rehearsals and performances as platforms for raising questions; to reimagine our musical performance as spaces of dialogic encounter; to problematize the very nature and existence of these ensembles; and to use ensembles to provoke, disrupt and challenge complacency. In this way, we can make the ensemble encounter a part of a student's intellectual, personal, aesthetic, *and ethical* transformation. Such a transformation in the grounding of world music ensembles would require an embrace of the problematics of performance studies, performance/conceptual art, and cultural studies more broadly.[162]

Averill challenges instructors of non-Western music ensembles to come up with a suitable pedagogical requirement that leads students to discuss the larger context of the music that they study, including issues of cultural representation, dialogue about cultural encounters, and so forth. Averill is quick to suggest, however, that playing the music should not be less fun or thrilling. This fun aspect might culminate at the end of semester when the ensemble launchs a public performance. During the semester, gamelan teachers must devote much of their time to preparing their group for this end-of-semester performance; this includes lessons for players of lead instruments, and additional rehearsal.

For the performance, the group might also invite "ringers" to strengthen the ensemble. In some university gamelan groups, the teacher organizes a group whose core members might not be students, but employees of the university, members of the community who happen to have experience playing gamelan during their college years, or alumni of a nearby university. Together with advanced students, this group is responsible for giving public performances. With the increased number of gamelan on campuses, the number of former students with gamelan experience has increased. This has sometimes resulted in a new kind of gamelan performance group, namely a nonprofit community group independent from the university program. A few have been able to maintain their presence in the community, notably the Balinese gamelan Sekar Jaya in the Bay area.

To recapitulate: in the context either of World's Fairs or academia, heterogeneity marks the reception of gamelan. Following Barbara Kirshenblatt-Gimblett, audience experiences can be grouped into two categories: those audiences who acquire authentic aesthetic experiences, and those who obtain

Figure 4.3. Professor Mantle Hood and his American and international students. *From left to right:* Hardja Susilo, Max Harrell, Viswanathan, Mantle Hood, Hormoz Farhat, Willem Adraansz, and Donald Sur. © 1973 the Regents of the University of California. Courtesy of the UCLA Ethnomusicology Archive.

ethnographically mediated experiences.[163] The first category is based on a notion that the audience does not acquire rational understanding of the art they experienced: such a condition will prevent them from receiving authentic aesthetic pleasure. The second category follows the notion of performance as an ethnographic show. That is, the audience's experience is mediated by information about ethnographic signifiers of what they saw. Commonly, visitors to World's Fairs were given all sorts of brochures about the fair in general, and specific information on cultural performances.

Ethnomusicology, through which the presence of gamelan has been expanded in Western universities, required students to be informed about the cultural context of non-Western music. This has gradually brought about cross-cultural perspectives in gamelan discourse. A search for homology between music and socio-cosmological order entered into ethnomusicological discourses, and metaphoric or iconic readings of gamelan, the topic of the next chapter, become one of the most important issues in the study of gamelan.

Chapter Five

Cross-Cultural Perspectives on Gamelan Theory

Metaphorical Readings of Gamelan

In the 1960s, ethnomusicology was commonly defined as the study of music in culture, and Alan Merriam's anthropological approach became the defining practice of the field.[1] Mantle Hood, however, emphasized the musicological side of ethnomusicology.[2] This anthropological-musicological divide is often described as the "Merriam-Hood split." In subsequent studies, a number of ethnomusicologists attempted to find the points of intersection, causation, or homologies between Merriam's three analytical levels—concept, behavior, and sound.[3]

The works of Steven Feld, Marina Roseman, and Judith Becker, to mention just a few, offer a new trajectory in the search for these connections, bridging the anthropological-musicological split and moving toward the unification of musical analysis and socio-ethnography.[4] This change of emphasis happened when the definition of ethnomusicology as "the study of music as culture" gained momentum. Recently, Ingrid Monson has proposed a more encompassing definition, namely "the interdisciplinary study of music as cultural practice."[5] Monson also feels that it is necessary to distinguish ethnomusicology from other fields, including cultural studies. It is important for her to include "interdisciplinary study" in her definition of ethnomusicology "in order to emphasize a practice-based anthropological conception of culture."[6] This definition resonates with the present study, the aim of which is a discourse that strikes a balance between musical processes and socio-ethnography. Before embarking this topic, a brief background of the development of gamelan theory is in order.

The exposure of gamelan at Western universities has led to an increase in its study and the publication of gamelan treatises. For example, whereas nineteenth- and early twentieth-century dictionaries contain only brief entries on gamelan, by the mid-twentieth century longer essays appeared in volumes such as *The New*

Harvard Dictionary of Music, *The New Grove Dictionary of Music and Musicians*, and *The Garland Encyclopedia of World Music*.[7] These entries have become important references for authors who deal with musical culture and theory.

Intercultural understanding of gamelan goes beyond ethnographic and cultural topics, and performance, to encompass cross-cultural music theory. One noticeable example is the entry under "Mode" in the *New Grove Dictionary*, in which a lengthy essay on *pathet* (gamelan modal system) is one of the main subentries. Authored by several music scholars, the entry on "Mode" encompasses modal practices around the world, in Western and non-Western music. Chief author Harold Powers is a towering figure in both musicology and ethnomusicology, and one of the few music scholars whose works reveal a significant cross-cultural perspective. In his essay "Language Models and Musical Analysis," Powers uses various linguistic models in the analysis of European music from different historical periods (from Gregorian chant onward), Indian music, Javanese gamelan, and Middle Eastern music.[8]

I should mention that the proliferation of gamelan theory in the last six decades or so has been made possible by an intimate relationship between Western scholars, their Indonesian counterparts, and Javanese musicians. As I have stated:

> The presence of Dutch and American musicologists in Java in the twentieth century has kept Euro-American perspectives in view during the formulations of contemporary gamelan theory by Javanese musicologists. Moreover, since the middle of the [twentieth] century, opportunities have arisen for Javanese gamelan students to study ethnomusicology in Western countries. From the 1960s, gamelan theory has entered a new phase: the direct involvement of some Javanese musicians in formulating it. And in the 1970s, Javanese theorists often had the opportunity to exchange ideas and to work with their Western counterparts.[9]

This intellectual atmosphere is conveyed in Marc Perlman's delightful study *Unplayed Melodies*. The main topic of his study—implicit melody—came to him from three Javanese practitioners of gamelan music (myself, Supanggah, and Suhardi); he himself is a well-versed practitioner of gamelan. Perlman ends his book with a chapter discussing several Western musical analyses (ranging from Zarlino's sixteenth-century treatises to Schenker's approach in the twentieth century), pointing to how these analyses are relevant to gamelan theory.

The work of pioneering ethnomusicologist Mantle Hood on pathet is also to a certain extent cross-cultural: he uses terms such as "tonic," "dominant," "subdominant," and "cadence," terms that are not indigenuous to the gamelan. He postulates that the cadential formula "serves as the framework of the whole gendhing, which, in short, is one of the strongest features in the identification and, consequently, the very preservation of the pathet concept itself."[10] Judith

Becker asserts even more strongly the notion of a formulaic system in gamelan: "Gamelan *gendhing* (pieces) are formulaic from beginning to end . . . and in all musical lines."[11]

Becker connects this notion of a formulaic concept to the Serbo-Croatian epic singing tradition studied by Albert Lord.[12] Based on the creative work of musicians in an oral tradition, she suggests that a musician "has mastered a *technique* of composition based upon *the manipulation of formulas*, which allows him to perform and compose at the same moment."[13] Adapting a similar line of thought, Sutton speaks of the parallels in musical processes between Gregorian chant and Javanese gamelan, which he describes as a "centonization" method, a process of stringing together standard patterns selected from a stock of formulas.[14]

Becker's contribution to the study of gamelan goes beyond the formulaic concept of the music. Written in collaboration with with her husband, Alton Becker, her study on gamelan as metaphor for socio-cosmological order has become a seminal part of the ethnomusicological literature.[15] The main point of their argument is that the multiple cyclic motions and their periodic coincidences are the principal governing mechanism of gamelan music, from which the meaning of the music is conveyed, and which is in parallel with calendrical and other cultural systems. This chapter continues the discourse that the Beckers have started.

Metaphorical Readings of Gamelan

It is useful to provide a background of the broad characteristics of traditional Indonesian music. The fundamental governing musical principle of much Indonesian music is the cyclic recurrence of the melodic-temporal unit.[16] Jose Maceda uses the terms "drone" or "ostinato" to explain this musical phenomenon in Southeast Asia; a drone that centers not on pitch (as in Indian and Western music), but on pulse and timbre.[17] Gong-type instruments often mark off the basic musical unit. Other types of percussion instruments (such as drums) provide rhythmic support (in some cases, such as in *gondang* music of the Batak people in Sumatra and the Burmese *hsaing waing* ensemble, a set of pitched drums play the melody). Other instruments (often vocally inspired instruments such as the trumpet, rebab, and flute) provide the melody. In Maceda's terms, this melody is a musical counterpart to the drone.[18]

Margaret Kartomi proposes that typical religious thought and practice require a belief in the essential unity of existence and in a dualistic aspect of reality.[19] This belief is reflected in "the main syntactical dualism . . . between the rigidly unvarying tunings and rhythmic patterns of the drums and metallophones on the one hand, and the ornamented, intonationally variable, rhythmically libertarian wind and vocal parts on the other."[20] As in the other iconic readings I mentioned earlier, which place emphasis on homologies between musical structure and social order, more needs to be said about the dynamics of gondang music and its representation of Bataknese social structure and interaction. In light of the importance of the kinship systems in Batak life and *adat* (custom and tradition), the music may be seen as a form of acting out kin relations and the qualities embodied in those relations.[21]

Becker and Becker define "iconicity" as "the nonarbitrariness of any metaphor," following Kenneth Burke's study in *The Rhetoric of Religion*.[22] Burke defines various realms to which words may refer: (1) words for the natural world; (2) words for the socio-political realm; (3) words about words; and (4) words for the "supernatural."[23] Inspired by these schemes, Becker and Becker suggest several things that are important about languages and musics:

> 1. That the epistemology appropriate for discussing things is different for each realm: that is a stone is "real" in a different way than a friend is "real" or divine grace is "real." . . .
>
> 2. In a given culture, at a given point in history, one "realm" may be given priority, in the sense that discourse is most convincing if it can be put in terms of one particular realm. . . .
>
> 3. Iconicity can be defined using Burke's categories as finding the image of something in another realm, for example, finding kinship (realm 2) in nature (realm 1): plants belong to "families"; finding ecological "truths" (realm 1) in human relations (realm 2).[24]

Timothy Rice identifies four common metaphors which have been used by ethnomusicologists and musicologists: (1) the music-as-art metaphor, which refers to music as being about the processes of performing and composing music; (2) music as social behavior metaphor, in response to the music-as-art metaphor; (3) music as symbolic system or text that can make reference not only to the music itself, but also to a world beyond music; and (4) the music-as-commodity metaphor.[25] In the scheme proposed by Rice, Becker's study falls in the third category: music can have referential meanings to things, ideas, worlds, and experiences outside music itself.

The topic of music and metaphor has a long and complex history as part of both musicology and ethnomusicology.[26] The main issue is the use of language to describe the properties and relationships of music through metaphorical descriptions.[27] Zbikowski goes on to say that "one of the primary functions of language is to manipulate the attention of another person within a shared referential frame," while "music is to manipulate the emotions of others."[28] In a broader sense, "music can manipulate the emotions through the way it shapes ritual, dance, and rendering of a text."[29] Although music and language "comprise different domains of experience . . . mappings between these domains would yield numerous possibilities for the sort of meaning construction associated with metaphor."[30]

In light of that discussion of music and metaphor, I should say that I use the Javanese kingship tradition, or social relations in general, as a metaphor for the gamelan musical system.[31] To begin, I will recount the following anecdotes:

> At a wedding celebration, each musician from the gamelan academy ASKI (now ISI) of Surakarta sat down before the instrument of his choosing. One of my teachers chose to play bonang, his favorite instrument. He then played *grambyangan* and *buka* (introductory melodies) of *gendhing bonang* (an instrumental piece). Carefully listening, we all were able to enter on the stroke of the large gong (marking the beginning of the piece) with the correct gong note. But a feeling of uncertainty emerged. Why? Most of us did not know the piece, except perhaps our other two teachers. Some of us, including the kendhang player, whispered to each other, trying to identify the piece. For the remainder of the performance of this piece, we were trying to rely on our teachers for guidance from their instruments. What a way to begin a performance!

* * *

> The event was a monthly informal gathering of musicians for a "jam" session. Two pieces, *ladrang Wilujeng* and *gendhing Kombang Mara*, were completed smoothly. Then a few players invited a senior rebab (bowed string instrument) player, who was sitting among the listeners, to play; he agreed. He played *senggrèngan* and buka of a piece in sléndro tuning. After the group joined in on the stroke of the large gong, the saron (one-octave metallophones) could not be heard—the players were having a hard time identifying the piece. Even the bonang player seemed uncertain what to play. The previous rebab player, who was sitting near the senior rebab player, stood up and walked towards the bonang. He grasped the bonang mallets from the present player and began playing. The ensemble continued playing, with fewer problems: the new bonang player knew the piece, enabling him to guide the other players.
>
> In the same "jam," out of respect the group invited me to play gendèr. I complied, and requested that the group play *gendhing Lobong*, a piece that has many *andhegan* (momentary pauses in the middle of a piece). As we entered the beginning of the second section of the piece, the kendhang player signaled for the piece to stop. As in any andhegan, at this juncture the solo pesindhèn sings, demonstrating her melodic dexterity. At the end of her line, the gamelan resumed playing. The drum was first to play, guiding the whole ensemble for an appropriate irama. But the 'flamboyant' drummer led the ensemble in an unusual way—instead of playing in irama wilet, he unexpectedly gave the signal to play in irama rangkep. The ensemble had to respond by playing accordingly. Musicians and listeners in the hall were laughing. It was a pleasant surprise for me, although I had to struggle to find my treatment of *gendèran rangkep*.

These musical events are contrary to the usually image of gamelan. The images of a harmonious musical society (*rukun*) and cooperative work (*gotong royong*), commonly used to portray gamelan, are fractured, replaced by demonstrations of power (the rebab and *bonang* player), displays of individual virtuosity (the pesindhèn and the kendhang player), and playfulness. This might have just been the wayward personalities of a few musicians wishing to show off their musical prowess (for which the bonang player in the first example is known), or to demonstrate a kind of musical mischievousness to get attention (for which the kendhang player in the second event is infamous). To a certain extent, this might be true, but I am going to assume that my anecdotes are of more significance. How do we account for these dramatic interactions? Before addressing this question, let us recall Becker's study:

> In Java, the fundamental governing principle in gamelan music is the cyclic recurrence of a melodic/temporal unit, which is a musical manifestation of the way in which the passage of time is also ordered. In Java, time is represented as cyclical. Furthermore, time in Java is not represented as a single recurrent cycle, but several concurrent cycles running simultaneously. Important days are reckoned as those points of coincidence between the different, continuously ongoing cycles (Geertz, 1973; Kartodirdjo, 1959).
>
> The five-day-week cycle and the seven-day-week cycle are two calendrical systems most used in Java for daily affairs. . . . Any given day must be reckoned by its position in both cycles. Every thirty-five days (5 x 7) the cycles coincide, and this point of conjunction always has special significance.[32]

In other words, coincidence is important in both music and calendrical time. For Becker, "the notion of coincidence and the meanings, the beauty, and the power it generates operate across different kinds of reality."[33]

Becker is also struck by the *rigid binariness* of the music.[34] This is realized in the ways that a gongan structure is symmetrically divided and subdivided: "A whole becomes a half, then each half is divided into halves, making quarters, then each quarter is again halved, making eighths, etc. Like the cyclical conception of time, the basic duality of this music reflects a dual system of classification in Indonesia," which extends from the macrocosmic to the microcosmic level.[35]

Becker's idea that gamelan should be understood in terms of its epistemological links is a good start. However, the rather selective musical examples presented in her study lead me to think that there is more to explore on this subject. Her musical illustrations are chosen to stress the point of cyclic subdivisions; hence, only a few instruments are featured, mainly gong, kenong and saron, exemplifying the instruments in the first, second, and third levels of subdivision. There is almost no mention of other instruments, such as rebab and gendèr. An excerpt of the score of the piece *Subakastawa*, which includes elaborating instruments and singing, is referred to only in passing. Becker's primary focus on gong and temporal structure may create the impression that the musical system of Javanese gamelan is rigidly regimented; such a focus, although important, leaves out much that is central to gamelan practice.

Before commenting on Becker's study further, I would like to mention another example of an iconic reading of gamelan. As reported by Jaap Kunst, the regent of Temanggung, R. A. A. Chakrahadikusuma, wrote a treatise considering the parallels between gamelan compositions and batik cloth. He classifies gamelan instruments into three categories corresponding to three stages of batik making: *kalowongan*, the outlines of the batik patterns, correspond to the colotomic instruments and instruments playing *balungan*, while other instruments are comparable to *plataran* (the background) and *hisen-hisen* (decorative filling).[36] Kunst also reports a bureaucratic iconic model of gamelan:

> According to a Javanese conception the rebab may be called the *raja*, and the kendang the *patih* (prime minister) of the gamelan community (the gong, which subdivides the composition according to fixed laws, may be called the *jaksa* (here =judge)); in other words, according to this view the rebab is admittedly the principal instrument, but it has delegated the real work, i.e. the leading of the orchestral society, to the kendang, which, as it were, translates the former's instructions into a form easily understood by the community, whilst the gong sees to it that all melodic phrases are equitably allowed the same length.[37]

In his provocative article "Musical Politics in Central Java," John Pemberton observes that this image of a musical model kingdom appears in a reduced, more streamlined version in Martopangrawit's treatises on gamelan theory. A former prominent court musician and gamelan theorist, Martopangrawit categorizes the functions of gamelan instruments into two groups: *pamurba* (those instruments which have authority) and *pamangku* (those instruments which support).[38]

The model bureaucracy image was also transposed into Indonesian national thought in the mind of a prominent nationalist, Dr. Soetomo. According to him, in gamelan music,

> each player is skilled in his own instrument: the kendang player in beating his kendang and likewise those who play the gambang, saron, kempul, gong, rebab, and those who sing. In addition, each performer has to know the melody; each has to know when to play and when to stop. . . . There must be teamwork in addition to each person's own competence. If each player performs expertly and understands and obeys the rules, players will produce harmonious music. If each player is expert, disciplined, and willing to work with others, the results will be pleasing.[39]

Soetomo adds that, aside from knowing how to play and being expert on their instruments, "by working harmoniously, following regulations (manut pranatan), to obey discipline," musicians "can work together, not jealous nor causing to show off one's own work, so as to be able to have a result which is harmonious, appropriate and not incongruent."[40]

Clearly, the above ideal image of gamelan is in contrast with the anecdotes I related earlier. Moreover, as Pemberton reported, based on stories told to him by older musicians from court circles (including Martopangrawit), many accomplished gamelan musicians were, and so remained during the period of his research in the 1970s, "a spunky lot, known for gambling, romancing, and drinking . . . Stories are studded with cigar-toting drummers, rival *rebab* players, gamelan jokesters, and musical revenge—all part of a lively dissonance rather than a model social harmony."[41]

This lively dissonance can also be found in musical practice. Even in gamelan performances held in a religious context, there occur shows of musical rivalry, such as in the performance of gamelan *sekatèn* (a special ensemble of remarkably large instruments, performed once a year to celebrate the life of the Prophet Muhammad.) The playing of a sekatèn piece begins with a long introduction performed by the bonang, but the choice of the specific piece for the ensemble is determined by the first *demung* player in the moment after the end of the bonang introduction. "Since the *bonang* player must lead the chosen piece, the *demung* player chooses carefully, either to expose the *bonang* 'master' with an obscure composition, or to hand him a lightweight piece (knowing full well that sooner or later positions will switch). Built in to this scene is the enticing possibility of subverting the 'master,' musically."[42]

Whereas in the religious context musicians can demonstrate this kind of musical game, they can do so to an even greater extent, either subtly or explicitly, in a regular gamelan performance. Pemberton's succinct description of this lively "dissonance":

> Although the *halus* [refined] gamelan orchestra may appear to be governed by a perfect regularity of uniform gong cycles and routine melodic formula, its music is riddled with moments of specific irregularity and structural contradiction. There are, for example, points in certain gamelan compositions where everyday melodic patterns are replaced by an idiosyncratic melody or a direct musical quotation; this gives the composition its character. Then again, there are melodic impasses, blind spots built into the very structure of gamelan music: points which require the sudden transformation of a two and one-half octave melody into one and one-half octaves; sudden modal shifts within a single composition; broad melodic leaps which, for the detailed workings of the gamelan's elaborating instruments, can create the sense that there is no way to get "there" from "here." These are moments where one either wings it with a show of confidence (which, when the results are less than successful, is called *ngawur*, "faking it") or draws from a traditional bag

of musical tricks, or both. It is the solving, or better yet, the playing out of these musical riddles that forms a musician's esoteric know-how: the crystallization from gamelan experience of all that does *not* fit the rules.[43]

Pemberton does not pursue the potential iconic reading of this cunning artistry of the musicians as a reflection of socio-cosmological order. Similarly, there has not been further discussion about the process of either batik making or bureaucratic operation as metaphoric readings of gamelan, although each is suggestive and invites more detailed consideration. As regards batik, for example, one might ponder more closely the process that gives each batik cloth its auspicious aura.[44] If one considers batik cloth only as an end product, it could be seen merely as a relentless repetition of the same design patterns. However, in examining the process of *batik tulis* (hand-written batik) making, one discovers that it is "the very process of repeating, ornamenting, or combining segments of known patterns which for Javanese gave batik its auspicious aura."[45] Philip Kitley further observes that, traditionally, the process is "an extended exercise in self control and an intimate involvement in stroking potent symbols. As the *canting* (waxing pen) moved in and around the shapes, the batik artist brought to life symbols and patterns which radiated auspiciousness through their traditional associations."[46] Thus, the significance of making batik lies in the central Javanese belief that repetition is also re-creation, a cyclical process of renewal.[47]

Also referencing batik, Weiss asserts that the quality of batik is assessed "by looking at the refinement of the marks on the cloth, the clearness of the colour, the intricacy and clarity of the detail as it leads the eye from aggregations of the minute to the larger repeating pattern."[48] Like gamelan, the important element in batik is the treatment and quality of detail.

But the batik analogy with gamelan goes only so far, since batik making is carried out by only one artist. The question is, therefore: what more can be said about the iconic relationships between the gamelan musical system and Javanese culture in general, if we take into account the overall, processual dynamic of the music?

The Bureaucracy Metaphor and the Networking Model

As has been noted, Chakrahadikusuma intriguingly conceptualizes gamelan in terms of a bureaucratic model—rebab is likened to the king; the king gives executive power to the drum (the prime minister); and the large gong, the chief justice, ensures that resources are distributed lawfully. However, the metaphor could easily be understood as a bureaucracy. What is needed is further elucidation of the dynamics of the kingship bureaucratic operation.

"Magico-religious" or "ritual state" have commonly been used to describe the character of the kingship tradition of seventeenth- and eighteenth-century

Mataram.[49] Harmony and ritual anchored the relationship between sovereign and people. Applying the analogy of cosmic order, the sovereign was regarded as the central star about which the whole society revolved. This paradigm required the absolute power of the king over his subjects, and thus the king was identified as a god or, in Islamized Java, *kalipatulah* (God's representative on the earth). This concept is known among anthropologists as transcendent kingship. Laksono explains that the premise of the transcendent model is to characterize kingship as "something ethereal," and "absolutely beyond the reach of the five senses."[50] The divine king's role "was absolute in guaranteeing the perpetuation of order in macrocosmos"; he was thus "the only true model of the universe and, by corollary, the one and only way of resolving life and death issues."[51] This structuring principle would create a diametrically opposed binary taxonomy, such as sacred-secular, lord-servant, good-evil, and even left-right (discussed below).

However, this "magico-religious" character or "ritual state" model of Javanese kingship represents an ideal structure or normative view of it.[52] In implementation, different dynamics come to the fore. It follows that the rigid binary taxonomy noted above often contradicts much that happens in the Javanese tradition. For example, Javanese people acknowledge a social stratification, but it is not in the pure form of the Hindu caste system, which emphasizes endogamy and heredity. Rather, tolerance is one of the salient traits of the Javanese.[53]

One of the hallmarks of Javanese tradition, the *slametan* (ritual feast), is an example of a ritual event that runs against the very premise of the principal of hierarchy. Performed in all sorts of rites of passage and other critical junctures in one's life, slametan is attended by the sponsor's neighbors regardless of their status in society. Slametan is a momentary bonding of members of the community in which, ideally, everyone is treated equally, although individual status is also acknowledged.

This kind of dynamic is well represented in many aspects of the shadow puppet performance, wayang. Anderson's definition of wayang points to the richness of this performance tradition: "Wayang, like any other metaphysical and ethical 'system,' is concerned to explain the universe. Though partially based on the Indian epics Mahaharata and Ramayana, the Javanese wayang mythology is yet an attempt to explore poetically the existential position of Javanese man, his relationships to the natural and supernatural order, to his fellow-men—and to himself."[54] This is achieved by Javanizing the Indian epics. Where the Hindu "*Mahabharata* rhetoric contained certain elements diametrically opposed to social relations," Javanese social structure "tended to favour the identical, reciprocal and equi-positioning of the various components making up the configuration of indigenous society."[55] For example, one of the most beloved characters in wayang, Semar, is a clown-servant of multi-paradoxical character and iconography.[56] "He is ornamented like a woman, his clothes are those of man, yet his face is that of neither man nor woman. He is the repository of the highest wisdom, yet this flashes from in between his gentle jokes, his clowning, and even his persistent uncontrollable farting."[57] More on Semar:

> What manner of creation is this, who stands leaning on his belly? or is it, who sits rocking on his buttocks?
>
> The mid-day sun is sallow beside the radiance of his face.
> How can such brilliance emanate from one as pallorous as a corpse?
>
> No parent, no children has he. His smile misted in tears.
> Bleak perils of humanity, softened in the gentle rain of his compassion.
>
> Goodness itself, this god made man, who
> Dominates the *satria* with servitude.
>
> Kings grovel before him; gods honour him;
> Even the Most-High does his bidding.
>
> Invincible through nondeeds, omnipotence in inertia.
> Here lies the source of his *sakti* (divine might).
>
> Dawn at dusk, sunset at daybreak.
> The perfect being: Ismaya.[58]

The paradoxical nature of Semar epitomizes a perfect democratic ideal, namely that the highest status is in perfect unity with the lowest status; *manunggaling kawula lan gusti* (a perfect union between the commoner and the lord) is a philosophical expression that captures well the meaning of this concept.

The complex picture of human relations is also conveyed in the seemingly insignificant division of puppet characters according to their left or right position in the screen—left associated with evil, right with good. In fact, this left-right division in wayang informs us that "the deeper complementarities and ambiguous interconnections of human existence are cunningly exposed by the irony that Left and Right are not absolute. Depending whether, at a wayang performance, one watches the puppets or their shadows, right becomes left and left right. Both are merely in the eye of the beholder."[59]

To fully understand the complexity of Javanese social relations, we should conceptualize those relations in terms of both transcendent and immanent aspects. Luc Nagtegaal does something similar when he argues that Javanese kingship should be defined in terms of a complex network of social relations. One of his points is that the Mataram state was a largely decentralized society: "The balance of power was constantly changing and was heavily dependent upon individual personalities."[60]

The mutual ties between those who possessed political power were strictly personal, and did not apply to an entire group. The average person in a position of power was both patron and client; his authority was based partly on the support of a number of subordinates and partly on the favours of his superior. All these ties together made up a complex network that was the official way, in the Java of the seventeenth and eighteenth centuries, of exercising political power. In other words, this network was itself 'the state.'[61]

Thus, the Mataram state was a complex "network state," having immense flexibility in its social structure, social networking, and ability to incorporate new, foreign elements.

Interactive Networking and Leadership

Three points have emerged from this discussion. First, the transcendent model has been revised by recognizing the importance of the immanent aspect of social relations. Secondly, dualism or binary classification should not be understood rigidly in the Javanese tradition, since it often contradicts the practice of Javanese tradition. Lastly, the networking model is better suited than a rigid bureaucratic model to describe the Javanese kingship tradition.

The importance of networking is the subject of Benjamin Brinner's study of competency and interaction in gamelan playing. He points out: "The flexibility of Javanese *gamelan* performance makes interaction fundamental to this tradition. Performance decisions ranging from the choice of pieces to be played to many aspects of the way in which these pieces will be performed can be spontaneous because the core competence includes extensive knowledge of interactive networks, systems, and structures."[62] Furthermore, "nearly every aspect of interaction depends on context, and interactive priorities are shuffled from one musical genre to the next. This variety is greater still when one considers individual musicians' preferences, strengths, and weaknesses and the interpersonal dynamics of performance."[63]

"Interactive network" is a key term here. As in the case of leadership in the Mataram political structure, there is a problem in defining leadership in the musical ensemble:

> Labeling one member of an ensemble "leader" implies that the others are "followers." Often enough this is true, but in many contexts this is an inappropriate term, since musicians may be musically or socially subordinate to a leader and interact with that leader without actually following. A possible alternative is the commonly invoked "accompanist," but this word carries connotations which are limiting or unfortunate. There may be many situations in which no term is needed at all, but when one is required "support" appears a likely candidate to contrast with "leader" or to distinguish those who are

not in the sonic foreground at a given moment. Analysis of supporting roles involves assessing how much room these roles allow for individual initiative and which domains are influenced or dictated by other performers.[64]

It is very common to categorize gamelan instruments according to a set of functions. But the interactive nature of the music has made any classification according to their function always incomplete. This is because the key of an interactive network "is more than a set of roles. It is also defined by the relationships between members of an ensemble and the musical domains in which these relationships are played out. A musician leads, follows, mediates, or supports with respect to other musicians and to particular aspects of sound-shaping. To tackle this part of the interactive equation, we need to ask to whom a musician relates in a particular role and in which domain(s) this relationship is played out."[65]

Brinner goes on to contrast the tasks of a conductor of a Western orchestra with the leadership of Javanese gamelan. While the symphonic conductor has unchallenged musical authority, leadership responsibilities in Javanese gamelan are shared among several musicians. Those responsibilities shift among instrumentalists and vocalists, each with his or her domain of influence. Melodic leaders in gamelan do not dominate like a Western conductor (for example, to pick a particular instrument to bring out a particular note), but influence other parts through musical idioms or passages.[66]

Gongan-Irama, a Structural Binary

How are we to combine this fluidity of leadership in gamelan with a division such as pamurba-pamangku (authority and supporter), which is common knowledge among musicians?

Becker pointed out that gongan structure is rigidly binary. This binary division reflects a dual system of Indonesian classification generally: sea-mountain, moon-sun, female-male, and so forth. In this regard, Weiss suggests that though many scholars assert "a tacit assumption of balanced stasis between pairs," we should "reexamine the dynamic relationship between binary pairs in Javanese culture."[67] Weiss illustrates this in terms of the juxtaposition between order and chaos as embodied in the story of Goddess of the South Ocean, Ratu Kidul: "She is associated with demons, death, and the dangerous sea, yet she also empowers those whose right it is to rule Java, bestows life and wealth, and nurtures prosperity on land."[68] Ratu Kidul is known as "a vacillation between the sea and the land," but she also has a "role as adviser and protector of rulers and also devastator of their realms and reigns."[69] Weiss makes a key point about what is important in this binary classification: "the juxtaposition between order and chaos . . . is not one of rigid opposition."[70]

One division is paired with its balanced opposite, one is in dialectical interaction with the other. To elaborate, let us examine the case of the interaction between gongan and *irama*.[71]

Gongan is an essential element, the structural framework of a gendhing—corresponding to the transcendent aspect in the kingship tradition. It is a subjective form that exists in the minds of musicians. In practice, however, this formal structure can be manipulated, modified, or enhanced. A concept that governs the shift of temporal flow, which has an effect on the gongan structure, is called irama—in the kingship tradition, this is the domain of the immanent.

In the narrower sense, irama is a temporal flow: *seseg* (fast), *sedheng* (moderate) and *tamban* (slow). In a wider sense, irama denotes a process of expansion or contraction of formal structure accompanied by a corollary change in density levels of the elaborating instruments. There are four levels of irama: *tanggung* (I), *dadi* (II), *wilet* (III), and *rangkep* (IV).[72] The transition from one irama to another is carried out by a gradual slowing down or speeding up of tempo, which is then followed by the increase or decrease of the density levels (i.e., by doubling or halving) of the elaborating instruments in proportion to the basic beat of a gendhing, often carried out by the balungan. When the irama of a piece changes, the pulse and the melody of balungan may or may not change, depending on the irama in which the melodic basis of the piece resides.

The drum (kendhang) governs irama. There are three drumming styles, each corresponding to the mood of the composition (or a section of it), to the mood of the theatrical performance, or to the characters of a dance. These drumming styles consist of rhythmic patterns, ranging from the repetition of a simple pattern with an underlying regular beat (kendhang *satunggal* and kendhang *kalih*) to elaborate patterns with elusive, but still regular, beats (kendhang *ciblon* and *wayangan*). In a medley presentation, two or more drumming styles may be used in different sections of the performance of a composition.

The change of irama has wider musical implications beyond the change of density and temporal flow. It allows a single piece to assume different lengths and different degrees of instrumental or vocal embellishment; as it usually requires different playing styles for some instruments, it affects melodic content, and thus also affects the mood of the piece.[73] For example, in playing the first section of *ladrang Pangkur*, the drum plays a less elaborate rhythmic pattern in the kendhang kalih style; gendèr plays in the less ornate *lomba* technique; and bonang plays a predictable, less elaborate pattern called *pipilan*. When the drum cues the ensemble to change to irama wilet (by guiding the ensemble to slow down with the more lively ciblon drumming style), the gendèr will change its playing from lomba to the lively rangkep style; and the bonang playing changes from pipilan to the animated *imbal* technique.

Here a metaphor with social relations can be drawn: the transcendent (an essential element that stands beyond the actual practice) is to be paired with its opposite, the immanent (an element that has direct relevance to the changing of the situation). The former is the gongan cycle (a subjective or formal reality), the latter, irama (the realm of existential or practical).

Rebab and the Lord-Servant Binary

The transition from one irama to another might be accompanied by a change of playing style, e.g., from soft to loud or vice versa. When the playing style changes from soft to loud, the rebab, vocalists, gendèr, and other soft-sounding instruments drop out. The question is, in light of the role of the rebab as melodic leader of the ensemble, who is then responsible for leading the ensemble?

It is true that Javanese musicians and theorists consistently label the rebab as the leader of the ensemble. The formal terms used by Sindusawarno and Martopangrawit to describe rebab's leading role is pamurba lagu, "that which serves as the supervisor of melody." Some musicians use a term that implies deeper meaning, namely, *pamurba yatmaka*, "that which gives authority over the soul." Sastrodarsono explains: "The word yatmaka derives from the [root] word 'yatma,' which means 'soul.' The melody and the wilet [ornament] of the rebab become the jewel of gamelan playing; thus it can be said that [rebab] becomes the 'soul' of gamelan playing. Here the soul refers to the melody and wilet of the rebab."[74]

Older writings on gamelan also mention the importance of the rebab. According to Soelardi, the rebab must "be competent in the treatment of melody, since it is the guidance of pesindhèn and gendhing. It is analogous to the feeling of a gendhing."[75] Notice that the rebab not only guides pesindhèn, but also the gendhing. Moreover, the rebab is seen to project one of the most important elements of the music, namely the feeling (*raosing*) of a gendhing.

With regard to rebab playing, the *Serat Centhini* (late eighteenth or early nineteenth century) also uses the term yatmaka.

9. The string was bowed, pitch *nem* was confirmed.
Then [the rebab] played a *sendhon* in *pathet sanga*,
complete with its cadenza.
Then a *gendhing* began:
Gambir Sawit was heard pleasantly and lightly.
Agreeable was the ornament of their playing,
well together,
all got the same feel.
Mrs. Kacer was singing lively in rising melody,
tightening the hearts,

10. intensely clear as the flute fills with essence.
Intertwining is the ornament in accompanying the *rebab*.
Hence significantly appealing
as all meticulous embellishing [their playing].
As sliced rattan in a half,
the sounds are encompassed in the string.
Rebab and *sindhèn* are sweet,
reaching a peak is the depth of the harmony.
The soul of (*yatmakaning*) *gendhing* and singing slices our hearts,
exciting is Kulawirya.[76]

To further illustrate the significance of gamelan networking and the ambiguity of the role of the rebab, let us examine the composition *Puspa Warna* (see ex. 5.1). The evidence shows that the *gérongan* (male chorus) melody underlines the piece,[77] which puts the rebab in a compromising position: its status as a melodic leader is weakened. It is true that the rebab part could still be conceived of as a melodic guide, bridging or anticipating the gérongan lines, but in practice the role of the rebab as a melodic leader is marginalized, to the extent that musicians would have no problem playing the piece even if the rebab were absent. This is because the melodic identity of the piece is already clearly presented in the gérongan.[78]

In summary, the role of the rebab is determined by the practice of networking. In certain irama—e.g., dadi and wilet in soft-style playing—the rebab is considered to be a melodic guide for the ensemble. However, the rebab becomes insignificant, performing unadorned melody, when the piece shifts to irama tanggung. In fact, in this irama, the rebab might drop out altogether. Here one may observe a transfer of power from rebab to bonang, or even to the saron group. This happens when the piece is presented in faster tempi and with loud-style playing. The rebab—the "king" according to the bureaucracy metaphor—must temporarily cede its authority to other instruments.

Elaboration of the Skeleton

Our discussion would be incomplete without mentioning another dynamic dualism, namely the concept of melodic skeleton (balungan) and its elaboration (*kembangan*). This deceptively simple concept has long been an important issue in gamelan discourse. However, the nature of the balungan itself is controversial. Early gamelan theorists assumed that balungan is contained in the melody of the one-octave instruments, the saron.[79] This notion has been corrected to prefer the notion of balungan as an abstraction of multi-octave melodies drawn from the multi-octave instruments or vocal parts.[80] This means that the balungan can be a form of melody existing only in the mind of the musicians since none of the instruments assigned to play balungan have the ambitus comparable to the multi-octave instruments or vocal parts.

Example 5.1. The Ngelik section of Puspa Warna (balungan, rebab, gérongan). The underlined melodies of rebab and gérongan (connected by arrows) indicate the ways in which rebab leads gérongan. Key: () = Gong; ⌢ = Kenong; ⌣ = Kempul.

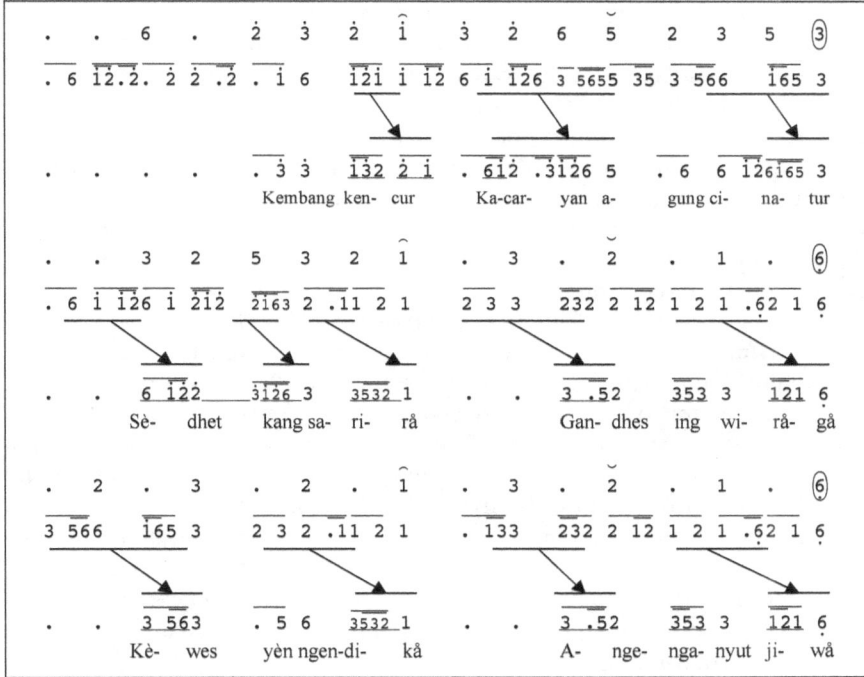

However, even after balungan has been redefined, the question persists: is it really used as a guide for melodic elaboration? Marc Perlman suggests that in the context of balungan as both abstract and concrete sense (polysemy) of 'gendhing,' "the balungan, more than any other part, is conceptually central to the idea of the composition."[81] Even given the varied contours of balungan (indicating their relationship with other parts, whether congruent or divergent with them),[82] balungan, as a form of implicit melody, "function[s] cognitively to make the melodic texture of *karawitan* [gamelan] more coherent and its melodic guidance more consistent"[83] However, even if the musicians considered balungan as "a purely conceptual guide, the basis for musical interpretation, the *balungan* often fails to offer a clear basis or point of reference for the elaborating parts."[84]

Why doesn't balungan always guide the melodic motion of the piece? Perlman has addressed this question intensively.[85] Here, I would like to answer the question from the perspective of the concept of dynamic dualism I mentioned above. Balungan is a reference to the "simplified world" (to borrow Perlman's term) of a complex musical process. It represents a subjective melodic framework—the transcendent or essential element. Yet its central role is not always consented to by other parts of the ensemble—the immanent or existential element.

The point about gamelan's musical processes is not so much that one part dictates another, but rather that one part interacts with and affects the other. Past and present gamelan discourses often emphasize musical interaction, minimizing the importance of balungan, though acknowledging its central role. In discussing a strategy for memorizing gendhing without gamelan, a senior and accomplished musician, the late Mitropradongga, told Perlman: "If you try to memorize the *balungan,* you'll easily forget it (*gampang lali*), but if you fill it with *rebaban, kendhangan, gendèran,* or whatever else you're familiar with, it will stick (*leket*) . . . you should sing (*ura-ura*) or hum (*rengeng-rengeng*), filling it with all sorts of stuff (*wrena-wrena*), whatever you need: *gendèran, sindhènan,* etc."[86] Martopangrawit proffered a similar response when Perlman asked him to hum a gendhing. Although the rebab part is prominently hummed, Martopangrawit hummed other instruments as well, including gendèr, pesindhèn, and *gérong* parts.[87] Supanggah sees this phenomenon as "miniature *klenèngan*": that is, when a musician memorizes a gendhing, or by extension when a composer composes a piece, he has the sound of the entire ensemble in his mind.[88] Elsewhere, Supanggah points out that Javanese gamelan devalues precision (*ketepatan dan kecermatan*), emphasizing instead dialogue; musicians give each other a chance to be visible.[89] The preceding discussion shows that in explaining the process of memorizing and conceptualizing gendhing, musicians do not place balungan in the forefront of their minds.

Discussion about the functionality of instruments in the ensemble is absent in the *Serat Centhini.* Instead, the authors use metaphor to describe interaction in gamelan playing, for example imagining a musical interaction as a sensual experience.

> 111. The musicians played with skill and the same feel for the piece. The tranquility of the irama vied with the melodic realizations (*wilet*) in arousing desire (*malatsih*). [Their rendition] was just the right length for a dalang's *janturan.*
>
> 112. They played so together [*that the feeling of the gendhing (rasaning gendhing)*] was obtained. So they played on and on. They played the gendhing for a long time. Then it sped up and moved into *inggah* section (*munggah*).
>
> 113. The longer it lasted, the more intimate with one another (*gulet*) the individual rendition became; they seized (*rebut*) the thrill of satisfaction. The musicians were all sexually aroused, eager and randy, feeling (*rasa-rasa*) as if they couldn't stand it any longer.[90]

Clearly "vied" (*adu*), "intimate with one another" (*gulet*), and "seized" (*rebut*) are key words for interaction. Sexual metaphor is expressed in the first and last verse—which finishes with a reference to sexual climax.

The Dynamic of Coincidence

I would like to end this chapter with another look at musical coincidences: what is its nature or character? Let us consider the following passages from *Serat Centhini*:

> 103. ... Come on, let's just play music (Jav. *klenèngan*), that would be nice.
>
> 104. But there is a saying which goes: If you make music (Jav. *klenèngan*) and use a kendhang but not a gong, it is rather improper and is called incomplete.
>
> 105. It is best to use a gong, but not loudly, just softly. Jayengraga said with a smile. Widiguna, is that so?
>
> 106. He answered politely: It is true what has been said. What Uncle Kulawirya says is the same as this maxim: In the time of your humble servant's father,
>
> 107. In the time of my older brothers and the elders, it was considered incomplete to use a kendhang which was not accompanied by a gong. If you don't use a gong, don't use a kendhang.
>
> 108. (Jayengraga) said gently: If that is so, I'll go along. A rough appearance is ugly. To be incomplete would not be good. So, let's get the gong used for wayang.
>
> 109. Those who were sent off got the gong and *kenong* and returned. Then Jayengraga began playing on the rebab, most beautifully, the *sendhon* for *pathet sanga*, while he sang the *suluk*.
>
> 110. Once the last phrase of the *sendhon* had been played, he began the buka (introduction) to the *gendhing Gambir Sawit* in [pathet] *sanga*. As the gong played everyone felt content and happy.[91]

The authors of the *Serat Centhini* point out that it is improper for gamelan playing not to use gong. The significance of the gong is immediately felt on the first stroke marking the end of *buka*, the introduction of the piece: "As the gong [of the buka] played everyone felt content and happy." From another manuscript, the beauty of the sound of a gong is described as follows: "Gong *jumeglug mandul-mandul / gumulung ombaking ririh*" (the booming and shimmering of the gong is as the rolling of the soft-sounding ocean tide).[92]

Like much of *Serat Centhini*'s passages on gamelan, these descriptions emphasize the experiential response to gamelan playing, not the functionality of the instruments. This kind of description is suitable for a musical experience that recognizes networking and the processual dynamic in multipart (vocal or instrumental) music. This is why Steven Feld avoided the term "heterophony"—a multipart relationship resulting from simultaneous performance of a slightly variant or elaborated version of the same basic text-melody-rhythm.[93] Such a concept excludes music, such as the music of Kaluli that Feld studied, where "the 'lead' part and 'follow' part(s) are completely free to switch roles at any point, and continually and playfully change order."[94] He argues that an analysis of Kaluli music needs to attend the crucial aspect of processual dynamics and the centrality of timbre and texture.[95] Feld's point applies also to gamelan.

As I mentioned earlier, "coincidences" are the most important processes in gamelan music. Coincidences involve both cyclic repetition and the playfulness of punctuations (see below); similarly, the gamelan musical process and other aspects of Javanese cultural systems also contain both static structures (the state of transcendence) and spirited play (the state of immanence).

Let us consider a coincidence that happens in the stroke of a large gong, the most potent coincidence in a gamelan composition. When playing pieces with shorter structures (lancaran, ketawang, ladrang) in irama tanggung, the gong is struck at a slight delay from the beat of the piece. In the playing of a piece in irama dadi, wilet, and rangkep, however, the gong stroke should be delayed more, and the delayed stroke also applies to kenong and kempul strokes. This delaying stroke is a matter of musical style or musical treatment: in the case of delaying kenong and kempul in *plèsèdan* (which literally means "slip," in which the pitch of kenong or kempul anticipates the succeeding note of the piece), this treatment guides the melodic flow of the piece.

The delaying of the stroke is expanded for pieces with longer structures (pieces with structures of 64, 128, or 256 pulses per gongan). The delayed gong-stroke is preceded by the slowing down of the whole ensemble, guided by the drum, calling the ensemble's attention to the coming of the gong. Other instruments play their gong tone at a slight delay from the gong beat.[96] This treatment of the gong "disorients" the rhythmic flow, requiring the musicians to feel momentarily "unsettled" before regrouping musical synchrony.[97] The moment before the gong stroke, the stroke itself, and the time after it, create the most intense point of coincidence, but also a sense of playfulness.

Ward Keeler offers one explanation for the delay in the sounding of the gong. He describes how short gendhing, including light pieces with catchy melodies and music for battle, have a quality of clear focus and aural clarity.[98] In contrast, long gendhing, with complex variations, have greater aural richness but less aural clarity. According to Keeler, the interruption of the steady rhythm as the ensemble slows down before the gong stroke "makes its effect particularly mysterious. The listener is deliciously surprised by this interruption in the steady but diffuse sound characteristic of longer *gendhing*. The *gong*, that is, fits into a *gendhing*'s diffuse context as a massive, form-determining stroke, contrasting with other instruments by the enormous range of its overtones. It thereby drives all the other instruments momentarily out of hearing. As its sound diminishes, the sense of diffuseness and equilibrium returns."[99]

For gamelan theorist-composer Supanggah, the slowing down of the tempo, delaying the gong stroke, and subsequently the pulse of the whole ensemble in regaining their synchrony, including the treatment of kenong stroke (plèsèdan or not), all create what he calls "togetherness, but not together." He explains:

> *Rampak-rempeg* is a concept involving cooperative work and togetherness, but not in synchrony (*bukan kesamaan*). Performing a gamelan ensemble follows a horizontal line. All musicians are aiming at or orienting themselves toward a definite end: *seleh* or gong, without paying attention too much to vertical lines in which all instruments must be in synchrony (*bersama* or *bareng*) following a rule of harmony . . . The examples of preference to non-synchrony can be seen in the practice of *jengglengan* in the Sekaten gamelan, ending (*suwuk*), also the existence of terms concerning the aesthetic and the treatment (*garap*) in *karawitan*, such as *nggandhul* (i.e., delayed in the treatment of *gong, kempul, kenong, sindhen, gender, rebab*, and so forth), *nungkak* (anticipation: *bedhug, rebab*), *mbanyu mili* (like the flow of water, for *gambang*), *nyela irama* (off beat for *keplok*, clapping), and others.[100]

Supanggah's elucidation parallels Feld's idea of "simultaneously in-synchrony while out-of-phase." By "in-synchrony," Feld means "that the overall feeling is of togetherness, of consistently cohesive part coordination in sonic motion and participatory experience. Yet the parts are also 'out of phase,' that is, at distinctly different and shifting points of the same cycle or phrase structure at any moment, with each of the parts continuously changing in degree of displacement from hypothetical unison."[101]

Feld's descriptions apply not only to musical circumstances surrounding the gong stroke, but also the overall processual dynamics of the multi-layered gamelan ensemble, a musical style that creates "nuances of *textural densification*—of attacks and final sounds; decay and fades; changes in intensity, depth, and presence; voice coloration and grain; interaction of patterned and random sounds; playful acceleration, lengthenings, and shortenings."[102]

Let us return to the relation of coincidences in calendars to coincidences in gamelan. Indonesians, especially Javanese and Balinese, employ a combination of lunar-solar and other calendrical cycles of varying length, ranging from five to ten day names per cycle. In this format, a periodic coincidence of days from different cycles will occur. For example, using three cycles of five, six, and seven days per week will produce a particular combination of name days every 210 days. Geertz explains the significance of this "permutational" (as he calls it) calendar: "The outcome of all this wheels-within-wheels computation is a view of time as consisting of ordered sets of thirty, thirty-five, and forty-two, or two hundred and ten quantum units ("days"), each of which units has a particular qualitative significance of some sort indexed by its trinomial or binomial name: rather like our notion of the unluckiness of Friday-the-Thirteenth."[103] For the Balinese and Javanese, calendrical markings don't tell you what time it is; instead, they (or more precisely, the days they define) tell you what *kind* of time it is.[104]

In the courts of Surakarta and Yogyakarta, *garebeg* is the most celebrated festival. The word garebeg means "cheering," referring to people cheering, surrounding, and escorting the king. The garebeg is a large royal slametan (ritual feast), which Geertz aptly describes as a kind of universal social coincidence, an event in which "friends, neighbors, fellow workers, relatives, local spirits, dead ancestors, and near-forgotten gods all get bound, by virtue of their commensality, into a defined social group pledged to mutual support and cooperation."[105]

There are four garebeg: *garebeg Pasa, garebeg Sawal, garebeg Besar*, and *garebeg Mulud*; each signifies a particular commemoration of a religious event in that month.[106] Of the four garebeg, the garebeg Mulud is the most celebrated festival, and is even bigger when it falls on the coinciding day of the Java-Islam calendars every eight years (*windu*): the twelfth day of Mulud in the year of Dal. It is both a show of the king's and kraton's power, and to honor the birth of the Prophet Muhammad. The week-long religious festival known as Sekatèn is marked by the daily performance of extraordinarily large gamelan instruments, as mentioned before. It is the fact that Javanese court and Islamic cultures are coincident which gives weight to the festival. The garebeg Mulud festival is full of coincidences.

Garebeg symbolizes an ideal of social harmony under the command of the king and his absolute authority. However, the word slametan reminds us of the reality of the world. Slametan derives from the root word "*slamet*," which means "safe and sound." It is intended to prevent any disturbances—"nothing is going to happen" if slametan is observed. There is in slametan a sense of momentary bonding of members of the community, like the moment of the stroke of the gong: people are united by a speech and religious prayer, followed by formal eating. The eating is "formal" because it is done only symbolically: each participant has only a few bites of food and a few sips of drink. The final stage of slametan consists of dividing the remainder of the food, to be brought home by participants. Pemberton even goes so far as to say that the distribution of exchanged food is the focus—slametan is a symbol of surplus production and its dissemination.[107]

The final day of the garebeg Mulud begins with a procession, including music and the marching of honor guards. The most distinctive element of the procession, however, is the offering of foods. The food is arranged in the shape of a mountain (*gunungan*): rice in a conical shape (the main object), vegetables, cookies, etc. The procession progresses from the kraton to the great mosque; after a religious ceremony, the mountain of food is carried out of the mosque. Soon after it reaches the front of the mosque gate, people fight with each other over the food. The belief is that the food symbolizes the king's contribution toward the harvest, and those who get food will receive blessings from the king (*berkah*). This event comprises many coincidences, punctuated by an element of chaos, disorder, and playfulness. This is analogous to the moment of coincidence in gamelan: the spirited play in the execution of temporal flow, the textural and timbral change, and the interactive activities among the instruments when the gong is struck to mark the end of the cycle of the piece.

To recapitulate: at the beginning of this chapter I mentioned the interdisciplinary expansion of ethnomusicology in the last three decades to the study of music and its relation to socio-cultural practices. Monson sees this as an exciting development, but also notes the decline of the number of studies devoted to musical processes, namely, the study of music as cultural practice.[108] A recent study of gamelan by Mark Benamou voices a similar concern. He observes that ethnomusicologists address musical meaning almost entirely in terms of the social and symbolic aspects of the music; consequently, less attention is given to the topic of the affect of musical process, the "aesthetic" (the topic of his book). He argues that the "aesthetic" deserves to have a central place in ethnomusicology. His study is an attempt "to bridge the notorious divide between music and context, between the aesthetic and the historical, between the musical and the social, between musicological and anthropological ethnomusicology."[109]

In chapter 5 of this work, I have tried to bridge this divide by tracing the development of gamelan theory in the context of ethnomusicology, the development that has brought about the notion of homology between musical process and musical context. My study in this chapter is an expansion of the treatment of the topic by Judith and Alton Becker.

By employing the concept of binary division—not as things diametrically opposed to each other, but as balanced opposites and dynamic complementaries—I have shown the ways in which musical structure and process can be seen to metaphorically express the socio-cultural order. For example, the orderly slametan ritual of the garebeg Mulud is marked by chaos and playfulness (rebutan) at the end, like the diffusion marking the end of the steady, orderly rhythm of the cyclic motion of a gongan; diffuseness and equilibrium coincide. For another example, the position of rebab as leader of the ensemble is a fluid phenomenon, as the rebab can cede his power to other instruments. The same phenomenon can be seen in the practice of leadership in Javanese society.

The complex networking of binary interactions in gamelan is captured in the term "*garap*." The term has been defined in a various ways—interpretation, treatment, working out of a particular instrument or singing.[110] I prefer to define garap in a wider sense of musical practice, namely "performance practice." This refers to all things that have an impact on the dynamic of the ensemble's interplay, including the choice of instrumentation, dynamic, tempo, melodic patterns, and notes.[111] Garap implies many levels of binary interactions (skeleton-elaboration, gongan-irama, lord-servant, etc.).

It seems that the term garap only arrived in the later development of gamelan theory, beginning in the mid twentieth century, but it captures the essence of the ensemble's interplay: a fixed structural pattern (for example gongan or balungan) is not only a static vessel within which structural freedoms operate; the formal structural pattern itself is also a subject for manipulation—the transcendent and immanent work hand in hand.

The kind of metaphor the Beckers propose—cyclic motion in both gamelan and calendrical systems—is a topic alien to Javanese musicians and gamelan connoisseurs, but by and large her hypothesis is persuasive. In Java, the common usage of metaphor is limited to musical description, such as *regu* (majestic) or *sigrak* (lively) for the *rasa* of a composition, and *ukel pancaran* (flowing curlicue) and *kembang tiba* (falling flowers) for the style of gendèr playing.[112]

Metaphor can disappear or be contested. For example, it is very common in the wayang puppet play (a performing art rich with metaphor) to find that the dhalang (puppeteer) represents God, and his creation is a set of shadows cast on screen. However, the authors of the nineteenth-century *Serat Centhini* argued that, because the relation between dhalang and puppet is an allusion to the conception of the universe, the relation between the Absolute and the Contingent, between God and man is indeed very complicated.[113] The author of another important nineteenth-century literary work, *Serat Gatholoco*, positioned the *blencong* (an oil lamp, the light source of the wayang performance) as being the oldest element (implying the Power) in the shadow play, not the puppeteer.[114]

As our discussion touches on wayang, it leads me to suggest that the dynamic relationship between musical process and musical context, between fixed structural patterns and structural freedom, transcendent and immanent, is analogous to the dynamic dualism conveyed in wayang performance. That is, in the wayang the world is not conceived of as moving in a linear trajectory, yet wayang can express the endless variety of human life. In the words of Claire Holt, wayang performance expresses "a stable world based on conflict."[115] Yet, as Anderson states, "the sense of underlying instability is no less important than the sense of permanence."[116]

Conclusion

I mentioned in the introduction that the nation-state, culture, and the performing arts are inextricably linked. This is especially true in Southeast Asia: throughout history, the state has been an important patron of the arts.[1] While the region has gone through interrelated chains of historical events—religious conversion, colonialism, and from revolution to independent state—it is inaccurate to define the state "as a finished product or structure that has existed in 'traditional,' 'colonial,' or 'modern' forms."[2] Rather, the state is the result of temporally interrelated human, social, and institutional practices. The history of Southeast Asia should be understood as "an overlapping series of localizing [hence hybridizing], transcultural processes differently distributed over the whole region [of Southeast Asia or even in Indonesia alone] and occurring over many centuries at different rates in different places."[3]

Underlying the cultural transformation process is transculturation, a complex process of cultural transition, occuring as a consequence of "the merging of cultures over time, incorporating resolution of their differences."[4] Hand in hand with the transcultural transformation process is the phenomenon of *networking*: interconnected chains of multiple agencies seen synchronically and diachronically. Both processes bring about cultural hybridization, transplantation, appropriation, adaptation, and cross-fertilization.

Heterogeneity, contestation, and ambivalence define the hybridization process. This is because the process involves all sorts of power negotiation in cultural relations. In the case of tanjidor, as the patronage and the performance context of the band changed—from colonialism to the modern nation state—the position of the genre in society became uncertain. During the colonial period, the music and the slave musicians were under the care of wealthy European traders or landowners, marking them as "special." In the twentieth century the music was banned by the state. And today, the state and some in the artistic community defend the existence of tanjidor, a source of pride and a distinct musical entity to the city of Jakarta.

Gendhing mares has experienced a similar predicament. The genre can be performed only if the court of Yogyakarta has enough resources. However, the recent atmosphere of rejuvenation of Western music-gamelan hybridization has encouraged the court to use gendhing mares to accompany bedhaya

Semang, the most refined, sacred, and symbolically powerful ceremonial dance. There is no assurance, however, that gendhing mares and the bedhaya Semang will survive as anything other than markers of the Yogyakarta court for their historical and musical distinction.

In the case of kroncong, in the late nineteenth century to early twentieth century it was associated with and performed for lowly members of the Indo community. Subsequently, it was elevated to the national music of Indonesia, known and enjoyed by many Indonesian people, regardless of their ethnic group. However, as other new genres of Indonesian popular music emerged, such as *dangdut* and *campursari*, the popularity of kroncong has declined.

The heterogeneous and contested nature of hybridization also appeared in contemporary *wayang* performances and musik kontemporer—musical and cultural hybrids that developed in postcolonial Indonesia. Modern technology—elaborate sound systems, electronic devices, computer-generated audio and images, and other kinds of pictorial backdrops—intensify the hybrid nature of cultural performances and their spectacularization.

Sardono's *Opera Diponegoro* can also be seen in this light. Aside from presenting all sorts of Javanese musical and theatrical idioms, the play employs many non-Javanese modes of production, including the Western modern dance, a written script, Sumatranese music and dance, a dance sequence modeled after a Middle Eastern belly dance, and Islamic chanting. The multiple theatrical and musical idioms in the play present a kind of liminoid genre (experimenting with variable repertoires as leisure activities and aesthetic pleasures) without disregarding liminality (the state of ambiguity, an experience in a ritual event).[5] The production of *Opera Diponegoro* was possible because of a network of individuals and institutions. The play was not produced by a permanent theatrical company, but rather an assembly of the best dancers, musicians, lighting designers, and painters from Jakarta, central Java, and even the United States.

Networking is also the basis for the presence of gamelan in the West, the subject matter of part 2 of this book. Various agencies, such as colonial and native individuals, academicians and private entrepreneurs, and performers themselves, have shaped the gamelan's representation in the West. The contexts in which gamelan appeared (detached from its place of origin) and the reception of gamelan by various segments of society can be understood in terms of deterritorialization.

Ambiguity and ambivalence were parts of the cultural performances in the World's Fairs. We recall a peculiar case in the 1883 Amsterdam exhibition, in which gamelan instruments were constructed according to European taste, and the Dutch national anthem was played on the gamelan. For another example, the encounter between central Javanese dancers and Sundanese musicians at the 1893 Columbian Exhibition brought about an unconventional, hybrid dance performance. Since the Columbian and Paris Expositions employed the same format and hosted the same performing group from West Java, most likely the same hybrid performance also took placte at the 1889 Paris exposition.

It is worth reiterating here that Debussy did not hear much gamelan from the court of Java: instead he heard mostly Sundanese music. Only occasionally did the group at the 1889 Paris World's Fair perform Javanese dance, accompanied by whatever music the Sundanese musicians provided. The position of Javanese gamelan and dance became ambiguous at these fairs. Did they represent primitive art, or nineteenth-century art? Public reception was equally ambiguous and unpredictable. Two contrasting public receptions can be noted: (1) an authentic aesthetic experience in which the audience was not required to know the background of performing arts that they saw; and (2) an enjoyment through ethnographic mediation consisting of written documents, such as pamphlets and program notes.

As the presence of gamelan shifted from the World's Fairs to the world of academia, the network changed and expanded, now adding academic institutions, scholars, students, learned societies, composers, and concert managers. Having taught gamelan in the United States for forty years, I have observed that the presence of gamelan in universities has brought about students' excitement and the fulfillment of an ideological inclination toward multicultural and intercultural perspectives. However, feelings of anxiety and ambivalence also came along with it: the question of the worthiness of music as part of the academic curriculum and the issue of how to teach and represent non-Western music in academic setting still arises from time to time.

The creation of university-based gamelan ensembles, or any non-Western ensemble, for that matter, also means changes in the institutional and curricular structure, changes in the distribution of resources, and competition among scholars. Nettl's work shows that the idea of the superiority of Western musical thought was still alive and well in the schools of music of Midwestern universities in the mid-1990s. The gamelan succeeds on campuses because it is a large ensemble, similar to a large Western ensemble.[6] In some cases, a native teacher is invited to teach gamelan on campus; in most cases, ethnomusicologists teach it. In teaching non-Western music, ethnomusicologists feel as if they have to go through a liminal state, common to the hybridization process in general: anxiety and ambivalence cannot be avoided, though the experience can also be fun and valuable. Solis aptly describes this feeling as follows:

> Each author is a sort of Noh Drama *shite*, undertaking and recounting a journey between worlds full of symbolic encounters. This journey, still in progress for us all, results in emotional and cognitive growth and conflict.... All [the authors] have undergone the exquisite agonies of cultural transplantation to the field, and the equally traumatic act of leaving it. In the field, our friends and research collaborators have unselfishly given us gifts we know we cannot repay.... Thus we labor mightily to engage our students and

to convey at least something of what we felt and feel, re-creating the field a little at each rehearsal. We know we cannot replicate the experience, yet we are determined to create a meaningful and coherent performative world. In *Performing Ethnomusicology* we share the lessons of our journeys and the challenges of our engaging, vital, bittersweet, and exhilarating task.[7]

It is commonly understood that ethnomusicology emphasizes the study of music as an ethnographic phenomenon. Instead of searching for the meaning of music from the sound structure alone, usually considered to be the domain of Western music theory (though this view has been changing),[8] ethnomusicologists seek to understand the musical structure in its relation to social and cosmological order: musical process as a reflection of cultural practice. In this regard, the structure of gamelan music is seen in homology with other Javanese cultural systems, such as the calendrical system, as proposed by Judith and Alton Becker. I extend this study to the traditional social order, employing one of the hallmarks of the Javanese worldview, namely a binary taxonomy of balanced opposites.

Certain interconnected themes emerge as constants in this study: transculturalism, hybridity, and networking. Musical genres from the colonial period of Java, the repertoire of musik kontemporer, the gamelan in the nineteenth-century world exhibitions, theatrical idioms in *Opera Diponegoro*, wayang kontemporer, the formulation of gamelan theory, and gamelan in the world of academia—all are hybrid cultural practices that have developed as a consequence of overlapping series of transcultural processes and networking.

Notes

Preface

1. Sumarsam, *Kendhangan Gaya Solo.*
2. Sumarsam, *Tjengkok Genderan.*
3. Sumarsam, *Gamelan.*
4. Sumarsam, "Inner Melody."
5. Perlman, *Unplayed Melodies.*
6. Sumarsam, *Gamelan*, 161–237.
7. Ibid., 144.
8. Perlman, *Unplayed Melodies*, 169.
9. Ibid., 4–5.
10. Ibid. 5.
11. Ibid., 6.
12. Benamou, *Rasa: Affect and Intuition*, xix.
13. Ibid., 88.
14. Perlman, *Unplayed Melodies*, 6–7.

Introduction

1. Pieterse, *Globalization & Culture*, 87.
2. White, "Introduction: Rethinking Globalization," 6.
3. Irving, *Colonial Counterpoint*, 45.
4. Ang, *On Not Speaking Chinese*, 197.
5. Anderson, "The Idea of Power," 58.
6. Wolters, *History, Culture, and Region*, 55.
7. Sumarsam, "Past and Present Issues of Islam," 45–64.
8. Andaya, *The World of Maluku*. Andaya points out that the aims of the Portuguese nobility in entering Asia were (1) to pursue the war against Islam; (2) to perform an outstanding service to their king on the battlefields; and (3) to enrich themselves, in their status and lifestyle. The first aim was neglected, however, and the last became the primary intention (ibid., 37).
9. Geertz, *The Interpretation of Culture*, 240.
10. Appadurai, "Grassroots Globalization," 7.
11. Holt, *Art in Indonesia*, 3.
12. When viewing history as temporally interrelated human, social, and institutional practices, categories such as "traditional," "colonial," and "modern" are irrelevant (See Day, *Fluid Iron*).
13. MacAloon, "Olympic Games," 1.
14. Sumarsam. *Gamelan*, 123.

15. Ibid., 123–24.

16. See Lombard, *Nusa Jawa: Silang Budaya* 1, 241–42, from which the discussion below is drawn.

17. Ibid., 241.

18. My perspective on this point is based on my involvement with the Indonesian cultural mission to be dispatched to the second New York World's Fair and Rumania (I was one of the gamelan musicians in the group). Because of political circumstances—a bad diplomatic relationship between Indonesia and the United States, and the 1965 tragedy of the alleged communist coup d'état—the cultural missions were canceled. Several weeks of training in Jakarta, including one rehearsal attended by President Sukarno, allowed me to learn from my Jakartan performing artist colleagues about cultural activities in Jakarta and the presidential palace.

19. Gathutkaca is one of the sons of Bima, the second of the five Pandhawa brothers—a story drawn from the *Mahabharata* epic. A prince of *gagahan* (strong) character, Gathutkaca is known for his ability to fly; the puppeteer even has a special narration for when he is preparing to fly. He attacks his enemies by pouncing on them from above.

20. Rusini, *Gathutkaca di Panggung Soekarno*, 53.

21. Vickers, *Bali: A Paradise Created*, 180.

22. Yampolsky, "Forces for Change," 700–25.

23. Becker, "Kroncong, Indonesian Popular Music," 14–19; Heins, "Two Cases of Urban Folk Music," 20–29; Kornhauser, "In Defense of Kroncong," 104–83; Yampolsky, "Kroncong Revisited," 7–56.

24. See Hatch, "Popular Music in Indonesia."

25. Monson, "Jazz as Political and Musical Practice," 22.

Chapter One

1. White, "The Promise of World Music," 195.

2. Weiss, "Permeable Boundaries," 209.

3. Ibid.

4. Yampolsky, "Indonesia: Cultural and Musical Geography," 274–83.

5. Guillot, *Kyai Sadrach*.

6. See Sumandiyo, *Seni dalam Ritual Agama*.

7. See Poplawska, "Wayang Wahyu," 194–202.

8. Sumarsam, *Gamelan*, 69–71, drawn from Kornhauser, "In Defence of Kroncong," Boxer, *The Dutch Seaborn Empire*, Taylor, *The Social World of Batavia*, and treatises from the courts of Surakarta).

9. Yampolsky, "Indonesian Popular Music."

10. See Kornhauser, "In Defence of Kroncong" and Heins, "Two Cases of Urban Folk Music."

11. Yampolsky, "Kroncong Revisited," 16–18. Yampolsky suggests the development of the music of Mardijkers as follows: "The most we can be (relatively) sure of it is that the Portuguese ships brought *cavaquinho* (which became the *kroncong* lute) and possible the frame drum (called *adufe* in Portugal, *rebana* in Indonesia), as well as a handful of melodies, the rudiments of chordal harmony as accompaniment to sung melody. Presumably these elements—perhaps mixed with others from India, Africa, and Malacca—became the basis for Mardijker music" (ibid., 17).

12. Cohen, *Komedie Stamboel*, 168.

13. Purbadipura, *Serat Sri Karongron*, 30–31.
    Mijil
    . . .
    sesambèn miyarsi
    pangrasaning piyul

    gitar suling tarebang mandholin
    panabuhé alon
    pra metengan lan kalawijané
    wiwit gendhing kembang kacang muni
    nganggo dèn bawani
    ing tembang megatruh

    suwuk nuli gendhing pinggir kali
    banjur muni kroncong
    gendhing bintang surabaya lèrèn
    sawatara nuli munya malih
    setambul awiwit
    siji loro telu

    ingkang nabuh ngiras nyindhèni
    dadi maju loro
    tangan cangkem milu nyambut gawé
    suprandéné katon seneng ati
    . . .
14. Woodfield, *English Musicians in the Age of Exploration*, 5–6.
15. Ibid., 5.
16. Yasadipura, quoted in Poedjosoedarmo and M. C. Ricklefs, "The Establishment of Surakarta," 101.
    Babad Giyanti. Dhandanggula.
    Tedhakira kangjeng kang siniwi
    pra prajurit kumpeni lan jawa
    urmat drèl atri swarané
    sinauran mriyem gung
    magenturan anggegeteri
    slomprèt tambur musikkan
    suling bendhé barung
    munggang kodhokngorèk ngangkang
    carabalèn pradongga munya ngrerangin
    horeg wong sanagara
17. For a complete report of different kinds of *prajuritan* music in the late-nineteenth century court of Yogyakarta, see Groneman 1895, 80–87.
18. Sumarsam, *Gamelan*, 68–74, drawn from Taylor, *The Social World of Batavia*; Atmadikara, *Babad Krama Dalem*; and *Serat Babad Nitik*.
19. Taylor, *The Social World of Batavia*, 107–8; Purbadipura, *Sri Karongron*, 2: 268.
20. Sumarsam, *Gamelan*, 75.
21. Ibid., 119.
22. Boonzayer, *Brass Unbound*, 10.
23. Furnivall, *Netherlands India*, 457–58.

24. Sumarsam, *Gamelan*.
25. *Babad Nitik Mangkunegaran wiwit taun Alip 1707 ngantos dumugi Je 1718*.
26. Ibid., 1. Sinom. 13b–16.
    Sampunnya sragni [srageni] priya
    anulya sragni èstri
    barondongan paringgitan
    kang ngabani Kangjeng Gusti
    rempeg sragni èstri
    kalah kang sragni kakung
    éram sakèh tumingal
    tambur éstri suling éstri
    . . .
27. Boonzayer, *Brass Unbound*, 92.
28. Ranger, *Dance and Society in Eastern Africa*, 10.
29. Ibid., 10.
30. My interest in writing about tanjidor and gendhing mares began when I had an opportunity to hear, for the first time, a recording of tanjidor from a CD of Indonesian music produced by Smithsonian Folkways. Almost immediately I noticed the flamboyant style of the music and the complete integration of Western instruments into an improvisatory ensemble. Soon after listening to the CD I was reminded that there is a repertoire in the Yogyakarta gamelan court, gendhing mares, that also requires the use of European wind instruments. However, the music is very controlled, reserved, and dignified, with only limited participation from the Western instruments. Comparison of these two genres and examination of their development and cultural contexts illustrates the differences of each cultural space in localizing and hybridizing foreign musical material and shaping the meaning of the new form in its new contextual zones.
31. Abdurachman, *Bunga Angin Portugis di Nusantara*, 48.
32. Yampolsky, "Betawi & Sundanese Music."
33. Boxer, *The Dutch Seaborne Empire*; F. de Haan, *Priangan*; Wall, *Indische Landhuizen*; Parani et al., *Tanjidor*. The last reference, *Tanjidor*, is a report based on fieldwork on tanjidor carried out by faculty members of the Jakarta Institute of Arts Education. This is the most extensive report on the history, function, and practice of the genre.
34. Augustin Michiels was also intimately known as "Majoor Jantje." An ancestor of his was a freed, Christianized slave from Bengal, whose descendants had a prominent status in the Mardijker community.
35. Quoted in Wall, *Indische Landhuizen*.
36. European music, gamelan, and Chinese music were present together in Michiels's house. Did the musicians of these three genres exchange their musical repertoire or idioms? Perhaps, but there is no evidence to support this assumption.
37. Lohanda, "Tanjidor Di Dalam Kehidupan Sang Seniman," 97–35.
38. Ibid., 103.
39. Yampolsky, "Betawi & Sundanese Music."
40. Abdurachman, *Bunga Angin Portugis di Nusantara*, 48.
41. The description of the instrumentation of tanjidor is based on Yampolsky's "Betawi & Sundanese Music."
42. Sumarsam, *Gamelan*.
43. Subuh, *Gendhing-Gendhing Mares*.

44. There is disagreement about the number of gendhing mares. According to Subuh, there are forty-four *gendhing*. Vetter ("Music for 'the Lap of the World,'" 243) mentions that the *Pakem Wirama* lists fifty pieces. My count of gendhing mares in *Pakem Wirama* ends up with thirty-eight pieces (Bima is listed twice: Bima Mares and Mares Bima). However, I only have access to a handwritten transliteration of *Pakem Wirama*, ordered by Th. Pigeaud in 1934. There are a number of pieces mentioned by Subuh that appear in *Pakem Wirama* as regular *gendhing*.

45. Vetter, "Music for 'the Lap of the World,'" 281.

46. Subuh, *Gendhing-Gendhing Mares*. As an undergraduate student of ISI, whose thesis is on gendhing mares, he interviewed the following musicians: R. W. Lokasari, R. L. Pustakamardawa, R. W. Kawindrasutikna, and R. W. Sasmintamardawa. He also mentions that the term "mares" was used in a court manuscript, *Buku Pesindhèn Badhaya Srimpi* (The book of singing Badhaya Srimpi dance), composed during the reign of HB VIII.

47. Lindsay. *Klasik, Kitsch, Kontemporer*, 207.

48. Geertz, *The Religion of Java*, 232–34.

49. Becker, "Earth, Fire, Sakti," 385.

50. See Boonzayer, *Brass Unbound*.

51. The strong execution of the *balungan* also strengthens the distinction between two styles of gamelan playing: soft- and loud-style musical presentation, one of the most important aesthetic elements in gamelan. In discussing these styles, we should recognize two categories of gamelan instruments: soft-sounding instruments, consisting of metallophones played with padded mallets, flutes, string instruments, and singing; and the loud-sounding instruments, consisting of drums, gong-type instruments, and metallophones played with unpadded mallets. In the soft playing style, the loud-sounding instruments are played softly; in a loud-style presentation, the soft-sounding instruments may drop out all together.

52. For a comparison between irama and Thai *Thaw*, see Judith Becker, "A Southeast Asian Musical Process," 453–64.

53. Ricklefs, *A History of Modern Indonesia*, 119.

54. Here is part of the poem, translated by Ben Anderson, in "A Time of Darkness and a Time of Light," 219.

> The luster of the realm
> Is now vanished to the eye
> In ruins the teaching of good ways
> For there is no example left
> The heart of the learned poet
> So coiled about with care
> Seeing all the wretchedness
> That everything is darkened
> The world immersed in misery
>
> The King kingly perfection
> The Chief Ministers chiefly in truth
> The *bupati* constant of heart
> The lower officials excellent
> Yet none can serve to stay
> The time of doom . . .

The Javanese text is written in a *macapat* sung-poetry, Sinom. It runs as follows:

Mangkya darajating praja
Kawuryan wus sunya ruri
Rurah pangrèhing ngukara
Karana tanpa palupi
Ponang para mengkawi
Kawilet ing tyas maladkung
Kongas kasudranira
Tidhen tandhaning dumadi
Ardayèng rat déning karoban rubéda

Ratuné ratu utama
Patihé patih linuwih
Pra nayaka tyas raharja
Panekaré becik-becik
Parandéné tan dadi
Paliyasing kala bendu
. . .

55. Ricklefs, *A History of Modern Indonesia*, 113.
56. Sumarsam, *Gamelan*, 100.
57. Pemberton, *On the Subject of "Java,"* 69.
58. Hostetler, "Bedhaya Semang." The following story of the origin of *bedhaya* Semang is based on Hostetler's account. She draws the story from *Serat Babad Nitik*, a manuscript about Sultan Agung.
59. The myth from the court of Surakarta names Panembahan Senapati, the founder of Mataram and Sultan Agung's grandfather, as a figure who met Ratu Kidul.
60. Suharti. "Bedhaya Semang," 38–52.
61. The following account is based on my personal communication with Suharti (2009).
62. Wolters, *History, Culture, and Region*, 55.
63. Weiss, "Permeable Boundaries," 206.
64. Ibid.
65. As I mentioned in the introduction, the other category that Weiss asserts is "intentional" fusion, which I will apply to Sardono's *Opera Diponegoro*, the topic of chapter 3.

Chapter Two

1. *Nusa Tenggara*, December 5, 1996. In my description of Monjaya, I have consulted other newspapers, including *Republika, Suara Pembaruan, Kompas*, and the weekly magazine *Gatra*.
2. Sumarsam, *Gamelan*.
3. Theodore et al., "Tokoh-Tokoh Perjalanan Musik," 123–24.
4. Anderson, *Imagined Communities*, 145.
5. See Vickers, *A History of Modern Indonesia*, 156–60.
6. Yampolsky, *Lokananta*, 45.
7. Weintraub, *Dangdut Stories*, 40–41.
8. Manuel, *Popular Musics of the Non-Western World*, 211.

9. Ibid., 212.
10. Weintraub, *Dangdut Stories*, 173–200.
11. Ibid., 11–12.
12. Mrázek, "Javanese Wayang Kulit in the Times of Comedy," pt. 1, 67.
13. Supanggah, "Campur Sari," 15–16.
14. Mrázek, "Javanese Wayang Kulit in the Times of Comedy," pt. 1, 67.
15. Perlman, "The Traditional Javanese Performing Arts," 8.
16. Sutton, "Popularizing the Indigenous or Indigenizing the Popular?" 25.
17. Ibid., 25–26.
18. Supanggah, "Campur Sari," 14.
19. Supanggah, *Bothèkan Karawitan I*, 3.
20. Ibid.
21. Cooper, "From the Land of a Thousand Peaks."
22. For a brief background of wayang, see chapter 3.
23. It is also called *gunungan*, which means "mountain," a name based on the shape of the figure itself.
24. Although there are a few female dhalang, the great majority are men.
25. Sumarsam, "Gamelan as a Vital Accompaniment," 105–16.
26. Traditional musicians considered *Ayak-ayakan Panjang Mas* one of the most beautiful gamelan pieces, and that being able to perform this piece was an artistic pinnacle; today it is rarely played.
27. From the root word *tanceb* (meaning to stick the puppet's rod onto the banana log at the base of the screen), *tanceban* connotes a sense of being stationary or remaining in place.
28. Mrázek, "Phenomenology of a Puppet Theater," 120.
29. Alton Becker states that the manner of presentation of the plot in wayang violates the ideals of Western dramatic plot structure, which emphasizes a clear connection between episodes and the presentation of cause and effect. "In wayang theater, coincidence motivates actions. There is no causal reason that Arjuna, the frail wayang hero, meets Cakil, a small demon, in the forest, as he (or a counterpart) does in each wayang. It is a coincidence; it happens (jadi), and because they are who they are, they fight and Cakil dies, but not forever; he will be killed over and over again in each wayang. When Arjuna and Cakil meet, two worlds, two epistemologies coincide for a moment. Cakil is purely physical. He attacks Arjuna because Arjuna makes him uncomfortable" (Becker, "Text Building, Epistemology, and Aesthetics," 219). Indeed, Becker effectively explains many aspects of wayang and wayang plot in terms of epistemological coincidences. My discussion focuses on the ways in which the scenes in a wayang performance are sequentially ordered in time and space.
30. Traditionally, gara-gara in the Yogyakarta wayang style differs from that of the Surakarta. In the Yogyakarta style, the gara-gara always initiates the beginning of the second plot division (pathet Sanga). Hence gara-gara can be found in every wayang performance. In the Surakarta style, gara-gara is traditionally presented only when the prince is in a state of introspection: his introspective power throws the world out of balance. However, gara-gara in contemporary Surakartan wayang follows the Yogyakarta style.
31. The term commonly used to describe the presence of a rock, dangdut, or campursari singer is *artist tamu* (guest star).
32. I should emphasize that, in spite of the emphasis on their sensuous nature, for the most part these singers are highly accomplished musicians.
33. Sumanto, *Narto Sabdo*, 61.

34. Kayam, *Kelir Tanpa Batas*, 119.

35. Ibid., 155–56. Actually, "*ngèli tapi ora kèli*" is a statement made by Ki Timbul Hadiprayitno, one of the best-known dhalang in Yogyakarta. The statement indicates the attitude of traditional dhalang in response to changing times: that the change should be selective so that the wayang will not sunk into hedonism (ibid., 151).

36. Mrázek, "Phenomenology of a Puppet Theater," 279.

37. A famous dhalang told me that he used to be able to deliver funny jokes in the clown scene, but that nowadays this role has been taken over by the comedian(s).

38. The set-up of wayang performance on a proscenium stage (such as in the monthly wayang performances at Radio Republik Indonesia) actually makes wayang unwatchable from the puppet side—only a narrow space remains behind the screen.

39. Ganasidi is an abbreviation of Lembaga Pembinaan Seni Pedalangan (Institution for Fostering the Art of Puppetry), created in 1969.

40. Kuwato, "Pertunjukan Wayang Kulit di Jawa Tengah."

41. Mrázek, "Phenomenology of a Puppet Theater," 476.

42. Ibid., 477.

43. Mrázek, "Javanese Wayang Kulit in the Times of Comedy," pt. 2, 114–15.

44. Murtiyoso et al., *Pertumbuhan & Perkembangan Seni*.

45. Ibid., 51.

46. MacAloon, "Olympic Games and the Theory of Spectacle," 247.

47. Hooker and Dick, introduction to *Culture and Society*, 14.

48. Ibid., 14–15.

49. Gamelan presentation in the hotels attracts tourism, but usually, the gamelan is only a small ensemble of three or four musicians and a singer. Even at those hotels with a full gamelan ensemble, such as the Kusuma Sahid Hotel, my recent observations indicate that they are rarely played by a full or competent group.

50. Kayam, *Kelir Tanpa Batas*.

51. Siegel, *Solo in the New Order*.

52. Umar Kayam, *Kelir Tanpa Batas*, 261–70.

53. Ibid., 270.

54. See Hardjana, "Catatan Music Indonesia," 13–14.

55. Yampolsky, "Forces for Change."

56. Ibid., 712. See also Amrih Widodo, "The Stages of the State," 1–35.

57. Yampolsky, "Forces for Change," 712.

58. Ibid., 714.

59. Acciaioli, "Culture as art," 148–72.

60. Yampolsky, "Forces for Change," 719. One may think that Yampolsky is optimistic about the future of traditional performing arts. Actually, he also notices a "graying out" of these arts, saying: "Most of these surviving traditions are now in the hands of ageing performers who see no one from the next generation emerging to take over. The reasons given are familiar: young people aren't interested in the past and the old arts, they want to know what's happening in Jakarta; they leave the villages and move to cities as soon as they possibly can. I believe there is a more basic reason as well: pervading the messages that come out of Jakarta, from government and media (both independent and state-run), is the premise that village life is backward and impoverished, and that villagers are boobs and bumpkins. What inducement does that offer to the young to commit themselves to village life and pour their energy into mastering a village art?" (ibid., 720).

61. McGraw, "Musik Kontemporer," 3.

62. Ibid.

63. Dewan Kesenian Jakarta, *Pesta Seni 1974*, 159–61.

64. Humardani, "Membina Kritik Musik," paper presented at the 1974 Music Conference in Taman Ismail Marzuki, Jakarta.

65. Rustopo, *Gendhon Humardani Sang Gladiator*.

66. Ibid., 205. Humardani was an influential leader in the development of traditional performing arts in Central Java. He was the director of the Indonesian Academy of Gamelan (ASKI, later STSI, now ISI) from 1972 to 1985, and concurrently served as head of the Center of Central Javanese Arts (PKJT, Pusat Kesenian Jawa Tengah). He encouraged composers at the academy to use musical elements from anywhere in Indonesia and the West to create new Indonesian music that could enrich the spiritual life and aesthetic experience (*pengalaman hayatan*) of the people. Although Humardani helped set the atmosphere for creating new performing arts, he had no direct input on the practice of composing new music for gamelan. Instead, he was involved more in the creation of new wayang and dance. This was particularly apparent in the practice of condensing wayang performance from an all-night to a two-hour performance, and shortening the traditional dance repertoire.

67. Raden, "Sketsa Kehidupan Musik Kontemporer di Indonesia," 65.

68. Ibid., 67.

69. Raden, "Dinamika Pertemuan dua Tradisi," 6–14.

70. Raden, "Music, Politics, and the Problems of National Identity in Indonesia."

71. Sjukur, "Mak Comblang dan Pionir Asongan," 15–19; Mack, "Sejarah, Tradisi, dan Penilaian Musik," 20–30; and Tambayong, "Niat Kembali Sonder Pergi, 31–40.

72. Regarding the development of new Indonesian music (or campursari for that matter), some composers, musicians, commentators, and listeners come up with the same reasons as Raden. Statements such as "new music is able to bridge Western and ethnic music" or "bridging diatonic and pentatonic music" are often heard in discussions at music conferences and in newspapers.

73. Sjukur, "Mak Comblang dan Pionir Asongan," 15; see also Dieter Mack, "Sejarah, Tradisi, dan Penilaian Musik," 22.

74. Rhodius and Darling, *Walter Spies and Balinese Art*, 21–23.

75. Ibid., 27. This latter is one of Spies' most interesting musical experiments. A report by Rhodius and Darling deserves a full mention here: "In the palace of Prince Paku Alaman VII, a great friend of the arts, he made the experiment, with the help of a lady friend, of rendering the music of the Javanese gamelan on two pianos tuned to the European scale. The attempt turned out to only unsatisfactory approximation, but meanwhile he had invented a notation which allowed the gamelan players to write down their parts. From these notes he put together a complete score of a Javanese composition, and from this made a piano reduction in *European* notation for piano tuned to the *Javanese* scale. Soon after, a concert was held in the Prince's palace with a piece scored for gamelan, singers, and pianos tuned to the Javanese scale. The Javanese orchestra began and the singers joined in. At a sign from the Prince, the gamelan ceased playing and the two grand pianos took over. The singers continued without missing a beat or showing any sign of being disconnected. At a second sign, the pianos fell silent and the gamelan resumed. The process was repeated several times with enormous success, clearly proving the accuracy of Spies' transcription and the theory that the European piano, suitably tuned, was interchangeable with the gamelan." Unfortunately, the score of this piece is lost, perhaps because of the Japanese invasion (ibid., 29).

76. Langen Gita is one of the nine pieces composed by Mangkunegara IV (r. 1853–81), based on poetic songs. Langen Gita can be performed in two ways, in the slow-

paced *gérongan* (chorus) style of a *ketawang* piece, or in the faster tempo of the *dolanan* (children's song) style.

77. Raden, "Dinamika Pertemuan dua Tradisi," 6.
78. Ibid.
79. Dewan Kesenian Jakarta, *Pesta Seni 1974*, 158.
80. At this time, according to Hill ("The Two Leading Institutions"), a longstanding budgetary conflict between the Center and the Jakarta state government (the agency responsible for the Center's budget) reached its peak. This is also the period when new venues in Jakarta—namely Taman Ancol and Taman Mini—began their operation. Consequently, the audience for the Center's performances declined, which made it more difficult to justify its annual budget.
81. The music is dominated by Javanese (Surakarta and Yogyakarta), Balinese (Denpasar), and Sundanese (Bandung) gamelan. The government-sponsored gamelan institutions are found in these regions.
82. See a list of the works and composers in Hardjana (*Enam Tahun Pekan Komponis Muda*). I would note that the dominant presence of gamelan at the festival had a wider impact. When Indonesia sponsored a performing arts festival in the U.S in 1990–91, STSI of Surakarta was selected to represent new Indonesian music. The one-year festival was headed by the former Minister of Foreign Affairs, Dr. Mochtar Kusuma-Atmadja, director of the Nusantara Jaya Foundation (the sole organizer of the festival). Supported by the governments of Indonesia and the United States, the festival consisted of performances of traditional and new performing arts from Indonesia, presented throughout the United States.
83. Sjukur, "Mak Comblang dan Pionir Asongan," 19.
84. Supanggah, "Gambuh" (original work, 1979).
85. Suwardi and Pande Made Sukerta, "Laras-Gender-Sebuah Proses," 314–15.
86. Hardjana, *Esai & Kritik Musik*, 90.
87. Santoso and Subono, "Sworo Pencon," 254.
88. Besides being an organizer of YGF, Sapto was the program director of the Geronimo radio station and a member of the Yogyakarta Arts Council. The festival was financed partly by the local government, but mostly by private donation. Sapto, with his Geronimo crew, was the sole organizer of the festival, gathering funds and providing publicity. Advertisements through Geronimo have been very effective, since the station caters to a large student community—Yogyakarta is home to the oldest and largest university in Indonesia, Gadjah Mada. Participants in the festival include performance groups and individuals from Indonesia and abroad, who come with their own financial support or assistance from their state government or private institution. The festival usually provides local accommodation. In its first five years (1995–99) the festival took place in the Purna Budaya concert hall of the Taman Budaya Arts Center, near the campus of Gadjah Mada University. In 2000, the committee moved the festival to the Kawasan Gayam community along Gayam Street, on which the Geronimo is located; the stage was built on a section of sidewalk in front of the radio station. Subsequently, the festival has alternated between Purna Budaya and Gayam.
89. Ferianto, liner notes of *Nang Ning Nong Orkes Sumpek*.
90. Earlier I mentioned Surjodiningrat as one of the composers who presented his work in the pre-YGF. He is a professor of Mathematics at Gadjah Mada, and has used computers to generate new gendhing. Unfortunately no trace seems to remain of these gendhing.
91. For a complete report on the life and work of Cokrowasito, see Wenten ("The Creative Work of Ki Wasitodipuro").

92. Becker, *Traditional Music in Modern Java*.
93. Mack, *Sejarah Musik*, 552.
94. Ibid., 570.
95. Ibid.
96. As discussed in the preface, people from the birthplace of campursari (the village of Gunung Kidul, near Yogyakarta) shared the same view—campursari represents modernity.
97. Geertz, *Negara*, 104.

Chapter Three

1. Three years later, economic crisis, corruption, and the abuse of power by Suharto's regime brought about the downfall of his New Order government.
2. The prelude of the recent production of *Opera Diponegoro* performed in Jakarta can be viewed at "Sardono W. Kusumo. Tari Opera Diponegoro.flv," YouTube video, posted by Salihara, May 31, 2010, http://www.youtube.com/watch?v=m2Uel1z5E8U.
3. At this symposium I presented a paper on the history of the introduction and impact of gamelan in the West (the seed of chapter 4). While participating in the symposium, I had an opportunity to see the debut of *Opera Diponegoro*. Since then, the play has been performed several times in different cities in Indonesia and abroad: Surabaya, Semarang, Solo, Yogyakarta, Singapore, and New York. My discussion is based only on the debut performance.
4. Geertz, *The Interpretation of Culture*, 6.
5. Lombard, *Nusa Jawa*, 111. The following brief background of Raden Saleh is drawn from Lombard.
6. Ricklefs, *A History of Modern Indonesia*, 115.
7. Carey, introduction to *Babad Dipanegara*, xl.
8. Ricklefs, *A History of Modern Indonesia*, 117.
9. Schechner, *Between Theater & Anthropology*, 8–9.
10. Brandon, *Theatre in Southeast Asia*, 146–47.
11. I would like to thank Waluyo Sastro Sukarno for making these documents available to me.
12. Brandon, *Theatre in Southeast Asia*, 147.
13. "Wayang kulit purwa" would be the most accurate term for the genre, but the term wayang purwa is sufficient and commonly used.
14. Sears, Laurie. "Transmission of Indian Epics," 12–15.
15. Born blind, the father of the Kurawa children, Dhestarastra, trusted his brother Pandhu (the father of Pandhawa brothers) to rule the kingdom. The cousins grew up in the same compound and under the same tutors, mainly their uncle Bisma and the priest Durna. However, there are clues that the Pandhawa brothers are actually semi-divine beings and not just charismatic humans (the oldest brother, Yudhistira, is the incarnation of the god Dharma; the second brother, Bima, is the incarnation of the god Bayu; the middle brother, Arjuna, is the incarnation of Wisnu; and the twins Nakula and Sadéwa are the incarnation of the gods Aswan and Aswin). In the course of their adolescence, the Kurawa brothers become arrogant and full of hatred toward their cousins, sparking rivalry and jealousy. After Pandhu dies, the Kurawa brothers, under the leadership of the eldest brother Duryudana, occupy the kingdom of Hastina. Using various

means, the Kurawas try to prevent their cousins from taking back the kingdom. The story ends with a final battle, and the Pandhawas are victorious.

16. The journey begins when Rama, accompanied by Sinta and Laksmana, is sent into exile by his father who, under pressure from his second wife, names Rama's half-brother as successor to the throne. During their exile in the jungle, Sinta is kidnapped by the ten-headed demon king Rahwana of Ngalengka. With the assistance of a monkey army under the command of the white monkey Anoman, Rama and Laksmana begin the search for Sinta. They must build a dam to cross the strait which leads to the kingdom of Rahwana, and after a grand battle between the two camps—Rama, Laksmana, and the monkeys against Rahwana and his army of giants—Sinta is found. In order to test her purity, Rama orders Sinta to be burnt. She escapes the fire unscathed and Rama, Sinta, Laksmana, and the monkey army all live happily ever after.

17. See Soedarsono, *Wayang Wong*; Jennifer Lindsay, *Klasik, Kitsch, Kontemporer*.

18. An exception was wayang wong in the court of Yogyakarta in the nineteenth century, which was held in an outdoor courtyard.

19. Soetrisno and Murgiyanto, personal communications, 1979 and 1987 respectively; Partohudoyo, "Bab Langendriyan"; Djakoeb and Wignyaroemekso, *Layang Anyumurupaké*.

20. Partohudoyo, "Bab Langendriyan."

21. Tondhakusuma, "Pakem Mondraswara."

22. Warsadiningrat, *Sacred Knowledge*, 155.

23. I would like to thank Philip Yampolsky for giving me access to these recordings, and for dating the phonographs. Yampolsky is one of the few ethnomusicologists who has an abundant collection of meticulously catalogued old recordings of Indonesian music. Many phonographs from 1920s and 1930s produced by Beka and Odeon that I have listened to, contain music for langendriyan.

24. Besides the recordings of langendriyan at the Mangkunegaran court, the companies also produced recordings of langendriyan music performed by kethoprak and wayang wong troupes outside the court, suggesting the popularity of langendriyan at the time. It seems that by the late nineteenth century, as wayang wong became a popular genre, the dancers of wayang wong (and later kethoprak) adapted the music of langendriyan, especially the key musical feature of the genre: the singing of poetry by the dancers accompanied by srepegan.

25. Susanto, *Ketoprak*, 12. See also Susanto, *Imaginasi Penguasa dan Identitas Postkolonial*.

26. Susanto, *Ketoprak*, 12.

27. Kartomi, "Performance, Music, and Meaning of Reyog Ponorogo," 165.

28. I have known Sardono since the 1960s, when I was a student at the gamelan conservatory in Solo. I was one of the musicians for the Ramayana ballet in Prambanan when he was one of the star dancers. In 1970, we were in the same group at the Indonesian performance at Expo '70 in Osaka, Japan: I was a gamelan musician, and he was artistic director. Returning from Japan, he began to produce experimental theater; one of his initial productions was *Samgita*, a play based on the Ramayana. He asked me to provide musical accompaniment with the use of a few gamelan instruments, so I put together a group of five musicians and we played musical passages and idioms drawn from the gamelan *sekatèn* repertoire, *palaran* singing, and a Balinese interlocking style of two drums. That was the only collaboration I have undertaken with Sardono, as I began my career abroad, first in Australia and then the United States. My interest in his work did not end, however, and I followed his activities from afar. I wrote a review (Sumarsam, "Sajian Politis Manusia Jawa-Indonesia) of his play, "Passage Through the Gong," which was presented at the Brooklyn Academy of Music in New York.

29. First performed in 1961, the production was originally called *Ballet Ramayana*, later changed to *Sendratari Ramayana*. *Sendratari* is an abbreviation for art (*seni*), drama, and dance (*tari*) in Indonesian. The Ramayana epic was performed in four nightly two-hour-long episodes; the spectacular production involved hundreds of dancers and musicians performing on a large outdoor stage with a very elaborate lighting and sound system. It is still performed, on a smaller scale, on a newer stage located on the right side of the Prambanan temple.

30. Kusumo, "Hanuman, Tarzan, Pithecanthropus Erectus."

31. Ibid.

32. Murgiyanto suggests that Erdman and Graham's style of modern dance influenced Sardono in creating his own work ("Moving between Unity and Diversity"). But according to Sardono himself (personal communication 2009), he only casually observed the classes of these two prominent modern choreographers and does not feel that they influenced his own work.

33. Murgiyanto, "Moving between Unity and Diversity," 346.

34. Ibid.

35. Lombard, *Nusa Jawa*, 175.

36. Ibid.

37. Carey, "The Cultural Ecology of Early Nineteenth Century Java," 4.

38. Ibid., 1.

39. Sumarsam, "Past and Present Issues of Islam," 52–64.

40. Carey, "The Cultural Ecology of Early Nineteenth Century Java," 10–11.

41. Ibid., 11.

42. Program notes for "Opera Diponegoro," performed at the Taman Ismail Marzuki, Jakarta Arts Center, September 29–30, 1995.

43. Ibid.

44. *Babad Diponegoro*, 167–68.

  Babad Diponegoro. Sinom.
  99. Sinambut sang lir Supraba
  binekta mring tilamsari
  Kangjeng Pangran nuli nendra
  supé solat dhahar iki
  sadinten ngantos ratri
  ajrih nunggu sang Retnayu
  mung tinengga kéwala
  wancinira tengah wengi
  nulya dhawah tandha bendhuning Hyang Suksma
  100. Ardi Mrapi murup ika
  anglir sundhul ing wiyati
  kadya kabekan Ngayogya
  kang ngakasa kadi geni
  kang swara nggegirisi
  jumegur lawan gumludhug
  brama pating pancurat
  kalangkung giris pan sami
  ting kudhandhang ngupados pangungsèn samya

45. Translated by Ann Kumar, in "Dipanegara (1787?–1855)," 99–100.
  Babad Diponegoro. Dhandhanggula.

1. Tambuh-tambuh kang samya dèn gungsi
ing ngawiyat langkung petengira
mangkana kang winarnèng rèh
Jeng Pangran dèrèng wungu
langkung éca dènira guling
sang Retna pan kawedan
èsmu maras iku
menawa tilar séda
mring kang raka arsa mungu langkung ajrih
mung tinengga kéwala
2. Sang Kusuma mangkana tyasnèki
maspaosken dhumateng kang raka
lamun lajeng séda mangké
mung nyipta béla iku
tuhu lamun tan nedya kari
mangkana tan winarna
sang Retnaning ayu
apan kagungan parekan
langkung dènya sembrana tan pirsa ajrih
bok Buang namanira
3. Langkung ajrih ningali wiyati
lan suwara tambuh solahira
dadya jerit-jerit baé
lawan parekan sagung
gustinira kaliyan nèki
maksih anèng jron tilam
mangkana winuwus
Kangjeng Pangran dhuk miyarsa
mring swaraning parekan samya anjerit
kagyat wungu tumulya
4. Aningali sang resmining putri
lenggah dagan Jeng Pangran atanya
ana apa ta nak anggèr
sang Dyah alon umatur
tan uninga kawula yekti
pan dèrèng medal-medal
Jeng Pangran nulyèku
miyos akekanthèn asta
lang sang Retna mring palataran wus prapti
ningali ing gegana
5. Lamun adi ingkang urub iki
lawan obahira kang bantala
mèsem Jeng Pangran kalihé
kalawan aturipun
para sagung parekan sami
mapan awarna-warna
mangkana nulyèku
Jeng Pangran nambut sang Retna
pan binekta wangsul mring tilam sari
dumugèkken san karsa

46. Translated by Kumar, ibid., 76–78.
Babad Diponegoro. Sinom.
17. Enjing anulya lumampah
lajeng andeder kang wukir
guwa Langsé kang sinedya
dirgama wus tan kaèsthi
samana sampun prapti
guwa Langsé lampahipun
Sèh Ngabdulrahkim nulya
nèng riku amati raga
awatara nèng guwa satengah condra
18. Ngeningaken inkang cipta
wus sirna sagung kaèksi
Sèh Ngabdulrahkim samana
mung kanun rumeksèng urip
urip rumeksèng dhiri
dhiri wangsul urip sampun
kang urip kaya-kaya
sampun tan kena winarni
kawarnaa kang ngedhaton ing samodra
47. Personal communication, Waluyo, 2009.
48. Schechner, *Between Theater & Anthropology*, 194.
49. Turner, *From Ritual to Theatre*.
50. Ibid., 52.
51. Ibid.

Chapter Four

1. I began researching this topic in 1995 when the committee of the Art Summit Indonesia 1995 invited me to present a paper entitled "Gamelan and the West: Cultural and Musical Interaction." Although I kept in mind some questions and ideas from that paper, this chapter grew out of my more recent research.
2. Boon, *Affinities and Extremes*, 35.
3. Forge, "Raffles and Daniell," 115.
4. Ibid., 147.
5. Ibid., 150.
6. Miller and Gerstle, "Recovering the Exotic," 1.
7. Ibid.
8. Ibid.
9. Raffles, *The History of Java*, 470.
10. Quoted in Quigley, "The Raffles Gamelan at Claydon House."
11. Ellis, "On the Musical Scale of Various Nations."
12. Quoted in Crawfurd, *History of Indian Archipelago*, 339–40.
13. For an analysis of the notations of the two *gendhing* from this collection, *Onang-Onang* and *Boyong*, see Benjamin Brinner, "A Musical Time Capsule from Java."
14. Raffles, *The History of Java*, 2:57.
15. Both sets are well protected as invaluable museum objects. Interestingly, one of the gamelan was tuned to a Western diatonic scale. It is not clear whether the gamelan

was retuned to the Western scale after the instruments' arrival in England, or whether Raffles commissioned the Javanese maker to tune the instruments this way (Quigley, personal communication, 1994).

16. Quigley, "The Raffles Gamelan at Claydon House."

17. The gamelan is considered an incomplete set (due to the absence of *bonang*). It seems that, judging from the size of the instruments (which are larger than regular gamelan), the ensemble is meant to present the loud style of music. Thus, the absence of *bonang*, standard instruments for the loud style, is a puzzle.

18. Quigley, "The Raffles Gamelan at Claydon House," 12–14.

19. It is worth mentioning an illustration of *celempung* (a plucked-stringed instrument) in the book. The tuning pegs of this instrument are commonly located on the top end of the instrument, but Raffles' illustration places the pegs on the right side. The illustration also includes a pair of European plectra. Is this a case of sloppiness, or did it aim to make the instrument more familiar to European eyes?

20. Raffles, *The History of Java*, 470.

21. Ibid., my emphasis.

22. Mendonça, *Javanese Gamelan in Britain*.

23. Woodfield, *English Musicians in the Age of Exploration*, 103–4.

24. Ibid., 276. The drawings suggest an ensemble similar to the *Monggang* or *Carabalèn* types of gong ensemble (minus drum) in the central Javanese courts of Surakarta and Yogyakarta, courts that were founded in the mid-eighteenth to early nineteenth century. Is it possible that in the sixteenth and seventeenth centuries this type of gamelan was commonly found in Javanese political and cultural centers? In the sixteenth century, Banten was such a center—a powerful court city with a large harbor. The court of Kasultanan Banten was founded by arrivals from Demak, another powerful center on the north coast of Java. Did this result in a musical transfer from Demak to Banten? The early drawing of a gong ensemble in Tuban (another center of trading near Demak) by a Dutch expedition in the late sixteenth century suggests a similarity, showing a Carabalèn type of gamelan.

25. See Kunst, *Music in Java*, 114–15.

26. Quoted in Kunst, *Music in Java*, 114.

27. Sumarsam, *Gamelan*, 20–22.

28. Kunst, *Music in Java*, 115.

29. Bloembergen, *Colonial Spectacle*, 13.

30. Ibid.

31. Corbey, "Ethnographic Showcases, 1870–1930," 364.

32. Breckenridge, "The Aesthetics and Politics of Colonial Collecting," 196.

33. Ibid., 200–201.

34. Bloembergen, *Colonial Spectacle*, 322–23.

35. Breckenridge, "The Aesthetics and Politics of Colonial Collecting," 203.

36. Groot, "Bijdrage tot de kennis van de zeden en gewoonten der Javanen"; See Kumar, "The Socialization of the People."

37. Wilken, "Sewaka, een Javaansch gedicht met eene vertaling en wordenboek."

38. Kusumadilaga, *Serat Sastramiruda*.

39. Pemberton, *On the Subject of "Java,"* 58.

40. Based on Fig. III. 14, Terwen identifies the instruments as *saron* and *peking*. I am inclined to think that both of them are actually *saron barung*, as their size is almost the same, conforming to modern gamelan *klenèngan* instrumentation. Terwen also thinks that there is *gong ageng* in the set, stating in a parenthesis "as far as can be seen in Fig.

III. 18"—referring to the difficulty of seeing it in the picture, because the *gong kemodhong* player blocks the view of the entire *kempul* behind him. With Fig. 111. 2 taken into consideration, I believe that *gong ageng* is not part of the set. In my experience, usually gongs hung behind the gong kemodhong player are kempul; this is corroborated by the presence of gong kemodhong, which has the same function as gong ageng.

41. It is common in European sources to use "ronggèng" as a generic term for any dancing girl hired to dance with males at a dance party, but each region might have its own term. "Talèdhèk" or "tandhak" are the terms commonly used by people in Central and East Java.

42. I consulted with Bambang Suryono, a dancer of the Mangkunegaran court, about my finding. He identifies the costumes as belonging to the dancers of *serimpi* Pandhelori.

43. Keller 1879, quoted in Terwen, *Gamelan in the 19th-Century Netherlands*, 88.

44. Ibid., 96.

45. Ibid.

46. Ibid., 97.

47. Ibid., 96.

48. Quoted in Terwen, *Gamelan in the 19th-Century Netherlands*, 99–100.

49. Ibid., 100.

50. Ibid., 101.

51. See ibid., 103–44.

52. Bloembergen, *Colonial Spectacle*, 30.

53. "*Kampong*" was how the Dutch spelled the word at the time, whereas the Javanese would spell it "*kampoeng*," or in the new spelling, "*kampung*."

54. Terwen, *Gamelan in the 19th-Century Netherlands*, 148.

55. Ibid., 51.

56. Ibid.

57. Terwen, *Gamelan in the 19th-Century Netherlands*, 147.

58. Figures from Greek mythology: the muses of music and singing, respectively, and a "barbarian" queen.

59. Ibid. The organizer in question was the engineer Daniel Veth, son of P. J. Veth, who was stationed in the East Indies to supervise the collection of ethnographic objects for the exhibition. His father was an esteemed scholar in the study of Orientalism (ibid., 146).

60. Ibid., 153–55.

61. De Vale, "A Sundanese Gamelan, 67.

62. There is no evidence showing when and how this diatonic tuning was carried out. De Vale reports that the 1883 gamelan was a pélog gamelan, but she also says that the gamelan is badly out of tune.

63. Quoted in Terwen, *Gamelan in the 19th-Century Netherlands*, 149–50.

64. Ibid., 154.

65. Bloembergen, *Colonial Spectacle*, 134. For the presence of Annamitic theater, its close proximity with Javanese kampong, and its influence to Debussy's works, see Fauser, *Musical Encounters*, 183–206.

66. Bloembergen, *Colonial Spectacle*, 134.

67. Burris, *Exhibiting Religion*.

68. Quoted in and translated by Fauser, *Musical Encounters*, 144.

69. Burris, *Exhibiting Religion*, 82–85.

70. Bloembergen, *Colonial Spectacle*, 116.

71. Ibid.

72. There are also subregional gamelan styles. Cirebon gamelan in the northeastern part of west Java is known for its distinct style, though closely related to Sundanese gamelan. The southern part of Central Java, Banyumas and its vicinity, is also known for its unique style. In central Java there are two major court styles, Yogyakarta and Surakarta, and there are different gamelan styles in each of the minor courts within the two court cities, Paku Alam in Yogyakarta and Mangkunegaran in Surakarta, although the styles are closely related. Also, the social hierarchy of Javanese society creates another musical distinction: between court and village gamelan.

73. Spiller, *Focus: Gamelan Music of Indonesia*, 131.

74. Thompson, "Rethinking the *Divine Arabesque*," 108.

75. Chazal, "Grand Succès pour les Exotiques."

76. Ibid.

77. Greenhalgh, *Ephemeral Vista*, 88.

78. Email to the author on March 12, 2010.

79. See Sumarsam, *Gamelan*, 7; 121–22.

80. For a brief description of langendriyan and its story, see chapter 3.

81. Claire Holt, *Art in Indonesia*, 160.

82. Pigeaud, *Javaanse Volksvertoningen*, 51.

83. Quoted in Fauser, *Musical Encounters*, 178.

84. I should mention that Heins's dissertation ("*Goong Renteng*") is concerned with the influence of the Javanese Mataram kingdom on Sundanese musical culture. His point about the close ties between the Mataram and Sundanese courts becomes an important reference for discussion on this historical link (see Williams, "Sunda"; and Sutton, Suanda, and Williams, "Java."); but he was discussing early to mid-seventeenth-century Mataram, about three hundred years before the Paris exposition. In fact, the cultural link between the Mataram and Sundanese regions was severed after the Dutch East Indies Company took control of Sundanese territory in the late seventeenth century (Ricklefs, *A History of Modern Indonesia*, 79).

85. Fauser, *Musical Encounters*, 168.

86. The right prince is Mangkunegara V (r. 1881–96).

87. Fauser, *Musical Encounters*, 168.

88. Mueller, "Javanese Influence on Debussy's *Fantaisie* and Beyond."

89. Ibid., 166–67.

90. Quoted in Mueller (ibid., 162).

91. Ibid., 158.

92. Ibid.

93. Groneman, *De Gamelan te Jogjakarta*; Hood, *The Nuclear Theme*.

94. Lockspeiser, *Debussy*, 114–15.

95. Spiller's email to the author on August 8, 2012.

96. Koesoemadinata, *Lagu-Lagu Gede Sunda*.

97. I should mention that in the level of melodic outline, there are some commonalities between Sundanese and Javanese Wani-Wani (Solonese Wani-Wani is closer to Sundanese). There must have been a time when Sundanese and Javanese musicians were sharing the same piece, but the piece has been so regionalized that similarities cannot be recognized anymore.

98. Fauser, *Musical Encounters*, 177n99. I am assuming here that Fauser refers to the transcription of Vani-Vani that is not Tiersot's.

99. Ibid.

100. I would like to thank Henry Spiller (email November 8, 2010) for identifying the name of this piece for me.
101. Fauser, *Musical Encounters*, 180, ex. 4.2.
102. I would like to thank Maho Ishiguro for playing this piece and other examples for me on the piano.
103. Fauser, *Musical Encounters*, 199. Regarding the *Nocturnes* and *La Mer* being described as "stylized gamelan," Fauser references this from the work of Constantine Brailoiu, which is cited in Lockspeiser, *Debussy*, 116.
104. Ibid., 199.
105. Thompson, "Rethinking the *Divine Arabesque*," 132–33.
106. Ibid., 133.
107. Ibid., 125.
108. Ibid., 126.
109. Sumarsam, "Inner Melody."
110. Debussy incorrectly identified the speaker in this passage as Portia, when in fact it was Lorenzo.
111. Debussy 1913, in Lesure and Smith, *Debussy on Music*, 277–78.
112. Ibid., 278.
113. Spiller, *Gamelan: The Traditional Sounds of Indonesia*.
114. Ibid., 164.
115. Ibid.
116. I will return to this issue in later discussion.
117. Fauser, *Musical Encounters*, 171.
118. Ibid.
119. Ibid., 173.
120. Kernoa, quoted in Fauser, 173.
121. Greenhalgh, *Ephemeral Vista*, 82.
122. Rydell, *All the World's a Fair*, 66, drawn from McDowell, "The World's Fair Cosmopolis." 412–14.
123. De Vale, "A Sundanese Gamelan," 93. The recordings have been preserved in the Library of Congress.
124. Quoted in De Vale, ibid., 258.
125. This singing can vaguely be heard in cylinder # 31, but it is clearer in cylinder #32.
126. Bloembergen, *Colonial Spectacle*, 163.
127. Ibid.
128. Mona 1938, quoted in and translated by Gouda, *Dutch Culture Overseas*, 209.
129. It is true that, during this period, Indonesia was under Dutch rule. However, the Indonesian national awakening had started early on, marked by the *Sumpah Pemuda* (Youth pledge) in 1928. Calling Matu Mona an Indonesian, as opposed to Javanese, novelist is based on this nationalistic fervor.
130. Bloembergen, *Colonial Spectacle*.
131. Ibid. 285–88.
132. Ibid., 313–14.
133. Quoted and translated by Gouda, *Dutch Culture Overseas*, 225.
134. Ibid., 226.
135. Bali had a different colonial experience than Java. Whereas Java had a long contact with Europeans (especially the Dutch), in commerce and politics, Bali took a rebellious stance toward European presence; such rebelliousness ended in the first decade of the twentieth century in internationally known ritual suicides called *puputan*.

136. Picard, "Dance and Drama in Bali," 129.
137. Ibid.
138. Bloembergen, *Colonial Spectacles*, 333.
139. Bradbury II, *Messian and Gamelan*, 34–88.
140. Artaud, *The Theater and its Double*.
141. The other scholar was Brandt Buys, who focused his study on music in the island of Madura.
142. Heins, "Letter to the Editor."
143. Ibid., 99–100.
144. Kunst, *Ethnomusicology*, 1.
145. Cohen, "Indonesian Performing Arts in the Netherlands," 112–13; Cohen, *Performing Otherness*, 6–12.
146. Ibid., 109–36.
147. Mensink, *Gamelan en andere gong-spel ensembles*, 22.
148. Hood purchased the gamelan for UCLA from its Chinese owner in Surakarta.
149. Hood, "The Challenge of Bi-Musicality," 55.
150. Even the members of gamelan groups at Indonesian embassies or consulates usually consist of a mixture of Indonesians and Americans. The only gamelan groups composed exclusively of Javanese immigrants are located in the South American nation of Suriname, which has been home to Javanese immigrants since the beginning of the twentieth century. Most of these were Javanese laborers sent by the Dutch colonial government to work on plantations.
151. Nettl, *Heartland Excursions*, 84–85.
152. Merriam, *The Anthropology of Music*, 6.
153. Solis, *Performing Ethnomusicology*.
154. Ibid., 1–2.
155. Trimillos, "Subject, Object, and the Ethnomusicology Ensemble," 52.
156. Howard, "Performing Ethnomusicology," 26.
157. Solis, *Performing Ethnomusicology*, 7.
158. Vetter, "A Square Peg in a Round Hole," 117.
159. Nettl, *Heartland Excursions*, 85.
160. Averill, "Where's 'One'?," 108.
161. Ibid.
162. Ibid., 109.
163. Kirshenblatt-Gimblett, "Confusing Pleasure."

Chapter Five

1. Merriam, *The Anthropology of Music*, 6.
2. Hood, *The Nuclear Theme as a Determinant of Pathet*.
3. Rice, "Toward the Remodeling of Ethnomusicology," 470.
4. Feld, "Sound Structure as Social Structure"; Roseman, "The Social Structuring of Sound"; Becker, "Time and Tune in Java"; Becker and Becker, "Musical Icon"; and Becker, "Responding to Feld and Roseman." John Shepherd explains: "If musical style has an inherent social significance, then it should be possible to demonstrate that significance by carrying out musical analysis in terms of the social reality which gave birth to and is articulated by a particular musical style" (Shepherd, *Music as Social Text*, 12). His further comments deserve mention here: "Such analyses are notably absent from both

the musicological and sociological worlds. Surface reasons for the scant attention given to the sociology of music (as opposed to the sociology of musical life) are not difficult to find. Few sociologists feel themselves to be competent in a discipline which requires a significant degree of technical knowledge as well as, preferably, some first-hand experience as a practitioner. Most musicologists and music theorists, on the other hand, repelled by what they see as unending waves of pseudo-scientific jargon, have apparently decided that the area should be left well alone. The art of musical analysis is well established, and musicologists and music theorists see in sociology no good reason for changing their methods or approaches where traditional analysis is concerned" (ibid).

5. Monson, "Jazz as Political and Musical Practice," 22.

6. Ibid.

7. Randel, *The New Harvard Dictionary of Music*; Sadie, *The New Grove Dictionary of Music and Musicians*; Miller and Williams, *Southeast Asia*, vol. 4 of *The Garland Encyclopedia of World Music*.

8. Powers, "Language Models and Musical Analysis."

9. Sumarsam, *Gamelan*, 131.

10. Hood, *The Nuclear Theme*, 242.

11. Becker, *Traditional Music in Modern Java*, 81.

12. Lord, *The Singer of Tales*.

13. Becker, *Traditional Music in Modern Java*, 20, second emphasis added.

14. Sutton, *Variation in Central Javanese Gamelan Music*, 24–26.

15. Becker, "Time and Tune in Java"; Becker and Becker, "Musical Icon."

16. Becker, "Time in Tune in Java," 198.

17. Maceda, "A Concept of Time," 12–13. Maceda's exposition about drone in Southeast Asian music deserves mention here: "Drone may be understood to be not only a sustained sound, a continuation of the long vibration of gongs, but also a constantly repeating phrase of one or more pitches played by one or several instruments for the duration of the music."

18. Ibid., 13.

19. Kartomi, "Dualism in Unity," 75.

20. Ibid., 77.

21. Rita S. Kipp, "The Thread of Three Colors"; see also Mary Steedly, *Hanging Without a Rope*.

22. Becker and Becker, "Musical Icon," 203.

23. Ibid., 204.

24. Ibid.

25. Rice, "Time, Place, and Metaphor," 166–67.

26. See Zbikowski, "Metaphor and Music"; Powers, "Language Models and Musical Analysis"; and Keil and Feld, *Music Grooves*.

27. Zbikowski, Metaphor and Music, 516.

28. Ibid., 519–20.

29. Ibid., 520.

30. Ibid.

31. I presented the seed of this idea at the Asian Pacific Society for Ethnomusicology (APSE) Symposium, University of the Philippines, February 17–23, 2002. I also presented a different version of the same paper at the New England Gamelan Weekend at Wesleyan University, April 19–21, 2002, and at the seminar on Indonesian Performing Arts at the Indonesian Institute of the Arts (STSI, now ISI) Surakarta, July 3–4, 2002.

32. Becker, "Time in Tune in Java," 198–99.

33. Becker and Becker, "A Musical Icon," 208.
34. Ibid., 202.
35. Ibid., 202–3.
36. Kunst, *Music in Java*, 248.
37. Ibid., 223.
38. Martopangrawit, *Notes on Knowledge*, 15.
39. Translated by Suharni Sumarmo and Paul W. van der Veur, in van der Veur, *Toward A Glorious Indonesia*, 235–36.
40. Translated by Scherer, in Scherer, "Harmony and Dissonance," 309.
41. Pemberton "Musical Politics in Central Java," 24–25. Pemberton goes on to say that, given the fierceness of musicians' gossiping about these matters, "it is surprising that Central Javanese musicians are capable of playing 'together' at all, unless of course, gamelan's intimate musical togetherness has very little to do with ideal social harmony" (24n16).
42. Ibid., 25. For another practice that heightens the nonharmonious end, the players of gamelan sekatèn are encouraged to play as loud a sound as they can possibly produce. If a player breaks one of the enormous bronze keys of his instrument, he receives an award from the court authority.
43. Ibid., 27.
44. For example, a batik bearing the design called "Sida Mukti" (becoming comfortable in life and powerful) is the most appropriate batik to be worn by a newlywed.
45. Kitley, "Ornamentation and Originality," 8.
46. Ibid.
47. Ibid.
48. Weiss, *Listening to an Earlier Java*, 43.
49. See Moertono, *State and Statecraft*, and Nagtegaal, *Riding the Dutch Tiger*.
50. Laksono, *Tradition in Javanese Social Structure*, 14.
51. Ibid.
52. Laksono, ibid.; Kumar, The Religious, Social and Economic Life of the Court"; and Nagtegaal, *Riding the Dutch Tiger*.
53. Anderson, *Mythology and the Tolerance*.
54. Ibid., 5.
55. Laksono, *Tradition in Javanese Social Structure*, 23.
56. Ibid.
57. Anderson, *Mythology and the Tolerance*, 23.
58. Mulyono 1978 (translated by E. G. Koentjoro), in Laksono, *Tradition in Javanese Social Structure*, 25.
59. Anderson, *Mythology and the Tolerance of the Javanese*, 6.
60. Nagtegaal, *Riding the Dutch Tiger*, 51.
61. Ibid., 51–52.
62. Brinner, *Knowing Music, Making Music*, 208.
63. Ibid.
64. Ibid., 173.
65. Ibid., 175.
66. Brinner's description of the roles of the drummer, contrasting it with the roles of conductor, deserve a full mention here: "The drummer, who takes a large portion of the responsibility in a Javanese *gamelan*, sits in the middle of the orchestra, roughly equidistant from the other players. They can all hear him, but those in the front row have their backs to him. His cues are exclusively aural and completely integrated in the texture of

the music; his leadership, like that of other leading members of the *gamelan*, is unobtrusive and largely unrecognized by the public—he takes no bow and receives no billing. Conductors, on the other hand, stand in full view of all members of the orchestra, convey their desires exclusively with visual cues that are extraneous to the musical product, and are accorded much attention by audience, management, publicists, and critics, clearly set above the other musicians in status. Finally the conductor's post is not up for grabs but is generally given after much deliberation to an individual who has developed a special competence through extensive specialized training. Many Javanese musicians, on the other hand, are capable of assuming leading roles within a *gamelan*, thanks to their well-rounded competence, and often do so at a moment's notice, perhaps trading places between pieces" (Ibid., 172).

67. Weiss, *Listening to an Earlier Java*, 80.
68. Ibid.
69. Ibid.
70. Ibid.
71. I must admit that it is not common for gamelan musicians and theorists to consider *gongan* and *irama* as a binary classification. But my research has led me to conclude that this pairing is in line with musical practice (see below).
72. Believed to be a recent development, irama rangkep has its own characteristic: it creates an animated atmosphere.
73. Becker, "Southeast Asian Musical Process," 454.
74. Sastrodarsono, *Teori Nabuh Gamelan*, 4.
75. Soelardi, *Serat Pradongga*.
76. *Serat Tjentini*, 5–6: 169.

> Dhandhang Gula.
> 9. Njenggrèng ngèk wus pakolih nemnèki
> nulya asasendhon pathet sanga
> anutug lih-ulihané
> lajeng agendhing talu
> Gambirsawit raras angrangin
> Samya pakolihira
> wileté nenabuh
> arempeg padha karasa
> biyang Kacer kumecer sindhèné ngelik
> mamethet-methet driya.
>
> 10. Bening merit lir suling wrat sari
> muket wileté barungan rebab
> apupunton nges manisé
> samya angungas besus
> lir penjalin sinigar palih
> swara mot jroning kawat
> rebab lan sindhèn rum
> atungtum lungiding raras
> yatmakaning gendhing gendhèng mbelèr ati
> rongèh Ki Kulawirya.

77. Mangkunegara IV, *Sendhon Langen Swara*.
78. *Puspa Warna* had a noticeable impact on the development of gamelan composition, namely the rise of compositions in which the gérongan part was used as the basis

for the piece (e.g., a genre of compositions called *panembrama* and *macapat*-based composition). In some instances new gérongan melodies were composed for compositions whose originals have no gérongan.

79. Kunst, *Music in Java*, and Hood, *The Nuclear Theme*.
80. Sumarsam, *Inner Melody*.
81. Perlman, *Unplayed Melodies*, 111. His argument is partly a response to some scholars who are of the opinion that the notion of balungan is a distorted concept inspired by Western modes of thought. He offers proof that terms other than "balungan" might have been used in the 19th century, such as "gendhing," "cengkok" (Perlman, ibid., 110–12), and "wiletan" (ibid., 556–58). My take on this is that the concept of the melodic skeleton as contained in the early 20th-century term balungan has been misinterpreted as a supreme melodic guide (ibid., 110; Sumarsam, *Gamelan*, 149).
82. Ibid., 146. He shows us four representations of balungan, based on its congruent and divergent relationships with the melodic parts: (1) maximal congruence in both sides (among balungan and other parts); (2) maximal divergence, with the other parts congruent to each other; (3) congruence between balungan and one instrument from the other parts, but divergence from the others; (4) the other parts congruent with each other (informing the true balungan), but the balungan divergent from them.
83. Ibid.
84. Ibid., 88.
85. Ibid., 87–116.
86. Ibid., 104.
87. Ibid., 105.
88. Supanggah, *Bothekan Karawitan II*, 13.
89. Supanggah, *Bothekan Karawitan I*, 132.
90. *Serat Tjentini* 1–2, 247, translated by Anthony Day, "Sound, Feeling, Knowledge," 25–26.

>Pucung.
>111. kabèh baud padha rasané nenabuh
>rereming irama
>adu wileting malatsih
>ukur jawil sejejanturaning dhalang
>112. langkung runtut rasaning gendhing pakantuk
>dadya ngantak-antak
>dangu dènira anggendhing
>tan antara aneseg gendhingé munggah
>113. pan adangu saya gulet wiletipun
>rebut nges kesaman
>nabuhé samya birai
>rahab bérag rasa-rasa yèn uwisa

91. *Serat Tjentini* 1–2, 246–47, translated by Anthony Day (ibid).

>Pucung.
>103 . . . payo padha klenèngan baé kepénak
>104. nanging iku ana kojahé kang muwus
>yèn wong kalenèngan
>nganggo kendhang lan dèn-gongi
>rada nora ilok ingaran kemaga
>105. becikipun nganggo gong ywa seru-seru
>lirihan kéwala

Jayèngraga mèsem angling
apa nyata Widiguna mengkonoa
106. alon matur leres pangandikanipun
paman jengandika
sami lan pituturnèki
jenatipun gebal sampéyan pun bapa
107. jenatipun kakang myang kang sepuh-sepuh
mestani kemaga
mawi kendhang tan dèn-gongi
tan amawi egong sampun mawi kendhang
108. lingira rum yèn mengkono yèngsun milu
wadhagané ala
lire kemaga tan becik
lah ya mara jupuka gong pewayangan
109. kang tinuduh mundhut gong kenong prapta wus
nulya Jayèngraga
angrebab langkung respati
asesendhon sinulukan pathet sanga
110. wusnya nutug sendhon lih-ulihanipun
apan lajeng buka
gendhing sanga Gambir Sawit
ingegongan lega tyasé samya suka

92. Tondhakusuma, *Serat Gulang Yarya*, 5.
93. Feld, "Aesthetics as Iconicity," 82.
94. Ibid.
95. Ibid.
96. For the most expansive structure (256 pulses per *gongan*), a slight slowing down of the ensemble and the delaying of the stroke applies in the level of kenong phrase and the stroke of the kenong.
97. The practice of delayed gong strokes presents many problems in teaching gamelan to Western students, prompting teachers to come up with ways to guide their students, such as listening carefully to the beats of the *peking* instrument after all instruments have played their delayed beats. This practice is useful and adds to the dynamic of ensemble's interaction, but it occurs to me that this practice is never explicitly spoken about by Javanese musicians. A similar case occurs with the finding of pulsation at the beginning of *sampak*, whose introduction consists of a single beat (made up of three rapid strokes). In this instance, older musicians often explicitly advise us to listen to the beats of the kempul for the proper flow.
98. Keeler, *Javanese Shadow Play*, 226.
99. Ibid., 227.
100. Supanggah, *Bothèkan Karawitan I*, 132.
101. Feld, "Aesthetic as Iconicity," 82.
102. Ibid.
103. Geertz, *The Interpretation of Culture*, 392–93.
104. Ibid., 393.
105. Geertz, *The Religion of Java*, 11.
106. Pasa, Sawal, Besar, and Mulud are month names of the Java-Islam calendar.
107. Pemberton, *On the Subject of "Java,"* 245.
108. Monson, "Jazz as Political and Musical Practice," 22.

109. Benamou, *Rasa: Affect and Intuition*, xv.

110. Benamou, *Rasa: Affect and Intuition*, 105–6. See also Weiss, *Listening to Earlier Java*, and Supanggah, *Bothèkan Karawitan II*.

111. Benamou uses the term in analogy with performance practice of Western classical music, though he also notes that its use in gamelan involves more leeway than in most classical music. He also observes that the further back in the history of Western musical practice one goes, the more prominent is the oral nature of the music, and hence closer to gamelan practice (*Rasa: Affect and Intuition*, 106n26).

112. Benamou, *Rasa: Affect and Intuition*, 183.

113. Zoetmulder, "The Wayang as a Philosophical Theme," 91–92.

114. The main figure in the story asks: which of the following four elements is the oldest one: dhalang, wayang puppets, bléncong (the light source for wayang performance), or *kelir* (the screen)? One *santri* (a student devoted to Islam) indicates that the screen exists first before anything else. Another student mentions dhalang as the oldest one: the screen and puppets all are his, and the lamp is lit and hung by him. The third student suggests that puppets should be the oldest. The main figure dismisses all three replies. He proposes that the oldest one is the lamp, the light. Even if the screen, puppets, and gamelan are set up, and the musicians ready to play, if all is still dark, the dhalang is at a loss, because he cannot give speech to any of the puppets; hence the lamp (the light) is the oldest and powerful one. For a delightful English translation of *Serat Gatholoco*, see Anderson, "The Suluk Gatoloco."

115. Anderson, *Mythology and the Tolerance*, 16.

116. Ibid.

Conclusion

1. Lindsay, "Cultural Policy and Performing Arts."
2. Day, *Fluid Iron*, 2.
3. Ibid., 32.
4. Irving, *Colonial Counterpoint*, 100.
5. Turner, *From Ritual to Theatre*.
6. Nettl, *Heartland Excursions*, 94.
7. Solis, *Performing Ethnomusicology*, 17.
8. For an instructive review of the methodological link between musicology and ethnomusicology, see Cook's "We are All (Ethno)musicologists Now."

Glossary

alus	The concept of Javanese refinement contained and revealed in the inner (batin) and external (lahir) realms of human experience.
angklung	An instrument made of bamboo tubes fastened loosely on a frame, which produces sound when shaken.
babad	A generic term for a genre of traditional writing of Javanese history.
balungan	Melodic skeleton of gendhing (gamelan composition).
batin	The inner realm of human experience (see alus).
bedhaya	A genre of ceremonial dances in the Central Javanese court tradition performed by seven or nine dancers.
bedholan	From "bedhol," to pull out. The removal of puppets after the conclusion of the first scene of the wayang puppet performance.
bendhé	A small gong to be played to signal or call attention for readiness or an emergency situation.
bléncong	An oil lamp, traditionally used for the light source of the shadow puppet performance.
bonang	A generic name for gamelan instruments consisting of a set of kettle gongs arranged in one or two rows.
budhalan	The departure of the army in the first plot-division (after the first scene) of the wayang puppet performance.
calonarang	A story performed in Balinese dance drama or wayang to protect a village against evil sorcery.
campursari	A hybrid ensemble consisting of a few gamelan and Western instruments, featuring solo singing and electric keyboard.
cara balèn	An archaic gamelan ensemble featuring instruments with only four pitches, playing interlocking patterns.
celempung	A plucked-stringed instrument set on four legs.
dangdut	An Indonesian fusion ensemble of Western rock, Middle Eastern, and Indian film music.

Damarwulan	One of the main characters of a story of East Javanese origin; the story itself is also named after him.
demung	A medium-sized metallapohone with six or seven keys, performing a melodic skeleton of gamelan composition.
dhalang (dalang)	Puppeteer of the wayang puppet play and the dance drama enacting the story from the puppet play.
dhodhogan	The sound of the wooden chest which holds the puppets as it is tapped with a mallet by the puppeteer (dhalang).
dolanan	Children's song or a light-hearted piece in gamelan.
gambang	A wooden xylophone.
gara-gara	A midnight scene in the wayang puppet play, symbolically portraying the world in turmoil.
garap	A gamelan term referring to the treatment and interpretation of gendhing by musicians in their instruments.
gapuran	From "gapura" (gate). A scene portraying a king admiring the beauty of a palace gate to the inner palace.
garebeg	Religious festivals to commemorate important religious events.
gatra	A unit of four notes in gamelan composition.
gendang melayu	A large circular drum in the orkes melayu ensemble in North Sumatra.
gendèr	A metallophone with ten to fourteen keys suspended by cords in a wooden frame over tube resonators.
gendhing	A generic term for a gamelan composition.
gendhing mares	A group of gamelan compositions whose performance require the use of European wind instruments and drum.
gongan	A fundamental rhythmic structure of gamelan composition defined by the punctuation of different sizes of gongs.
gunungan	From "gunung," mountain. 1. A puppet figure with the shape of mountain (also called kayon); 2. A royal offering consisting of of food arranged in the shape of mountain.
imbal-imbalan	An interlocking playing technique of bonang or saron in gamelan.
irama	1. Tempo. 2. The doubling or halving of the density level of certain instruments in relation to the basic pulse, adjusting to the slowing down or speeding up of the piece. There are four levels of irama: tanggung, dadi, wilet, and rangkep.

janger	A twentieth-century Balinese theatrical genre combining many different elements, such as circus stunts and military drill.
janturan	Narration of a scene in wayang performance, with a soft accompaniment of gamelan.
jejer	The first scene of the Javanese wayang puppet play.
jineman	A genre of light-hearted gamelan pieces featuring solo pesindhèn singing.
jengglong	A Sundanese instrument: a set of horizontal kettle gongs arranged vertically in a wooden frame.
kaherva	The name of the most popular rhythm in Indian film music, adapted as the drum rhythm of Indonesian dangdut.
karawitan	A Javanese court term for gamelan and vocal music as fine art.
Kasunanan	The major court of Surakarta.
kayon	From "kayu," wood or tree. A puppet representing the tree of life; also called gunungan.
kebiar (kebyar)	The most renowned genre of Balinese gamelan ensemble, it emerged in the beginning of the twentieth century.
kecapi	A Sundanese plucked zither.
kecrèk	A Sundanese instrument consisting of a set of metal plates.
kedhatonan	Inner palace scene in the Javanese wayang puppet play.
kemodhong	The name of a pair of bossed-flat gongs, suspended by cord attached to a wooden box over a resonator.
kempul	Small hanging gongs in Javanese gamelan marking important structural points of the music for certain gongan structures.
kempyang	A small gong kettle, in pair with kethuk, marking structural points of a composition.
kendhang	A generic term for two-headed drums in gamelan. There are a number of kendhang; each can be identified according to its size, style, and function.
kenong	A set of medium-size horizontal gong-kettles, marking important structural points of the music.
kepyak(an)	A set of metal plates beaten by the dhalang's foot or mallet to accentuate puppet or dance movements.

ketawang	The name of one of the gongan structures of gamelan composition.
kethoprak	A folk drama enacting indigenous Javanese stories and history.
kethuk-kempyang	A pair of horizontal gong-kettles, subdividing the music into shorter phrases.
klenèngan	Traditional gamelan sessions for the sake of listening the music, not for accompanying any theatrical performances.
kodhok ngorèk	An archaic ensemble, featuring instruments with only two pitches.
komedie	An urban folk theater developed during the nineteenth century.
kraton	Court or palace.
kreasi baru	"New creation," a generic term for gamelan pieces composed in the mid-twentieth century onward.
kroncong	A genre of Indonesian popular music the origin of which can be traced back to Portuguese music introduced in Java in the sixteenth century.
kulantèr	A Sundanese small, two headed barrel-shaped drum.
lancaran	The name of one of the gongan rhythmic structures (the most compact) of gamelan composition.
Ladrang	One of the gongan rhythmic structures.
lagu gede	Older Sundanese gamelan compositions composed in a longer gongan structure.
lahir	External realm of human behavior related to the Javanese concept of refinement (see alus).
langendriyan	Javanese dance opera in which the dialogue is in the form of sung poetry and is sung by the dancers with gamelan accompaniment.
langgam	A style of kroncong defined by a particular form of song sung in Javanese, using the diatonic-based pélog tuning system.
laras	A tuning system.
legong	A Balinese court dance performed by two or three young girls.
macapat	A genre of sung poetry. Each *macapat* song follows a fixed number of lines per stanza, a fixed number of syllables per line, and a fixed vowel at the end of each line.

GLOSSARY 173

manasuka	A musical program, originating from a radio broadcast, that takes musical requests from home listeners, home viewers, or audience members.
Mangkunegaran	The minor court of Surakarta.
Mataram	The name of the kingdom and dynasty, the predecessor of the present-day courts and courtiers in Surakarta and Yogyakarta.
Ménakjingga	One of the main characters, an antagonist, in the Damarwulan story.
mestizo	Derived from the Portuguese word, meaning a person of mixed blood; it also refers to a culture made up of different cultural influences.
musik pop	Popular music.
orde baru	"New order," referring to President Suharto's regime (1966–97) as they identified themselves.
orde lama	"Old order," referring to Presiden Sukarno's regime (1945–66) as Suharto's regime calls them.
orkes melayu	A Sumatra-Western hybrid popular music developed in North Sumatra.
Panji	The main character (protagonist) of the East Javanese Panji story.
pantap	An acronym of Panitya Tetap Apresiasi dan Pengembangan Seni Pewayangan Jawa Tengah (The Permanent Committee for the Appreciation and Development of Central Javanese Wayang)
pantun	A quatrain in Indonesian or Javanese song.
paseban jawi	The outer hall palace scene in the first plot-division of the wayang puppet performance.
pathet	A Modal classification of gamelan composition. There are three main pathet for each of the tuning systems.
peking	The smallest saron (metallophone) instrument with the highest octave.
pélog	One of the main tuning systems in gamelan consisting of seven pitches, although used pentatonically.
pencon	A generic term for a knobbed gong instrument (from pencu, a protruding surface).
perang gagal	An inconclusive battle between two armies in the first plot-division of wayang performance.

perang kembang	The midnight battle between the prince and a group of ogres in the second plot division of wayang performance, featuring elaborate movements of the puppets.
pesantrèn	An Islamic boarding school.
pesindhèn	A Solo female singer in Javanese gamelan.
pogogan	A type of headdress for Javanese dancers of a male character.
pujangga	A Javanese court poet and chronicler.
puwi-puwi	A Javanese wind instrument (originally from Sulawesi) in a traditional marching band of the Yogyakarta court.
Ratu Kidul	The goddess of the southern ocean, the most powerful spiritual entity in the Javanese myth and belief system.
rebab	A two string bowed lute.
ronggèng	A generic term for a professional dancing girl hired to dance with male guests at a party. Each region might have its own term (see tandhak and taledhèk).
sabrangan	From "sabrang," overseas or foreign. A drumming style for gendhing mares of the Yogyakarta court gamelan.
saluang	A Sumatranese vertical flute from the region of Minangkabau.
sampak	A compact formal structure, and the name, of a composition.
sampir	A scarf-like cloth worn around the neck.
saron	A generic name for a metallophone with six or seven keys resting on a wooden frame.
saron barung	A medium-size, high-octave saron.
serimpi (srimpi)	1. A genre of female court dance. 2. A term used by laymen referring to any female dances.
simpingan	Puppets arranged symmetrically for decoration on the left and right sides of the screen.
sirepan	A soft-playing style featuring a dancer or singer in solo singing.
slenthem	A metallophone with six to seven large keys suspended by cords over tube resonators.
srepegan (srebegan)	A compact formal structure, and the name, of a gamelan composition.
stambul	1. An urban folk theater developed during the colonial Java. 2. A genre of kroncong repertoire.

suling	An end-blown flute in gamelan, made of bamboo.
sulukan	A generic term for songs sung by the dhalang of the wayang performance, with the accompaniment of a small ensemble of gamelan.
Sunda(nese)	An word referring to the people and cultural tradition of a region of West Java.
tanceban	A stationary position of puppets in wayang performance.
talèdhèk	A Javanese term for a professional dancing girl hired to dance with male guests at a party.
tandhak	See talèdhèk and ronggèng.
tanjidor	A European wind ensemble, sometimes mixed with Sundanese instruments, performing European marches and Sundanese songs.
tayuban	A dance party in which the males in attendance take turns dancing with professional tandhak (taledhèk) dancers.
tekes	A headdress of Javanese dancers in a semicircular shape.
tembang	Javanese sung poetry.
wahyu	A divine boon.
wali	Javanese Islamic saints believed to spread Islam.
wayang	1. A play whose dramatis personae are puppets of human actors. 2. A shadow play using flat leather puppets.
wayang gedhog	A puppet play using flat leather puppets presenting the East Javanese Panji story.
wayang golèk	A puppet play using three-dimensional wooden puppets presenting Islamic or Hindu stories.
wayang krucil	A puppet play using flat wooden puppets presenting the East Javanese Damarwulan story.
wayang purwa	A shadow puppet play using flat leather puppets presenting stories based on the Hindu Mahabharata and Ramayana epics.
wayang wahyu	A puppet play using flat leather puppets presenting stories from the Bible.
wayang wong	A Javanese dance drama with characters and stories from the wayang purwa.
zapin	A dance song of Middle Eastern origin that has been practiced and developed in the Melayu world, including Sumatra.

Selected Discography

This discography does not list all of the musical works discussed in the book, but many of them can be listened to online, particuarlly on YouTube, by searching for the key terms and names mentioned in the text.

Betawi and Sundanese Music on the North Coast of Java: Topeng Betawi, Tanjidor, Ajeng. Smithsonian/Folkways SF40421, 1994.
Frozen Brass Asia: Anthology of brass band music #1. PAN 2020CD, 1993.
Gamelan de Solo–Le jeu des Sentiments (A Garland of Moods). Maison des Culture du Monde, Inédit W 260125, 2006.
Indonesia Popular Music: Kroncong, Dangdut, & Langgam Jawa. Smithsonian/Folkways SF40056, 1991.
Langendriyan: Music of Mangkunegaran Solo II. World Music Library, King Record Co., 1995.
Shadow Music of Java. Rounder CD 5060, 1996.

Bibliography

In addition to published sources, this list includes manuscripts from the court of Kasunanan (KS) and the minor court of Mangkunegaran (MN), both in Surakarta. The manuscripts (preserved in microfilms) can be accessed at Cornell University, with catalogue identification "SMP" (Surakarta Manuscript Project).

Abdurachman, Paramita R. *Bunga Angin Portugis di Nusantara: Jejak-Jejak Kebudayaan Portugis di Indonesia.* Jakarta: LIPI Press, 2008.
Acciaioli, Greg. "Culture as Art: From Practice to Spectacle in Indonesia." *Canberra Anthropology* 8, no. 1/2 (1985): 148–72.
Andaya, Leonard Y. *The World of Maluku: Eastern Indonesia in the Early Modern Period.* Honolulu: University of Hawai'i Press, 1993.
Anderson, Benedict. "The Idea of Power in Javanese Culture." In *Language and Power: Exploring Political Culture in Indonesia,* edited by Claire Holt, 1–69. Ithaca: Cornell University Press, 1972.
———. *Imagined Communities: Reflection on the Origin and Spread of Nationalism.* London: Verso, 1991.
———. *Mythology and the Tolerance of the Javanese.* Ithaca: Modern Indonesian Project Southeast Asia Program, Cornell University, 1965.
———. "The Suluk Gatoloco." *Indonesia* 32 (1981): 109–50.
———. "A Time of Darkness and a Time of Light: Transportation in Early Indonesian Nationalist Thought." In *Perceptions of the Past in Southeast Asia,* edited by Anthony Reid and David Marr, 219–48. Hong Kong: Heinemann, 1979.
Ang, Ien. *On Not Speaking Chinese.* London: Routledge, 2001.
Appadurai, Arjun. "Grassroots Globalization and the Research Imagination." *Public Culture* 12, no. 1 (2000): 1–19.
———. *Modernity at Large: Cultural Dimensions of Globalization.* Minneapolis: University of Minnesota Press, 1996.
Artaud, Antonin. *The Theater and its Double.* New York: Groves Press, 1958.
Atmadikara, R. *Babad Krama Dalem Ingkang Sinuhun Kangjeng Susuhunan Paku Buwana Kaping Sanga ing Nagari Surakarta-Adiningrat.* Surakarta, 1867. Manuscript KS 85/SMP 104/4.
Averill, Gage. "Where's 'One'?: Musical Encounters of the Ensemble Kind." In *Performing Ethnomusicology: Teaching and Representation in World Music Ensembles,* edited by Ted Solis, 93–111. Berkeley: University of California Press, 2004.
Babad Nitik Mangkunegaran wiwit taun Alip 1707 ngantos dumugi Je 1718. Surakarta, 1791. Manuscript SMP/RP#696/697.
Babad Diponegoro. Jakarta: Department Pendidikan dan Kebudayaan, 1983.
Becker, Alton. "Text Building, Epistemology, and Aesthetics in Javanese Shadow Theater." In *The Imagination of Reality: Essays in Southeast Coherence System,*

edited by A. L. Becker and Aram A. Yengoyan, 211–43. Norwood, NJ: Ablex Publishing Corporation, 1979.
Becker, Judith. "Earth, Fire, Sakti and the Javanese Gamelan." *Ethnomusicology* 32, no. 3 (1988): 385–91.
———. "Kroncong, Indonesian Popular Music." *Asian Music* 7, no. 1 (1975): 14–19.
———. "Responding to Feld and Roseman." *Ethnomusicology* 27, no. 3 (1984): 454–56.
———. "Southeast Asian Musical Process: Thai *Thaw* and Javanese *Irama*." *Ethnomusicology* 24, no. 3 (1980): 453–64.
———. "Time and Tune in Java." In *The Imagination of Reality: Essays in Southeast Coherence System*, edited by A. L. Becker and Aram A. Yengoyan, 197–210. Norwood, NJ: Ablex Publishing Corporation, 1979.
———. *Traditional Music in Modern Java*. Honolulu: University Press of Hawai'i, 1980.
Becker, Judith, and Alton Becker. "A Musical Icon: Power and Meaning in Javanese Gamelan Music." In *The Sign in Music and Literature*, edited by Wendy Steiner, 203–15. Austin: University of Texas Press, 1981.
Benamou, Marc. *Rasa: Affect and Intuition in Javanese Musical Aesthetics*. New York: Oxford University Press, 2010.
Bhaktin, Mikhail. *Dialogic Imagination: Four Essays*. Edited by Michael Holoquist and translated by Caryl Emerson and Michael Holoquist. Austin: University of Texas Press, 1981.
Blacking, John. *Music, Culture, & Experience*. Chicago: University of Chicago Press, 1995.
Bloembergen, Marieke. *Colonial Spectacle: The Netherlands and the Dutch East Indies at the World Exhibitions, 1880–1931*. Singapore: Singapore University Press, 2006.
Boon, James. *Affinities and Extremes: Crisscrossing the Bittersweet Ethnology of East Indies History, Hindu-Balinese Culture, and Indo-European Allure*. Chicago: University Of Chicago Press, 1990.
Boonzajer, Robert Flaes. *Brass Unbound: Secret Children of the Colonial Brass Band*. Amsterdam: Koninklijk Instituut Voor de Tropen, 2000.
Born, Georgina. *Rationalizing Culture: IRCAM, Boulez, and the Institutionalization of the Musical Avant-Garde*. Berkeley: University of California Press, 1995.
Boxer, C. R. *The Dutch Seaborne Empire 1600–1800*. New York: Alfred A. Knopf, 1965.
Bradbury, William, II. "Messiaen and Gamelan: An Analysis of Gamelan in the Trangalila-symphonie." DMA diss., Cornell University, 1991.
Brandon, James R. *Theatre in Southeast Asia*. Cambridge, MA: Harvard University Press, 1967.
Breckenridge, Carol. "The Aesthetics and Politics of Colonial Collecting: India at World Fairs." *Comparative Studies in Society and History* 31, no. 2 (1989): 195–216.
Brinner, Benjamin. *Knowing Music, Making Music: Javanese Gamelan and the Theory of Musical Competence and Interaction*. Chicago: University of Chicago Press, 1995.
———. "A Musical Time Capsule from Java." *Journal of the American Musicological Society* 46, no. 2 (1993): 221–60.
Burns, Robert. "Rameau's Gambang (Response to Andre Schaeffner): Music and Cultural Relativity in Eighteenth-Century France." MA thesis, Wesleyan University, 1983.

Burris, John. *Exhibiting Religion: Colonialism and Spectacle at International Expositions 1853–1893*. Charlottesville: University Press of Virginia, 2001.
Carey, Peter B. R. *Babad Dipanegara: An Account of the Outbreak of the Java War (1825–30)*. Kuala Lumpur: The Malaysian Branch of the Royal Asiatic Society, 1981.
———. "The Cultural Ecology of Early Nineteenth Century Java: Pangeran Diponegoro, a Case Study." Occasional paper 24. Singapore: Institute of South-east Asian Studies, 1974.
Chazal, Jean-Pierre. "Grand Succès pour les Exotiques: Retour sur les spectacle javanais de l'Exposition Universelle de Paris en 1889." *Archipel* 63 (2002): 109–52.
Clayton, Martin, Trevor Herbert, Richard Middleton, eds. *The Cultural Study of Music: A Critical Introduction*. New York: Routledge, 2003.
Clifford, James. *The Predicament of Culture Twentieth Century Ethnography, Literature and Art*. Cambridge, MA: Harvard, 1988.
Cohen, Matthew. "Indonesian Performing Arts in the Netherlands, 1913–1944." Unpublished paper presented at the International Symposium Musical Encounters between Indonesia and the Netherlands, Leiden University, 2010.
———. *Komedie Stamboel: Popular Theater in Colonial Indonesia, 1891–1903*. Athens: Ohio University Press, 2006.
———. *Performing Otherness: Java and Bali on International Stages, 1905–1952*. Hampshire: Palgrave Macmillan, 2010.
Cook, Nicholas. *Music, Imagination & Culture*. New York: Oxford University Press, 1992.
———. "We Are All (Ethno)musicologists Now." In *The New (Ethno)musicologies*, edited by Henry Stobart, 48–70. Lanham, MD: Scarecrow Press, 2008.
Cooper, Nancy. "From the Land of a Thousand Peaks: Campur Sari Gunung Kidul A mixture of Old Musical Essences." Unpublished paper presented at the Forty-Second Annual Meeting of the Society for Ethnomusicology, 1997.
Corbey, Raymond. "Ethnographic Showcases, 1870–1930." *Cultural Anthropology* 8, no. 3 (1993): 338–69.
Crawfurd, John. *History of Indian Archipelago Containing an Account of the Manners, Arts, Languages, Religions, Institutions, and Commerce of its Inhabitants*. 3 vols. Edinburgh: Archibald Constable, 1820.
Day, Anthony. *Fluid Iron: State Formation in Southeast Asia*. Honolulu: University of Hawai'i Press, 2003.
———. "Sound, Feeling, Knowledge." Unpublished manuscript, n.d.
De Vale, Su. "A Sundanese Gamelan: A Gestalt Approach to Orgonalogy." PhD diss., Northwestern University, 1977.
Dewan Kesenian Jakarta. *Pesta Seni 1974*. Jakarta: Dewan Kesenian Jakarta, 1975.
Djakoeb and Wignyarumeksa. *Layang Anyumurupaké Pratikelé Bab Sinau Nabuh Sarta Panggawéné Gamelan*. Batavia: Drukkerij Eertijd H. M. van Dorp, 1913.
Ellis, Alexander. "On the Musical Scale of Various Nations." *Journal of the Society of Arts* 33 (1885): 485–527.
Erlmann, Veit, ed. *Hearing Culture: Essays on Sound, Listening and Modernity*. Oxford: Berg, 2004.

Fauser, Annegret. *Musical Encounters at the 1889 Paris World's Fair.* Rochester: University of Rochester Press, 2005.

Feld, Steven. "Aesthetic as Iconicity of Style, or, 'Lift-up-Over-Sounding': Getting into the Kaluli Groove." *Yearbook for Traditional Music* 20 (1988): 76–113.

———. "Communication, Music, and Speech about Music." *Yearbook for Traditional Music* 16 (1984): 1–18.

———. "Sound Structure as Social Structure." *Ethnomusicology* 28, no. 2 (1984): 383–409.

Ferianto, Djaduk. Liner notes of *Nang Ning Nong Orkes Sumpek.* Yogyakarta: Djaduk Ferianto dan Kua Etnika, 1997.

Findling, John and Kimberly Pelle, eds. *Historical Dictionary of World's Fairs and Expositions, 1951–1988.* New York: Greenwood Press, 1990.

Florida, Nancy. *Javanese Literature in Surakarta Manuscripts*, vol. 2. Ithaca: Southeast Asian Program Cornell University, 2000.

Forge, Anthony. "Raffles and Daniell: Making the Image Fit." In *Recovering the Orient: Artists, Scholars, Appropriations*, edited by Andrew Gerstle and Anthony Milner, 109–50. Chur, Switzerland: Harwood Academic Publishers, 1990.

Furnivall, John Sydenham. *Netherlands India: A Study of Plural Economy.* London: Cambridge University Press, 1939.

Gamelan of Java: An Introduction. 1983. Hawaii: The East-West Center & The University of Hawaii at Manoa. Video Documentary.

Geertz, Clifford. *The Interpretation of Culture.* New York: Basic Books, 1973.

———. *Negara: The Theater State in Nineteenth-Century Bali.* Princeton, NJ: Princeton University Press, 1980.

———. *The Religion of Java.* Chicago: University of Chicago Press, 1960.

Gouda, Frances. *Dutch Culture Overseas: Colonial Practice in the Netherlands Indies 1900–1942.* Amsterdam: Amsterdam University Press, 1995.

Greenhalgh, Paul. *Ephemeral Vista: The Expositions Universlles, Great Exhibitions and World's Fairs, 1851–1939.* Manchester: Manchester University Press, 1988.

Groneman, J. *De Gamelan te Jogjakarta.* Amsterdam: Johannes Muller, 1895.

Groot, Cornet A. D. de. "Bijdrage tot de kennis van de zeden en gewoonten der Javanen." *Tijdschrift voor Nederlandsch-Indie* 14, no. 2 (1852): 257–80; 346–67; 393–424.

Guillot, Claude. *Kyai Sadrach: Riwayat Kristenisasi di Jawa.* Jakarta: Pustaka Utama Grafiti, 1985.

Haan. F de. *Oud Batavia: Gedenkboek.* Bandung: A. C. Nix & Co., 1922.

———. *Priangan: De Preanger-Regentschappen onderhet Nederalndsch Bestuur tot 1811*, volume 4. Batavia: Bataviaasch Genootschap van Kunsten en Wetenschappen, 1912.

Hardjana, Suka, ed. *Enam Tahun Pekan Komponis Muda 1979–1985: Sebuah Alternatif.* Jakarta: Dewan Kesenian Jakarta, 1986.

———. *Esai & Kritik Musik.* Jakarta: Galang Press, 2003. First published 1984.

Hardjonegoro. "The Place of Batik in the History and Philosophy of Javanese Textile: A Personal View." In *Indonesian Textiles*, edited by Patricia L Fiske, Mattiebelle Stimson Gittinger, and Nina W Gwatkin, 223–34. Washington: The Textile Museum, 1980.

Haryadi, Franz. "Tanjidor Sebagai Ungkapan Musik." In *Tanjidor*, 97–134. Jakarta: Departemen Tari Lembaga Pendidikan Kesenian Jakarta, 1980.
Hatch, Martin. "Popular Music in Indonesia." In *World Music, Politics, and Social Change*, edited by Simon Frith, 47–67. Manchester: Manchester University Press, 1989.
Heins, Ernst. "*Goong Renteng*: Aspects of Orchestral Music in a Sundanese Vilage." PhD diss., University of Amsterdam, 1977.
———. "Letter to the Editor." *Ethnomusicology* 20, no. 1(1976): 97–101.
———. "Two Cases of Urban Folk Music in Jakarta." *Asian Music* 7, no. 1 (1975): 20–29.
Hill, David. "'The Two Leading Institutions': Taman Ismail Marzuki and Horison." In *Culture and Society in New Order Indonesia*, edited by Virginia Matheson Hooker, 243–62. Kuala Lumpur: Oxford University Press, 1993.
Holt, Claire. *Art in Indonesia: Continuities and Change*. Ithaca: Cornell University Press, 1967.
Hood, Mantle. "The Challenge of Bi-Musicality." *Ethnomusicology* 4, no. 2 (1960): 55–59.
———. *The Nuclear Theme as a Determinant of Pathet in Javanese Music*. Djakarta, 1954. Reprint, New York: Da Capo, 1977.
Hooker, Virginia and Howard Dick. "Introduction." In *Culture and Society in New Order Indonesia*, edited by Virginia Matheson Hooker, 1–23. Kuala Lumpur: Oxford University Press, 1993.
Hostetler, Jan. "Bedhaya Semang: The Sacred Dance of Yogyakarta." *Archipel* 24, no. 1 (1982): 127– 42.
Howard, Keith. "Performing Ethnomusicology: Exploring How Teaching Performance Undermine the Ethnomusicology within University Music Training." In *Musiké* 3 (2006): 21–31.
Humardani, Gendon. "Membina Kritik Musik." Unpublished paper presented at the 1974 Music Conference in Taman Ismail Marzuki, Jakarta.
Irving, D. R. M. *Colonial Counterpoint: Music in Early Modern Manila*. Oxford: Oxford University Press, 2010.
Kartomi, Margaret. "Dualism in Unity: The Ceremonial Music of the Maandailing Raja Tradition." *Asian Music* 12, no. 2 (1981): 74–123.
———. "Performance, Music, and Meaning of Reyog Ponorogo." *Indonesia* 22 (1976): 85–130.
Kayam, Umar. *Kelir Tanpa Batas*. Yogyakarta: Gama Media for Pusat Studi Kebudayaan UGM, 2001.
Keeler, Ward. *Javanese Shadow Play, Javanese Selves*. Princeton, NJ: Princeton University Press, 1987.
Keil, Charles and Steven Feld. *Music Grooves*. Chicago: University of Chicago Press, 1994.
Kipp, Rita. "The Thread of Three Colors: The Ideology of Kinship in Karo Batak Funerals." In *Art, Ritual and Society in Indonesia*, edited by Edward Bruner and Judith Becker, 62–95. Athens: Ohio University Center for International Studies Southeast Asia Program, 1979.

Kirshenblatt-Gimblett, Barbara. "Confusing Pleasure." In *Destination Culture: Tourism, Museum, and Heritage*, 203–48. Berkeley: University of California Press, 1998.
Kitley, Philip. "Ornamentation and Originality: Involution in Javanese Batik." *Indonesia* 53 (1992): 1–19.
Koesoemadinata, R. M. A. *Lagu-Lagu Gede Sunda*. Bandung: Yayasan Daminatila, 1989.
Kornhauser, Bronia. "In Defense of Kroncong." In *Studies in Indonesian Music*, edited by Margaret J. Kartomi, 104–83. Melbourne: Center of Southeast Asian Studies Monash University, 1978.
Kors, Ninja. "Networks & Islands: World Music & Dance Education." *Musiké* 3 (2006).
Kumar, Ann. "Dipanegara (1787?–1855)." *Indonesia* 13 (1972): 69–118.
———. "Javanese Court Society and Politics in the Late Eighteenth Century: The Record of a Lady Soldier. Part 1: The Religious, Social and Economic Life of the Court." *Indonesia* 29 (1980): 1–46.
———. "The Socialization of the People: 'Becoming Javanese.'" In *Java and Modern Europe: Ambiguous Encounters*. Surrey: Curzon Press, 1997.
Kunst, Jaap. *Ethnomusicology*. 3rd ed. The Hague: Martinus Niyhoff, 1959.
———. *Music in Java: Its History, Its Theory and Its Techniques*. 2 vols. The Hague: Martinus Nijhoff, 1973. Originally published as *De Toonkunst van Java*, 2 vols. (The Hague: Martinus Nijhoff, 1949).
Kusumadilaga, Kangjeng Pangeran Harya. *Serat Sastramiruda*. Solo: De Bliksem, 1930. First published 1879.
Kuwato. "Pertunjukan Wayang Kulit di Jawa Tengah Suatu Alternatif Pembaharuan: Sebuah Studi Kasus." MA thesis, Institut Seni Indonesia Surakarta, 2001.
Laksono, P. M. *Tradition in Javanese Social Structure: Kingdom and Countryside*. Yogyakarta: Gadjah Mada University Press, 1986.
Lesure, François and Richard Langham Smith, eds. *Debussy on Music: The Critical Writings of the Great French Composer Claude Debussy*. New York: Alfred A. Knopf, 1977.
Lindsay, Jennifer. "Cultural Policy and Performing Arts in Southeast Asia." *Bijdragen* 151, no. 4 (1991): 656–71.
———. *Klasik, Kitsch, Kontemporer: Sebuah Studi Tentang Seni Pertunjukan Jawa*. Yogyakarta: Gadjah Mada University Press, 1991.
Lockspeiser, Edward. *Debussy: His Life and Mind*. Vol. 1, *1862–1902*. London: Cassell, 1962.
Lohanda, Mona. "Tanjidor Di Dalam Kehidupan Sang Seniman." In *Tanjidor*, 46–59. Jakarta: Departemen Tari Lembaga Pendidikan Kesenian Jakarta, 1980.
Lombard, Denys. *Nusa Jawa: Silang Budaya*. Vol. 1. Jakarta: PT Gramedia Pustaka Utama, 1996.
Lord, Albert. *The Singer of Tales*. Cambride, Mass: Harvard University Press, 1960.
Lucier, Alvin. "Notes on the Program." *Making Music 1997: Alvin Lucier*. New York: Carnegie Hall Stagebill, 1997.
MacAloon, John. "Olympic Games and the Theory of Spectacle in Modern Societies." In *Rite Drama, Festival, Spectacle: Rehearsals Toward a Theory of Cultural*

Performance, 241–80. Philadelphia: Institute for the Study of Human Issues, 1984.
Maceda, Jose. "A Concept of Time in a Music of Southeast Asia (A Preliminary Account)." *Ethnomusicology* 1, no. 3 (1986): 11–53.
Mack, Dieter. *Sejarah Musik*, vol. 4. Yogyakarta: Pusat Musik Liturgi, 1995.
———. "Sejarah, Tradisi, dan Penilaian Musik." *Kalam* 2 (1994): 20–30.
Mangkunegara IV, K. G. P. A. *Sendhon Langen Swara*. Kediri: Tan Koen Swie, 1940. Original manuscript composed in Surakarta in the mid- to late nineteenth century.
Manuel, Peter. *Popular Musics of the Non-Western World: An Introductory Survey*. Oxford: Oxford University Press, 1988.
Martopangrawit, Raden Lurah. "Notes on Knowledge of Gamelan Music." Translated by Martin Hatch. In *Karawitan: Source Readings in Javanese Gamelan and Vocal Music*, edited by Judith Becker and Alan H. Feinstein, 1:1–121. Ann Arbor: Center for South and Southeast Asian Studies, University of Michigan, 1984.
McDowell, Edward. "The World's Fair Cosmopolis." *Franks Leslie's Popular monthly*. Oct. (1893): 407–16.
McGraw, Andy. "Musik Kontemporer: Experimental Music by Balinese Composers." PhD diss., Wesleyan University, 2005.
Mendonça, Maria. "Javanese Gamelan in Britain: Communitas, Affinity and Other Stories." PhD diss., Wesleyan University, 2002.
Mensink, Onno. *Gamelan en andere gong-spel ensembles van Zuidoost-Azie*. Den Haag: Haags Gemeentemuseum, 1982.
Merriam, Alan. *The Anthropology of Music*. Evanston, IL: Northwestern University Press, 1964.
Miller, Terry and Sean William, ed. *Southeast Asia*. Vol. 4 of *The Garland Encyclopedia of World Music*. New York: Garland Publishing, 1998.
Milner, Anthony and Andrew Gerstle. "Recovering the Exotic: Debating Said." In *Recovering the Orient: Artists, Scholars, Appropriations*, edited by Andrew Gerstle and Anthony Miller, 1–6. Chur, Switzerland: Harwood Academic Publisher, 1994.
Moertono, Soemarsaid. *State and Statecraft in Old Java*. Ithaca: Cornell Modern Indonesia Project, 1968.
Monson, Ingrid. "Jazz as Political and Musical Practice." In *Musical Improvisation: Art, Education, and Society*, edited by Gabriel Solis and Bruno Nettl, 21–37. Urbana: University of Illinois Press, 2009.
Mrázek, Jan. "Javanese Wayang Kulit in the Times of Comedy: Clown Scenes, Innovation, and the Performance's Being in the Present World." Pts. 1 and 2. *Indonesia* 68 (1999): 38–128; 69 (2000): 107–72.
———. *Phenomenology of a Puppet Theater: Contemplations on the Art of Javanese Wayang Kulit*. Leiden: KITLV, 2005.
Mueller, Richard. "Javanese Influence on Debussy's *Fantaisie* and Beyond." *19th-Century Music* 10, no. 2 (1986): 157–86.
Murgiyanto, Sal. "Moving between Unity and Diversity: Four Indonesian Choreographers." PhD diss., New York University, 1991.

Murtiyoso, Bambang, Waridi, Suyanto, Kuwato, and Harijadi Tri Putranto. *Pertumbuhan & Perkembangan Seni Pertunjukan Wayang.* Surakarta: Citra Etnika, 2004.
Nagtegaal, Luc. *Riding the Dutch Tiger: The Dutch East Indies Company and the northeast coast of Java, 1680–1743.* Leiden: KITLV Press, 1996.
Nettl, Bruno. *Heartland Excursions: Ethnomusicological Reflections on Schools of Music.* Urbana: University of Illinois Press, 1995.
New Webster's Dictionary of the English Language. The Delair Publishing Company, 1971.
"Pangeran Diponegoro." *Program Notes.* Jakarta: Art Summit Indonesia, 1995.
Parani, Yulianti, Frans Haryadi, Mona Lohanda, Siswandhi, and Suwandi Mangkudilaga. *Tanjidor: Sebuah Laporan Pengamatan Lapangan Kesenian Tanjidor di Daerah Jakarta dan Sekitarnya Mei-Oktober 1979.* Jakarta: Departemen Tari Lembaga Pendidikan Kesenian Jakarta, 1980.
Partohudoyo, Raden Ngabehi. "Bab Langendriyan." Surakarta, 1924–44. Manuscript MN 650/SMP 193/14.
Pemberton, John. "Musical Politics in Central Java (Or How Not to Listen to a Javanese Gamelan)." *Indonesia* 44 (1987): 17–29.
———. *On the Subject of "Java."* Ithaca: Cornell University Press, 1994.
Perlman, Marc. "The Traditional Javanese Performing Arts in the Twilight of the New Order: Two Letters from Solo." *Indonesia* 68 (1999): 1–37.
———. *Unplayed Melodies: Javanese Gamelan and the Genesis of Music Theory.* Berkeley: University of California Press, 2004.
Picard, Michel. "Dance and Drama in Bali." In *Being Modern in Bali: Image and Change,* edited by Adrian Vickers, 115–57. New Haven: Yale University Southeast Asia Studies, 1996.
Pieterse, Jan Nederveen. *Globalization & Culture: Global Melange.* Lanham: Rowman & Littlefield Publishers, Inc, 2004.
Pigeaud. Theodore G. *Javaanse Volksvertoningen.* Batavia: Volkslectuur, 1938.
Poedjosoedarmo, Soepomo, and M. C. Ricklefs. "The Establishment of Surakarta, a Translation from the Babad Gianti." *Indonesia* 24 (1967): 88–109.
Poensen, C. "De Wayang." *Medelingen van wege het Nederlandsch Zendelingen Genootschap* 16 (1872): 75–116, 218–20.
Poplawska, Marzanna. "Wayang Wahyu as an Example of Christian Forms of Shadow Theatre." *Asian Theatre Journal* 21, no. 2 (2004): 194–202.
Powers, Harold. "Language Models and Musical Analysis," *Ethnomusicology* 24, no. 1(1980): 1–60.
Powers, Harold, Frans Wiering, James Porter, James Cowdery, Ruth Davis, Richard Widdess, Marc Perlman, Stephen Jones, and Allan Marett. "Mode." In *The New Grove Dictionary of Music and Musicians,* edited by Stanley Sadie, 16:775–860. 2nd ed. Oxford: Oxford University Press, 2001.
Purbadipura, R. Ng. *Serat Sri Karongson.* 3 vols. Surakarta, 1913. Manuscript KS 140/SMP 113/5.
Quigley, Sam. 1996. "The Raffles Gamelan at Claydon House." *Journal of the American Instrument Society* 22 (1996): 5–41.
Raden, Franki. "Dinamika Pertemuan dua Tradisi: Music Kontemporer Indonesia, di Abad ke-20." *Kalam* 2 (1994): 6–19.

———. "Music, Politic, and the Problems of National Identity in Indonesia." PhD diss., University of Wisconsin–Madison, 2001.

———. "Sketsa Kehidupan Musik Kontemporer di Indonesia." In *Perjalanan Musik di Indonesia.* Jakarta: Pensi, 1983.

Raffles, Thomas Stamford. *The History of Java.* 2 vols. 1817. Reprint, Kuala Lumpur: Oxford University Press, 1982.

Randel, Don Michael, ed. *The New Harvard Dictionary of Music.* Cambridge, MA. Belknap Press of Harvard University Press, 1986.

Ranger, Terence. *Dance and Society in Eastern Africa. 1890–1970: The Beni Ngoma.* London: Heinemann Educational, 1975.

Rhodius, Hans and John Darling. *Walter Spies and Balinese Art.* Amsterdam: Tropical Museum, 1980.

Rice, Timothy. "Time, Place, and Metaphor in Musical Experience and Ethnography." *Ethnomusicology* 47, no. 2 (2003): 151–79.

———. "Toward the Remodeling of Ethnomusicology." *Ethnomusicology* 31, no. 3 (1987): 469–88.

Ricklefs, Merle Calvin. *A History of Modern Indonesia since c. 1300.* 2nd ed. Stanford, CA: Stanford University Press, 1993.

———. *Jogjakarta under Sultan Mangkubumi 1749–1792.* London: Oxford University Press, 1974.

Risdell, Marcus. "Javanese Gamelan: A Human Cannonball and the Missing Link." *Balungan* 13, no. 1 (2005): 6–10.

Roseman, Marina. "The Social Structuring of Sound: The Temiar of Peninsular Malaysia." *Ethnomusicology* 28, no. 2 (1984): 411–45.

Rusini. *Gathutkaca di Panggung Soekarno.* Surakarta: STSI Press, 2003.

Rustopo. *Gendhon Humardani Sang Gladiator: Arsitek Kehidupan Seni Tradisi Modern.* Yogyakarta: Yayasan Mahavhira, 2001.

Rydell, Robert. *All the World's a Fair: Visions of Empire at American International Expositions, 1876–1916.* Chicago: University of Chicago Press, 1984.

Sadie, Stanley, ed. *The New Grove Dictionary of Music and Musicians.* 2nd ed. Oxford: Oxford University Press, 2001.

Santoso and Subono. "Sworo Pencon." In *Enam Tahun Pekan Komponis Muda 1979–1985: Sebuah Alternatif.* Jakarta: Dewan Kesenian Jakarta, 1986.

Sastrodarsono, Soekanto. *Teori Nabuh Gamelan,* volume 1. Surakarta: Kemudawati, 1966.

Schechner, Richard. *Between Theater & Anthropology.* Philadelphia: University of Pennsylvania Press, 1985.

Scherer, Sawitri. "Harmony and Dissonance: Early National Thought in Java." MA thesis, Cornell University, 1975.

Sears, Laurie. "Epic Voyage: The Transmission of the *Ramayana* and *Mahabharata* from India to Java." In *Aesthetic Tradition and Cultural Transition in Java and Bali,* edited by Stephanie Morgan and Laurie Jo Sears, 1–30. Madison: University of Wisconsin Center for Southeast Asian Studies, 1988.

Serat Tjentini. Batavia: Ruygrok, 1912–15. First published 1814.

Shepherd, John. *Music as Social Text.* Cambridge: Polity Press, 1991.

Siegel, James. *Solo in the New Order.* Princeton, NJ: Princeton University Press, 1986.

Sjukur, Slamet Abdul. "Mak Comblang dan Pionir Asongan: Musik Kontemporer Itu Apa?" *Kalam* 2 (1994): 15–19.

Slobin, Mark. *Retuning Culture: Musical Changes in Central and Eastern Europe.* Durham, NC: Duke University Press.

Soedarsono. *Wayang Wong: The State Ritual Dance Drama in the Court of Yogyakarta.* Yogyakarta: Gadjah Mada University Press, 1984.

Soelardi, Raden Bagoes. *Serat Pradongga.* Weltevreden: Widya-Poestaka nr. 2, 1918.

Solis, Gabriel and Bruno Nettl. *Musical Improvisation: Art, Education, and Society.* Urbana: University of Illinois Press, 2009.

Solis, Ted, ed. *Performing Ethnomusicology: Teaching and Representation in World Music Ensembles.* Berkeley: University of California Press, 2004.

Spiller, Henry. *Focus: Gamelan Music of Indonesia*, 2nd edition. New York: Routledge, 2004.

Steedly, Mary. *Hanging Without a Rope: Narrative Experience in Colonial and Postcolonial Karoland.* Princeton, NJ: Princeton University Press, 1993.

Subuh. *Gendhing-Gendhing Mars atau Gati Kraton Yogyakarta.* Thesis S-1 Institut Seni Indonesia Yogyakarta, 1986.

Sudarko. *Pakeliran Padat: Pembentukan dan Penyebaran.* Surakarta: Citra Etnika, 2002.

Suharti, Theresia. "Bedhaya Semang: Dimensi Spiritual Dinasti Kesultanan Yogyakarta Sebuah Karya Rekonstruksi." *Jurnal Seni* 9, no. 1 (2002): 38–52.

Sumandiyo, Hadi. *Seni dalam Ritual Agama.* Yogyakarta: Yayasan untuk Indonesia & Lembaga Penelitian Institut Seni Indonesia, 2000.

Sumanto. *Narto Sabdo: Kehadirannya dalam Dunia Pedalangan.* Surakarta: STSI Press, 2002.

Sumarsam. "Gamelan as a Vital Accompaniment of Javanese Wayang." In *Aesthetic Tradition and Cultural Transition in Java and Bali*, edited by Stephanie Morgan and Laurie Jo Sears, 105–16. Madison: University of Wisconsin Center for Southeast Asian Studies, 1988.

———. *Gamelan: Cultural Interaction and Musical Development in Central Java.* Chicago: University of Chicago Press, 1995.

———. "Iconic Reading of Gamelan Revisited." In *A Search in Asia for a New Theory of Music*, edited by José S. Buenconsejo, 439–53. Manila: University of the Philippines Center for Ethnomusicology, 2003.

———. "Inner Melody in Javanese Gamelan." MA thesis, Wesleyan University, 1979. Reprinted in *Karawitan: Source Readings in Javanese Gamelan and Vocal Music*, edited by Judith Becker and Alan H. Feinstein, 1:245–304. Ann Arbor: Center for South and Southeast Asian Studies, University of Michigan, 1984.

———. *Kendhangan Gaya Solo.* Surakarta: Akademi Seni Karawitan Indonesia, 1976.

———. "Past and Present Issues of Islam within the Central Javanese Gamelan and Wayang Kulit." In *Divine Inspiration: Music & Islam in Indonesia*, edited by David D. Harnish and Anne K. Rasmussen, 45–79. New York: Oxford University Press, 2011.

———. "Sajian Politis Manusia Jawa-Indonesia." *Kompas Minggu*, November 28, 1993.

———. *Tjengkok Genderan.* Surakarta: Akademi Seni Karawitan Indonesia, 1971.

Supanggah, Rahayu. *Bothèkan Karawitan I.* Jakarta: MSPI, 2002.

———. *Bothèkan Karawitan II: Garap.* Surakarta: ISI Press, 2007.

———. "Campur Sari: A Reflection." *Asian Music* 34, no. 2 (2003): 1–20.

———. "Gambuh." In *Enam Tahun Pekan Komponis Muda 1979–1985: Sebuah Alternatif.* Jakarta: Dewan Kesenian Jakarta, 1986. First published 1979.

Supriyanto, Mathias. *Inkulturasi Tari Jawa.* Surakarta: Citra Etnika, 2002.

Surjodiningrat, Vijay Khandelwal, F. Soesianto. *Gamelan dan komputer: analisa patet dan komposisi gendhing Jawa laras slendro.* Yogyakarta: Universitas Gadjah Mada, 1977.

Susanto, Budi. *Imaginasi Penguasa dan Identitas Postkolonial: Siasat Politik (Ketoprak) Massa Rakyat.* Yogyakarta: Kanisius, 2000.

———. *Ketoprak: The Politics of the Past in the Present-Day Java.* Yogyakarta: Penerbit Kanisius, 1997.

Sutton, Anderson. "Popularizing the Indigenous or Indigenizing the Popular? Television, Video and Fusion Music in Indonesia." *Wacana Seni: Journal of Arts Discourse* 1 (2002): 13–31.

———. *Variation in Central Javanese Gamelan Music: Dynamics of a Steady State.* DeKalb: Northern Illinois University Center for Southeast Asian Studies, 1993.

Sutton, Anderson, Endo Suanda, Sean Williams. "Java." In *Southeast Asia*, edited by Terry Miller and Sean William, 630–728. Vol. 4 of *The Garland Encyclopedia of World Music.* New York: Garland Publishing, 1998.

Suwardi, A. L. and Pande Made Sukerta. "Laras-Gender-Sebuah Proses." In *Enam Tahun Pekan Komponis Muda 1979–1985: Sebuah Alternatif.* Jakarta: Dewan Kesenian Jakarta, 1976.

Tambayong, Yapi. "Niat Kembali Sonder Pergi: Pelbagai Pergulatan Musik (di) Indonesia." *Kalam* 2 (1994): 31–40.

Tanjidor. Jakarta: Departemen Tari Lembaga Pendidikan Kesenian Jakarta, 1980.

Taylor, Jean Gelman. *The Social World of Batavia: European and Eurasian in Dutch Asia.* University of Wisconsin Press, 1983.

Terwen, Jan Willem. *Gamelan in the 19th-Century Netherlands: An Encounter Between East and West.* Utrecht: Koninklike Vereniging voor Nederlandse Muziekgeschiedenis, 2009.

Theodore, K. S, Kadjat Adrai Dono, Yudhi N. H., Darmoyo S. S., and Harzufri Suleiman. "Tokoh-Tokoh Perjalanan Musik di Indonesia." In *Perjalanan Musik di Indonesia: Sebelum dan Sesudah Perang*, 119–98. Jakarta: Pensi, 1983.

Tondhakusuma, Raden Mas Harya. "Pakem Modraswara: Lampahan Damarwulan Ngarit." In *Javanese Literature in Surakarta Manuscripts*, compiled by Nancy Florida. Ithaca: Southeast Asia Program Cornell University, 2000.

———. *Serat Kyahi Gulang Yarya.* Surakarta, 1870. Manuscript MN 80/3/SMP 618.

Trimillos, Ricardo. 2004. "Subject, Object, and the Ethnomusicology Ensemble: The Ethnomusicological 'We' and 'Them.'" In *Performing Ethnomusicology: Teaching and Representation in World Music Ensembles*," edited by Ted Solis, 23–52. Berkeley: University of California Press, 2004.

Thompson, Rachel. "Rethinking the *Divine Arabesque*: A Critical Approach to Claude Debussy and the Javanese *Kampong* from the 1889 *Exposition Universelle.*" BA thesis, Wesleyan University, 1999.

Tiersot, Julien. *Musiques pittoresques: promenades musicales à l'Exposition de 1889.* Paris: Fischbacher, 1889.

Turino, Thomas. *Music as Social Life: The Politics of Participation.* Chicago: University of Chicago Press, 2008.
Turner, Victor. *From Ritual to Theatre: The Human Seriousness of Play.* New York: Performing Arts Journal Publication, 1982.
van der Kroef, Justus. 1954. "Dualism and Symbolic Antithesis in Indonesian Society." *American Anthropologist* 56: 847–62.
van der Veur, Paul W., editor. *Toward A Glorious Indonesia: Reminiscences and Observations of Dr. Soetomo.* Athens: Ohio University Center for International Studies Center for Southeast Asian Studies, 1987.
Vetter, Roger R. "Music for 'the Lap of the World': Gamelan Performance, Performers, and Repertoire in the Kraton Yogyakarta." PhD diss., University of Wisconsin–Madison, 1986.
———. "A Square Peg in a Round Hole: Teaching Javanese Gamelan in the Ensemble Paradigm of the Academy." In *Performing Ethnomusicology: Teaching and Representation in World Music Ensembles,* edited by Ted Solis, 115–25. Berkeley: University of California Press, 2004.
Vickers, Adrian. *Bali: A Paradise Created.* Victoria: Penguin, 1989.
———. *A History of Modern Indonesia.* New York: Cambridge University Press, 2005.
Wall, V. I. van de. *Indische Landhuizen en hun geschiedenis.* Batavia: G. Kolff & Co. 1932.
Kusumo, Sardono W. "Hanuman, Tarzan, Pithecanthropus Erectus." August 2001. Accessed July 1, 2012. http://www1.u-netsurf.ne.jp/%7Emie_y/suigyu/hondana/hanuman.html.
Warsadiningrat, Radèn Tumenggung. *Sacred Knowledge About Gamelan Music.* Translated by Susan Walton. In *Karawitan: Source Readings in Javanese Gamelan and Vocal Music,* edited by Judith Becker and Alan H. Feinstein, 2:23–170. Ann Arbor: Center for South and Southeast Asian Studies, University of Michigan, 1987.
Weintraub, Andrew N. *Dangdut Stories: A Social and Musical History of Indonesia's Most Popular Music.* New York: Oxford University Press, 2010.
Weiss, Sarah. *Listening to an Earlier Java.* Leiden: KITLV Press, 2006.
———. "Permeable Boundaries: Hybridity, Music and the Reception of Robert Wilson's *I La Galigo.*" *Ethnomusicology* 42, no. 2 (2008): 203–38.
Wenten, I. Nyoman. "The Creative Work of Ki Wasitodipuro: The Life and Work of a Javanese Gamelan Composer." PhD diss., University of California Los Angeles, 1996.
White, Bob W. "Introduction: Rethinking Globalization through Music." In *Music and Globalization: Critical Encounters,* edited by Bob W. White, 1–14. Bloomington: Indiana University Press, 2012.
———. "The Promise of World Music: Strategies for Non-Essentialist Listening." In *Music and Globalization: Critical Encounters,* edited by Bob W. White, 189–217. Bloomington: Indiana University Press, 2012.
Widodo, Amrih. 1995. "The Stages of the State: Arts of the People and Rites of Hegemonization." *Rima* 29, no. 1/2 (1995): 1–35.
Wilkens, J. A. "Sewaka, een Javaansch gedicht met eene vertaling en wordenboek." *Tijdschrift voor Nederlandsch-Indie* 2 (1850): 7–12, 383–461.

Williams, Sean. "Sunda." In *Southeast Asia*, edited by Terry Miller and Sean Williams, 699–725. Vol. 4 of *The Garland Encyclopedia of World Music*. New York: Garland Publishing, 1998.

Wolters, O. W. *History, Culture, and Region in Southeast Asians Perspective*, revised edition. Ithaca: Southeast Asia Program Cornell University in cooporation with The Institute of Southeast Asian Studies Singapore, 1999.

Woodfield, Ian. *English Musicians in the Age of Exploration*. Stuyvesant, N.Y.: Pendragon Press, 1995.

Yampolsky, Philip. "Betawi & Sundanese Music of the North Coast of Java." Liner notes of *Music of Indonesia*. Vol. 5. Washington DC: Smithsonian/Folkways, 1994.

———. "Forces for Change in the Regional Performing Arts of Indonesia." *Bijdragen* 151, no. 4 (1995): 700–25.

———. "Indonesia: Cultural and Musical Geography." In *The New Grove Dictionary of Music and Musicians*, edited by Stanley Sadie, 12:274–83. 2nd ed. Oxford: Oxford University Press, 2001.

———. "Indonesian Popular Music: Kroncong, Dangdut, & Langgam Jawa." Liner notes of *Music of Indonesia*. Vol. 2. Washington DC: Smithsonian/Folkways, 1991.

———. "Kroncong Revisited: New Evidence from Old Sources." *Archipel* 79 (2010): 7–56.

———. *Lokananta: A discography of the National Recording Company of Indonesia*. Madison: University of Wisconsin Center for Southeast Asian Studies, 1987.

Zbikowski, Lawrence M. "Metaphor and Music." In *The Cambridge Handbook of Metaphor and Thought*, edited by Raymond W. Gibbs Jr., 502–24. Cambridge: Cambridge University Press, 2008.

Zemp, Hugo. "Aspects of 'Are' are Musical Theory." *Ethnomusicology* 23, no. 1 (1979): 5–48.

Zoetmulder, P. J. "The Wayang as a Philosophical Theme." *Indonesia* 12 (1971): 85–96.

Zon, Bennett. *Representing Non-Western Music in Nineteenth-Century Britain*. Rochester: University of Rochester Press, 2007.

Index

Page numbers in italics indicate illustrations or musical examples.

Abdurachman, Paramita, 17, 18
academia: ethnomusicology programs, 4; gamelan education and groups in, 4, 109–14, 141; mid-twentieth-century studies of gamelan, 108–14
Acciaioli, Greg, 42
Adraansz, Willem, *114*
Africa, European bands in, 16, 21
alus concept, 20
alusan style, 63
Andaya, Leonard Y., 143n8(2)
Anderson, Benedict, 83, 124, 138, 147–48n54
Ang, Ien, v, 11
angklung, 94
angkok, 18
anticolonialism, xiii, 106–8
Arjunawiwaha (twelfth-century work), 5
Arndt, Jurgen, 99
Art Nouveau, 101
Artaud, Antonin, 108
Atmadarsana, 44
Averill, Gage, 112–13
Ayak-Ayakan Panjang Mas, 33, 149n26

babad, 65
Babad Diponegoro, 65, 66–68, 69–70
Babad Giyanti, 14–15
Babad Krama Dalem, 18
Babad Nitik Mangkunegara, 16
Babar Layar, 109
Balinese culture: colonial experience of, 161n135; displayed at International Colonial Exposition (1931), 107–8; gamelan, 6, 113; state ceremonials, 53; Sukarno's support of, 6

balungan: Debussy's interpretation of, 101–2; elaboration of, 130–33; fixed nature of, 138; performance of, 21–22, 121, 128, 147n51; as term, xii; of "Wani-Wani," 98; Western misinterpretation of, 166nn81–82
Bandara, Linda, 45, 46
bangsawan, 28
bawa, 13
Becker, Alton, 117, 118, 137, 138, 142, 149n29
Becker, Judith, 51, 115, 116–17, 118, 120–21, 127–28, 137, 138, 142
bedhaya, 20, 86–87, 95
bedhaya Ketawang, 23
bedhaya Semang, 23–24, 139–40
bedholan scene in *wayang*, 32
bedhug, 5
Benamou, Marc, xiii, 137, 168n111
bendhé, 15
Benedictus, Louis: *Danse javanaise*, 98, 99, 100
beni ngoma, 16–17, 21
Berlin exhibition (1880), 85
Bernard, M., 95
Bhaktin, Mikhail, 25
bi-musicality concept, 110, 141
binary division concept, 120, 126–33, 137–38, 142
Bloembergen, Marieke, v, 82, 89, 108
bonang, 13, 52
Boon, James, 77
Brandon, James, 57–58
brass bands. *See* military music and brass bands in Indonesia
Brata, Surya, 109

Breckenridge, Carol, 83
Brinner, Benjamin, 126–27, 164–65n66
British in Indonesia, 78–82
British Museum, gamelan set in, 79–80
budhalan scene in *wayang*, 32
Budi Utomo, 107
Burke, Kenneth, 118
Burma, *hsaing waing* ensemble of, 117
Burris, John, 82

Calonarang, 108
campursari, 15, 29–31, 140, 151n72, 153n96
cara balèn, 81, 158n24
Carey, Peter, 65–66
celempung, 158n19
"centonization" method, 117
Chakrahadikusuma, R. A. A., 121, 123
Chazal, Jean-Pierre, 95, 97
Chinese music complex in Indonesia, 11
Christianity in Indonesia, 2, 12
church music in Indonesia, 12
ciblon, 71
Claydon House, gamelan set in, 79
Clifford, James, 78
Cohen, Matthew, 13
Cokrowasito, 50; "Jaya Manggala Gita," 51–52
Committee of the 1995 Art Summit Indonesia, 55
comparative musicology, 109
Cooper, Nancy, 31
Corbey, Raymond, 82
Crotch, William, 79
Crystal Palace Exhibition (London, 1851), 83–84
cultural policy in Dutch East Indies, 88–89
cultural policy in Indonesia: of Suharto, 6, 27, 42–53; of Sukarno, 5–6, 7, 27, 42, 144n18
cultural studies, 115

dangdut, 15, 18, 27–29, 140
Daratista, Inul, 28–29
Darling, John, 151n75

Darwin, Charles, 92
de Leeuw, Ton, 48
de Vale, Su, 90
Debussy, Claude: *Fantasie*, 98–100; gamelan heard by, 94, 98–100, 106, 141; *La Mer*, 100; *Nocturnes*, 100; non-Western influences on, 100–101; *Pagodes*, 100; shared aesthetic with gamelan music, 101–2
Dewantara, Ki Hadjar, 108
dhalang: adjustments made by, 32, 33, 34–35; bond with puppets, 37; central role of, 59; changes in role of, 36–37; female, 149n24; metaphorical role of, 138; nicknaming of, 41–42; nontraditional elements incorporated by, 36; Sukarno's support of, 5, 33; *wayang kolosal* and, 39–40
dhodhogan, 34
Dick, Howard, 40
Diponegoro: arrest depicted by Saleh, 54, 56, 73; *Babad Diponegoro*, 56; as character in *Opera Diponegoro*, 54–59; chronicles written on, 65; interest in *wayang*, 65–66; life of, 55, 56–57
Dipura, Raden Rana, 79, 80
Djajadiningrat, 107
Doren, 17
Drake, Francis, 81–82
Drake expedition, 14
drone, 117
Dutch in Indonesia: colonial policy in Dutch East Indies, 88–89; Javanese courts' reactions to, 22–23, 78; musical imports, 6–7, 12, 14–15; nineteenth-century independence movements against, 4, 60; seizure of trading control, 13; *tanjidor* orchestras, 17–19; trading as focus of, 2

édan nickname, 41–42
Ellis, Alexander, 79
emic vs. etic perspectives, xiii
Erdman, Jean, 64, 155n32
ethnomusicology: academic programs, 4, 110–14, 137; hybridization and,

141; Merriam vs. Hood's approaches to, 115; music and metaphor as topic, 117–23; as term, 109
ethnotheory, xiii
European music complex in Indonesia, 11–12
evolutionary theory, 92
Expo '70 (Osaka, Japan), 6, 154n28
Exposition Universelle (Paris, 1878), 85, 93
Exposition Universelle (Paris, 1889), 88, 92–106; Dutch participation in, 92, 93; identity of gamelan and repertoire used at, 94–106; Javanese dance performances, 95–98, 103–6, 140–41; theme of, 92–93

Farhat, Hormoz, *114*
Fauser, Annegret, 96–98, 99–101, 103, 105
Feld, Steven, 115, 134, 135
Ferianto, Jaduk, 50–51
Forge, Anthony, 77
Furnivall, John, 16

gambang, 80
gambang kromong, 18
gamelan. *See* Balinese culture; Javanese gamelan; Sundanese gamelan; *categories below*
gamelan klenèngan, 86, 132, 133, 158n40
gamelan sekatèn, 84, 122, 154n28, 164n42
gamelan theory: bureaucracy metaphor, 123–26; cross-cultural perspectives on, 115–38; development of, 115–17; dynamic of coincidence in, 133–38; elaboration of skeleton, 130–33; formulaic concept, 117; *gongan-irama* binary, 127–29, 138; interactive networking and leadership metaphors, 126–27, 130, 134, 140, 164–65n66; metaphorical readings, 117–23, 142; *rebab* and the Lord-Servant binary, 129–30; sexual metaphor, 132–33
Ganasidi organizations, 38–40

gapuran scene in *wayang*, 32, 33
gara-gara subscene in *wayang*, 33–34, 35, 149n30
garap, 137–38
garebeg festival, 85, 136–37
Garuda statue (Bali), 26
gatra, 101–2
Gautier, Judith, 103
Geertz, Clifford, 55, 135, 136
gendang melayu, 28
gendèr, 48–49, 72, 79, 81, 94
gendhing: compositional structure, 101–2, 116–17, 128, 129–35; computer-generated, 152n90; in Jaya Manggala Gita, 51–52; as term, 19; in *wayang*, 32, 84
gendhing bonang, 119
gendhing dolanan, 36
gendhing Kombang Mara, 119
gendhing Lobong, 86, 119
gendhing mares, 11, 17, 19–24; colonial conflict and, 22–23; function of, 20; hybridization of, 139–40; incompatible musical elements in, 20–21; instrumentation, 19, 21; *irama* concept, 22; localization and, 25; number of, 147n44; origin, 19; performance of, *20;* structure in, 21–22; *tanjidor* compared with, 146n30
GengGong group, 52
Gilman, Benjamin, 103, 104–5
globalization, 2–3; *musik kontemporer* and, 46–53
Goens, Rijcklof van, 82
Golkar political party, 38–40
gondang, 117–18
gong ageng, 158–59n40
gong angkog, 18
gong kemodhong, 159n40
gongan cycle, 21, 105–6, 120, 127–29, 138, 165n71, 167n96
Graham, Martha, 64, 155n32
Groot, Cornets de, 84

Hadiprayitno, Ki Timbul, 150n35
Hadiwidjojo, Ki Djoko, 41, 107
Hamengku Buwana V, King, 19

Hamengku Buwana VII, King, 19
Hamengku Buwana VIII, King, 19
Hamengku Buwana XII, King, 24
Hardjana, Suka, 44, 48, 49
Harrell, Max, *114*
Heins, Ernst, 97, 109, 160n84
Het Soerabajasch Handelsblad, 107
heterophony, 134
Hill, David, 152n80
Hindu culture in Indonesia, 1–2, 24–25
Holt, Claire, 3, 96, 138
Hood, Mantle, 109–10, 111, *114*, 115, 116
Hooker, Virginia, 40
Howard, Keith, 111
hsaing waing ensemble of Burma, 117
Humardani, Gendon, 43, 151n66
hybridization: anxiety and ambivalence associated with, 25; ethnomusicology and, 141–42; globalization and, 2–3; during Indonesia's colonial period, 11–25; loss of local meaning and resonance through, 42; nation-state, culture, and cultural performance shaped by, 3, 139, 142; in *Opera Diponegoro*, 54–73; in post-independence Indonesia, 26–53; processes of, 11, 139; as term, 1, 11; of Western music in Indonesia, 2, 7

identity issues in post-independence Indonesia, 2, 4–5, 15, 26–27
Ijzerdraat, Bernard, Jr. *See* Brata, Surya
imbal-imbalan, 13
India, European bands in, 16
Indonesia: colonial period, 11–25, 78–82, 88–108; cultural greying out in, 150n60; geographical and ethnic diversity of, 3; globalization in, 2–3, 151n72; hybridity concept for, 1; independence of, 2; national identity formation, 2, 4, 15, 106–8, 161n129; nineteenth-century independence movements, 4, 60; revolution, 2; Suharto's cultural policies, 6, 27, 42–53; Sukarno's cultural policies, 5–6, 7, 27; time cycles in, 135–37; urbanization, 150n60. *See also* Balinese culture; Java; Sumatra; *specific topics*
Indonesian Communist Party, 107
Indonesian Youth Organization, 107
Institut Kesenian Jakarta (IKJ), 44
International Colonial and Export Trade Exhibition (Amsterdam, 1883), 88–92, 140
International Colonial Exposition (Paris, 1931), 106–8
Irama, Rhoma, 28
irama concept, 22, 127–29, 165n71
Islamic culture in Indonesia, 1–2, 11–12, 28

Jabung, Sawo, 52
jaipongan, 18
Jakarta Arts Center, 44, 47, 55, 58, 64
"Jamuran," 46
janger, 108
janturan, 32
jathilan, 63
Java: *batik* cloth compared with gamelan compositions, 121, 123, 164n44; concept of time in, 120, 135–37, 142; courts in, 78; early contact with European traders, 78; gamelan education in, 3–4, 5; historical overview, 3–7; incorporation of Europeans into royal culture, 22–23; as Indonesia's power locus, 3, 5; *kampong* village culture displayed at world's fairs, 88–92, 93; kingship tradition as metaphor for gamelan system, 119–24. *See also specific topics*
Javanese dance: at Amsterdam exhibition, 91; at Arnhem exhibition, 86–87; *bedhaya*, 20; at Chicago Exposition, 104–5, 140–41; at Paris 1889 exhibition, 93–98, *97*, 103–6, 140–41; *serimpi*, 20, 23; Sukarno's support of, 5. *See also specific types*
Javanese gamelan: at Amsterdam Exhibition (1883), 90–92, *91*, 140; at Arnhem Exhibition (1879), 84, 85–88; *batik* cloth compared with,

121, 123, 164n44; bureaucracy metaphor, 123–26; *campursari* performances, 30, 31; decline in popularity in Indonesia, 40; differences with Sundanese gamelan, 93–94, 102–3; Drake's encounter with, 81–82; drummer in, 164–65n66; Dutch group Babar Layar, 109; Dutch national anthem played on, 90, 91–92, 140; dynamic of coincidence in, 133–38; elaboration of skeleton, 130–33; ethnomusicological studies of, 115–17, 141; European enthusiasts, 109; *gatra* in, 101–2; *gongan* cycle, 21, 120, 127–29, 138, 167n96; heterogeneity of Western reception, 113–14; instrumentation, 21–22; interactive networking and leadership metaphors, 126–27, 130, 134, 140, 164–65n66; kingship tradition as metaphor, 119–24; in *langedriyan* genre, 61; mixed East/West groups, 110, 162n150; modernization and, 31; music compared to Scottish music, 79, 80; *musik kontemporer* and, 42, 48–50; necessity of gong in, 133–38, 167n97; nineteenth-century European accounts, 84–85; performances for tourists, 150n49; public performance by Western student groups, 110–14; Raffles's English imports, 78, 79–82, 157–58n15, 158n17; at Royal Aquarium (Westminster), 84, 88; subregional styles, 160n72; Suharto's support of, 6; Sukarno's support of, 5; Surakarta court style, 4, 5; UCLA's *Kyai Mendhung* set, 109–10; wax-cylinder recordings, 103, 104–5; Western academia's interest in, 4, 108–14, 141; World's Fair performances, 4, 6; Yogyakarta court style, 4, 5; youth views on, 30

Javanese theater: *Opera Diponegoro*, 54–73; Western theater compared with, 57–58. *See also wayang*

Jayadipura, Raden Mas, 108

jejer scene in *wayang*, 32
jineman, 36
Jodjana, 109

kaherva, 28
kampong culture: *dangdut* and, 28; displayed at Amsterdam Exhibition (1883), 88–92; displayed at Chicago Exposition (1893), 104–5, 140–41; displayed at Paris Exposition (1889), 93, 101, 140–41
karawitan, 131
Kartomi, Margaret, 117–18
Kayam, Umar: *Kelir Tanpa Batas*, 36–37, 41
kebiar, 108
kecapi, 49
kecrèk, 18
kedhatonan scene in *wayang*, 32, 33–34, 35
Keeler, Ward, 134–35
Kehrer (Dutch colonist), 87
kembangan, 130–33
kendhang, 15, 90, 121, 128
kendhang ciblon, 13
kenong, 18, 135
keprak, 48, 61
kepyakan, 34
Kernoa, Jean, 99
ketawang, 86
kethoprak, 59, 62–63, 71, 73, 154n24
kethuk, 18
Kilian, Godlieb, 60–61
Kirshenblatt-Gimblett, Barbara, 113–14
Kitley, Philip, 123
kodhok ngorèk gamelan, 72–73
Kodrat, Raden, 108
Koesoemadinata: *Lagu-Lagu Gede Sunda*, 99, *100*
komedie stambul, 13, 28
Koninklijk Nederlands Aardrijkskundig Genootschap, 85
kreasi baru, 43, 50, 51–52
kroncong, 11, 12–15; bahasa Indonesian song texts for, 15; *campursari* performance, 29; form and harmony, 12; instrumentation, 12; as natural

hybridity, 25; Portuguese influence on, 6; promoted as national music form, 15; societal position, 12–13, 140; at Surakarta court, 13–14
Kua Etnika ensemble, 50–51
kulantèr, 18
Kunst, Jaap, 82, 108–9, 121
Kusuma-Atmadja, Mochtar, 152n82
Kusumadilaga, Prince Pangeran Harya, 84
Kusumo, Sardono W.: background of, 63–65, 69, 154n28; *Opera Diponegoro*, 53, 54–73, 140
Kuwato, 38–40
Kyai Tentrem gong, 26

ladrang, 24, 86
ladrang Pangkur, 128
ladrang Wilujeng, 119
lagu gede, 99, 103
Laksono, P. M., 124
lancaran, 86, 103, 105
Lange, Daniel de, 87–88, 91–92
"Langen Gita," 46, 151–52n76
langendriyan, 59, 60–62, 96–98, 99, 103–6, 154n24
langgam Jawa, 13
legong, 108
lenong, 18
limbukan subscene in *wayang*, 33–34
localization: of church worship, 12; of European brass bands in East Africa, 16–17, 21; of Hindu culture in Indonesia, 24–25; of Hinduism and Islam in Indonesia, 1–2; in Southeast Asia, 139; as term, 1; of Western music in Indonesia, 2, 7, 11
Lockspeiser, Edward, 99
Lombard, Denys, 56, 58, 64
Lord, Albert, 117
Lucier, Alvin, 52–53; *Music for Gamelan Instruments, Microphones, Amplifiers and Loudspeakers*, 53

MacAloon, John, 40
macapat, 54, 60–61, 65, 68, 97, 148n54, 166n78

Maceda, Jose, 117
Mahabharata: reenactments in Indonesia, 1; stories used in *wayang*, 59, 60, 63, 144n19
manasuka, 31
Mangkunegara I, King, 16
Mangkunegara IV, King, 60, 61, 151–52n76
Mangkunegara VII, King, 108
Manuel, Peter, 28
mardijkers, 13, 144n11
Martopangrawit, Raden Lurah, 121, 129, 132
Mataram court: division of, 60; European contact with, 78, 82; Javanese-European musical hybrid at, 14–15; kingship tradition, 122–26; Sundanese culture influenced by, 160n84
McDowell, Edward, 104
McGraw, Andy, 43
McPhee, Colin, 45, 46
melayu, 18
Melayu music complex in Indonesia, 11, 28
mercu suar policy, 6
Merriam, Alan, 115
Messiaen, Olivier: *Turangalîla Symphony*, 108
Michiels, Augustijn, 17, 146n34, 146n36
military music and brass bands in Indonesia, 14–16; *gendhing mares*, 17, 19–24; marginalization, 23; popularity of, 16; *tanjidor*, 17–19, 21, 24–25; training, 16
Mitropradongga, 132
monggang, 71, 158n24
Monjaya statue (Surabaya), 26
Monson, Ingrid, 115, 137
Mrázek, Jan, 29, 37, 39
Mueller, Richard, 98
multiculturalism, 110–14
Murgiyanto, Sal, 155n32
Murtiyoso, Bambang, 39–40
musik kontemporer, 42–53; composers of, 44, 45–53, 152n82; globalization and, 46–47; hybridization of, 140; in New Order period, 44–53; in Old

Order period, 44; as term, 43, 44, 46; Young Composers' Week (1979) and, 47–50
musikan kumpeni, 15
Muslim music complex in Indonesia, 11

Nagtegaal, Luc, 125
Napoloenic wars, 78
Nartosabdo, 36
National and Colonial Industrial Exhibition (Arnhem, 1879), 84, 85–88
national anthem of Indonesia, 4, 27
national awakening in Indonesia, 2, 4, 27, 106–8, 161n129; Diponegoro as national hero, 56–57
Nepal, European bands in, 16, 21
Nettl, Bruno, 112, 141
networking: in gamelan theory, 126–27, 130, 134, 140, 164–65n66; hybridization and, 139
New Grove Dictionary, 116
New York World's Fair (1964), 64
ngamèn, 18
ngeng, 51

Opera Diponegoro (Kusumo), 54–73, *55;* audience for, 71–72; choreographer of, 63–65; confrontation scenes, 66, 71–72; dialectic in, 57–59; Diponegoro depicted in, 54; as ethnographic interpretation, 55; identity struggle scenes, 66; Islamic elements, 72–73; *kethoprak* in, 71, 73; love scene, 54, 66–69; Mount Merapi eruption scene, 54, 66–67, 68; Mozart's Requiem in, 54, 55; multiple genres used in, 58, 73, 140; opening scene, 54, 66; Ratu Kidul encounter, 66, 69–71; Sardono's monologue and commentary, 56–57; *terbangan* used in, 71, 72–73; term "opera" and, 58
opera productions in Indonesia, 28
orkes melayu, 27–28
ostinato, 117

Pakem Mondraswara: Lampahan Damarwulan Ngarit, 62

Paku Buwana IX, King, 18
Paku Buwana X, King, 13–14
pamurba yatmaka, 129–30
Pane, Sanusi, 5
panembrama, 166n78
Pantap committee, 38
pantun, 12
Pasaribu, Ben, 50
paseban jawi scene in *wayang*, 32
pathet modal system, 84, 116
peking, 158–59n40
pélog tuning system, 19, 72, 84, 86, 87
Pemberton, John: "Musical Politics in Central Java," 121, 122–23, 136, 164n41
perang gagal scene in *wayang*, 32
perang kembang, 38
Performing Ethnomusicology, 110
Perlman, Marc, xii–xiii, 30, 116, 131–32, 166n81
Pertemuan Musik conference (1974), 43, 47
pesindhèn, 35–36, 38, 129
Phillipines, European bands in, 16
Picard, Michel, 108
Pigeaud, Theodore G., 96
Pike, Kenneth, xiii
Poedjosoemarto, Soepomo, 5, 33
Poensen, C., 84–85
Poerbotjaroko, 5
Poetro, Soerjo, 44, 45, 46
Portuguese in Indonesia: church music and, 12; *kroncong* genre and, 6, 11, 12–15; Malacca conquest, 12–13; *musik kontemporer* and, 44; objectives of, 143n8(2); trading as focus of, 2
Powers, Harold, 116
"Prit Peking," 46
Pudjosumarto, Ki. *See* Poedjosoemarto, Soepomo
Purbacaraka, 108
Puspa Warna, 130, *131*, 165–66n78
Pustakamardawa, 19
puwi-puwi, 15

Quigley, Sam, 79–80

racism in nineteenth-century European worldview, 92–93
Raden, Franki, 44–46, 151n72
Raffles, Sir Thomas Stamford: gamelan sets brought to England, 78, 79, 90, 157–58n15, 158n17; *The History of Java*, 77, 78–80, 158n19
Rahardjo, Sapto, 44, 50, 51, 152n88
Ramayana: reenactments in Indonesia, 1, 155n29; stories used in *wayang*, 59, 60, 63
rampak-rempeg, 135
Ranger, Terence, 16–17
Rasta, Otong, 99
rebab, 18, 35, 49, 85, 94, 103, 121, 129–30, 137
Recovering the Orient (conference proceeding), 77–78
Reeves, Ron, 52
Reki, 86–87
réyog, 63, 71
Rhodius, Hans, 151n75
Rice, Timothy, 118
Ricklefs, Merle Calvin, 22
Rijks Ethnographisch Museum (Leiden), 85
Roestopo, 48
ronggèng, 86–87, 95, 159n41
Ronggowarsito: "Kalatidha," 22
Roseman, Marina, 115
Royal Aquarium (Westminster), 84, 88
Rusman, 5
Rydell, Robert, 104
Ryle, Gilbert, 55

sabrangan scene in *wayang*, 32
Said, Edward: *Orientalism*, 77–78
Saleh, Raden, 54, 55–56, 73
saluang, 49, 72–73
sampak, 86, 167n97
Santoso: "Sworo Pencon," 49
Sarekat Islam, 107
saron, 21–22, 158–59n40
Sastrodarsono, Soekanto, 129
Schechner, Richard, 57, 72
Scott, Edmund, 81
sekar ageng, 103

Sekatèn festival, 136
Serat Catholoco, 138, 168n114
Serat Centhini, xiv, 108, 129–30, 132–34, 138
Serat Pakem Wirama, 19, 108
Serat Srikarongron, 13–14
Seriem, 94, 97–98, 103
serimpi, 20, 23, 86–87, 91, 95, 104–5
sètan nickname, 41–42
Shepherd, John, 162–63n4
Siegel, James, 40–42
Sindusawarno, 129
Siwojo, Prince Pangeran Hario Gondo, 86
Sjukur, Slamet Abdul, 44, 45, 46, 50, 52
slametan, 124, 136, 137
slendang, 87
sléndro tuning system, 84, 86, 87, 103, 106
slenk nickname, 41–42
slenthem, 49
Smeding, H., 84–85
Smithsonian Folkways, 146n30
Soedharsono, Manteb, 41
Soekia, 94, 97–98, 103
Soelardi, Raden Bagoes, 108, 129
Soetomo, 121–22
Solis, Gabriel, 112, 141–42
Spies, Walter, 45–46, 151n75
Spiller, Henry, 99
srageni, 16
srepegan, 32, 61–62, 86, 87, 154n24
srimulat, 40–42
Sriwedari *wayang wong* dance drama troupe, 5
Storebeker, A. W., 89
Subakastawa, 120–21
Subono: "Sworo Pencon," 49
Subuh, 19, 147n44, 147n46
Sudjadi, 38
Suhardi, 116
Suharti, Theresia, 24
Suharto and Suharto regime: criticism of, 71; cultural support by, 6, 42–53; New Order period, 27, 40–46, 54; Western popular culture and, 7, 27, 40
Sukarno, Waluyo Sastro, 58

Sukarno and Sukarno regime: Balinese mother of, 6; cultural policies, 5–6, 7, 27, 44, 144n18; downfall, 27; Western popular culture and, 42
suling, 72
sulukan, 32, 59, 60
Sumanto, 36
Sumatra: 1870s Dutch ethnographical expedition, 85; *gondang* music of Batak people, 117–18; nineteenth-century independence movements against Dutch, 4; *orkes melayu* in, 27–28
Sumpah Pemuda, 4, 161n129
Sundanese gamelan: at Chicago Exposition (1983), 104–5, 140–41; differences with Javanese gamelan, 93–94, 102–3; Mataram court's influence on, 160n84; Parakan Salak plantation ensemble, 93, 94; at Paris Exposition (1889), 93–106, 140–41
Supanggah, Rahayu, xiv, 29, 30, 48, 116, 132, 135
Sur, Donald, *114*
Surakarta court: *bedhaya Ketawang* at, 23; dancers at Paris Exposition (1889), 93, 94; Dutch colonization and, 78; Dutch national anthem played at, 15; gamelan style, 4, 5, 86–88, 109–10, 158n24, 160n72; *garebeg* festival, 136–37; *kroncong* at, 13–14; *tanjidor* at, 17–18; *wayang* at, 149n30
Suriname, 162n150
Surjodiningrat, Wasisto, 50, 152n90
Suryono, Bambang, 96, 159n42
Susanto, Budi, 62
Susilo, Hardjo, 110, *114*
Sutton, Anderson, 30, 117
Suwardi, A. L., 48; "Gendèr," 48–49

tabla, 28
Taman Budaya Arts Center, 152n88
Taminah, 94, 97–98, 103
tamu scene in *wayang*, 32
tandak, 87, 95
tanjidor, 11, 17–19, 139; Batavian repertoire, 18; contexts for, 21; current status, 23; *gendhing mares* compared with, 146n30; instrumentation, 18; localization of brass bands through, 24–25; as natural hybridity, 25; Sundanese repertoire, 18–19; term derivation, 17
tayuban, 86, 87
tehian, 18
tembang, 97
terbangan, 71, 72–73
terompèt, 18
Terwen, Jan Willem: *Gamelan in the 19th-Century Netherlands*, 84–85, 86, 158–59n40
Thailand, European bands in, 16
Thompson, Rachel, 95, 101–2
Tiersot, Julien: gamelan transcription by, 98–101, *100*
Tijdschrift voor Nederlandsch Indie, 84
tingalan ageng, 16
Tondhakusuma, Raden Harya, 61, 62
transculturation, 139
Trimillos, Ricardo, 111
trumpet, 14
tuning systems: in *campursari*, 29–30; *pélog*, 19, 72, 84, 86, 87; *sléndro*, 84, 86, 87, 103, 106; Spies's experiment, 151n75
Turner, Victor, 73

UCLA, 109–10
ukuleles, 12

Valentijn, François, 82
"Vani-Vani." *See* "Wani-Wani"
Veth, C. D., 85, 90, 159n59
Veth, P. J., 85, 129n59
Vetter, Roger, 19, 112, 147n44
Vie parisienne, La, 92
Viswanathan, *114*
Vleuten, J. M. van, 95

Wahid, Abdulrachman, 29
Wakiem, 94, 97–98, 103
Wall, V. I. van de, 17
"Wani-Wani," 98–100, *100*, 103, 160n97
Warseno, 41

Warsi, 86–87
Warsodiningrat, 62
wayang: anachronistic effects in, 71; *Arjuna Wiwaha*, 69–71; audience position, 37–38; clowns in, 33–35, 124–25; contemporary performance, 30, 31–42; *dhalang* in, 5, 32, 33, 34–35, 36–37, 41–42, 59, 138, 149n24; Diponegoro's knowledge of, 65–66; as genre, 58, 59–61; hybridization of, 140; illustrations in Raffles's book, 77, 78, 158n19; Javanese ecology and, 66–71; *langendriyan* used in, 154n24; light source used, 37–38; metaphor in, 138; as mixed media genre, 32–33; nontraditional elements incorporated into, 35–36, *36*, 37, 41–42; performances at Amsterdam exhibition (1883), 90–91; performers at Paris Exposition, 96; plot structure, 31–36, 149n29; social relations in, 124–25; spectacular, 38–40; stories portrayed in, 59; Sukarno's support of, 5; Western instruments in, 31
wayang gedhog, 96
wayang golèk, 94
wayang krucil, 91
wayang kulit. See *wayang*
wayang purwa, 59–60, 62, 90, 153n13
wayang wahyu, 12
wayang wong, 59–60, 95–96
Weintraub, Andrew, 28, 29
Weiss, Sarah, 11, 25, 123, 127–28
Wesleyan University, 52–53
Western culture in Indonesia, 1, 2; *campursari*, 29–31; *dangdut*, 27–29; European composers, 45–46; hybridity and, 11–25; long history of, 4, 78–82; military music and brass bands, 14, 15–16, 19–24; music education, 44; *musik kontemporer*, 42–53; popular, 6–7, 26–27, 42; Suharto's New Order and, 40–46, 54. *See also* British in Indonesia; Dutch in Indonesia; Portuguese in Indonesia
Wheatstone, Charles, 79

Wilkens, J. A.: "Sewaka," 84
Willem III, King of the Netherlands, 90
Wirjosuparto, Sutjipto, 5
Wolters, O. W., 24–25
wong cilik, 62
Woodfield, Ian, 81
World's Columbian Exposition (Chicago, 1893), 88, 92, 103, 104–5, 140–41
world's fairs and exhibitions: Amsterdam exhibition (1883), 88–92, 140; Arnhem exhibition (1879), 84, 85–88; Berlin exhibition (1880), 85; centrality of economic interests in, 93; Crystal Palace Exhibition (London, 1851), 83–84; early fairs, 82–85; Expo '70 (Osaka, Japan), 6, 154n28; Exposition Universelle (Paris, 1878), 85, 93; Exposition Universelle (Paris, 1889), 88, 92–106; as imagined communities, 83; International Colonial Exposition (Paris, 1931), 106–8; Javanese performing arts at, 4, 82–108, 113–14, 140–41; *kampong* village culture displayed at, 88–92, 93; World's Columbian Exposition (Chicago, 1893), 88, 92, 103, 104–5, 140–41

Yampolsky, Philip, 11–12, 13, 42, 144n11, 150n60, 154n23
yatmaka, 129–30
Yogyakarta Art Festival, 50
Yogyakarta court: *bedhaya Semang* at, 23–24; Dutch colonization and, 78; European orchestra of, 45–46; gamelan style, 4, 5, 84, 158n24, 160n72; *garebeg* festival, 136–37; *gendhing mares* at, 17, 19–24, 139–40; *wayang* at, 149n30
Yogyakarta Gamelan Festival, 30, 50–53, 152n82
Young Composers' Week (1979), 47–50
Yudanegara, Bandara Raden Ayu, 24

zapin, 58
Zbikowski, Lawrence M., 118
Zemp, Hugo, xiii

www.ingramcontent.com/pod-product-compliance
Lightning Source LLC
Chambersburg PA
CBHW030651230426
43665CB00011B/1044